S0-AAI-801

mainline churches and the evangelicals

a challenging crisis?

RICHARD G. HUTCHESON, Jr.

John Knox Press
ATLANTA

Library of Congress Cataloging in Publication Data

Hutcheson, Richard G., 1921–
   Mainline churches and the evangelicals.

   Includes bibliographical references and index.
   1. Evangelicalism—United States.   2. Protestant
churches—United States.   3. United States—Church
history—20th century.   I. Title.
BR164.2 U5H87   280′.4′0973   80-84648
ISBN 0-8042-1502-2 (pbk.)   AACR2

© copyright John Knox Press 1981
10 9 8 7 6 5 4 3 2 1
Atlanta, Georgia 30365

Printed in the United States of America

To My Mother
Tess Hutcheson

preface

The next few years may present mainline American Protestantism with a crisis rivaling that of the twenties, symbolized by the famous Scopes Monkey Trial. A vigorous and growing evangelicalism now confronts the divided and declining mainline churches with a challenge for leadership and control. After six years of observation from a front row seat, I am convinced that a critical testing period is before us.

As Chairman of the Office of Review and Evaluation of the Presbyterian Church in the United States, I have been labeled by some as my denomination's "official watchdog." I have followed developments at every level, from the local congregation to central headquarters. Although mine is a relatively small denomination, it is considered a leader in ecumenical affairs. It works closely, through a network of interrelationships, with most other mainline denominations. My responsibilities to my own church have required me to keep up, at least in general terms, with developments in others throughout the last half of the seventies and the beginning of the eighties.

These have not been the best of times for mainline Protestantism. Steadily declining membership, radically slashed denominational budgets, shrinking agency staffs, waning influence on a secularized society—this has been the picture in every one of the Protestant denominations usually labeled mainline. Sunday School enrollments have plummeted since the flourishing fifties. Youth programs are moribund. The average age of members has climbed steeply. Churches are polarized internally, and a widely-noted gap has developed between clergy and laity. An even greater gap—alienation, in fact—has developed between social activist, denominational agency bureaucrats and many of the people in the pews.

Each year since I joined it in 1975, the Office of Review and Evaluation has made a report (a "Program Audit") to the General Assembly of the Presbyterian Church, U.S. Not only have these reports evaluated in orthodox managerial fashion "the effectiveness of the General Assembly's agencies in meeting their goals," but they have also dealt with "general trends and indices affecting the health and work of the church." A number of the crisis points and problem areas listed above (as well as others covered in the present book) have thus been delineated. Some concerned church people have taken these reports seriously. The trends—particularly those which seem to be trends downward—have led many to ask, Why? What does it all mean? Where is it leading? What can be done about it?

The Office of Review and Evaluation has not addressed these questions. Our program audits have necessarily been limited to straightforward reporting of data. My colleagues and I are employed neither to engage in speculative analysis of reasons nor to prescribe solutions. Besides, we have not always agreed regarding reasons and solutions.

Nonetheless, finding the answers to those questions may be one of the most urgent tasks before the church today; and this book, though a personal, off-duty undertaking, may be the most important thing to come out of my years in the PCUS Office of Review and Evaluation. It offers a descriptive analysis of the challenge to mainline churches now being mounted by the evangelical wing of Christianity. Based in a massive parachurch movement (which is startling both in its range and its vigor) evangelicalism has already established itself as that part of the church which is growing, in contrast to the shrinking mainline. It has already, to a considerable extent, captured mainline youth, it is already dominating Protestant overseas mission work, and it has moved vigorously into the former liberal preserves of social and political action.

None of this, of course, is new to the informed observer of American Christianity. This book seeks to make a fresh contribution to the understanding of our situation by pulling the various strands together into a comprehensible overall picture. But what lies ahead? How are we to move beyond shock, dismay, and confrontation, toward a positive and constructive response? How are we to transcend our lethargic past and our polarized present? Is it possible to greet some of the surprising changes thrust upon us by the 1970s and early 80s not with panic, but with wonder and openness? Is it possible that the mainline, instead of toppling over, may regain its balance?

The picture of mainline Protestantism emerging in this book may seem in some ways a gloomy, pessimistic one. Yet optimism or pessimism is largely a matter of perspective. Certainly the old liberal-ecumenical coalition which has dominated the mainline establishment through most of this century is no longer leading a strong and unified constituency. But the wave of evangelical and charismatic Christianity sweeping in on that constituency may be exactly what it labels itself—a renewal. Perhaps the Holy Spirit is telling us something. In any event, meeting the evangelical challenge is one of the most compelling tasks before ministers and lay leaders of mainline congregations today. This book seeks to help in understanding and confronting that task.

Many have assisted in its preparation. I wish to express my special thanks to Dr. Martin E. Marty of the University of Chicago Divinity School, President James I. McCord of Princeton Theological Seminary, Dr. James H. Smylie of Union Theological Seminary in Virginia, Dr. Robert K. Johnston of Western Kentucky University, and Mr. D. A. Sharpe of the Covenant Fellowship of Presybterians, who read the manuscript and offered valuable comments and suggestions. Not all the suggestions were accepted, and the responsibility for the result is entirely mine. The book is, however, a far better one than it would have been without those comments, and I am deeply grateful to them. Finally, I am grateful to my wife, Ann Rivers, for her continuing help, encouragement, and support.

Richard G. Hutcheson, Jr.

contents

part one

the
developing
challenge

chapter 1
confrontation:
mainline churches
and the evangelicals

Minor events can become symbols of major turning points. At the end of the 1970s, King College, a small but venerable liberal arts institution in Bristol, Tennessee, became such a symbol for one mainline denomination. King had long been affiliated with the Presbyterian Church, U. S., known colloquially as the Southern Presbyterian Church. It was the college of the Synod of Appalachia, serving primarily the mountain region made up of parts of Virginia, West Virginia, eastern Tennessee, and western North Carolina. Its endowment was small, and its financial condition had long been precarious; but its academic standards were high, and its reputation was good, particularly in the physical sciences. It had an attractive, well-equipped campus. It was a bit more conservative than most Presbyterian colleges, but so was its region. However, with a combination of loyal support from its Presbyterian constituency in Appalachia, and good old-fashioned trust in the Lord, it managed to survive and even flourish in a modest way.

Then came the seventies. The forces which brought nearly all small, financially pressed denominational colleges into question in that period hit King especially hard—the inflationary spiral that lifted operating costs to stratospheric heights; the heavy burden of complying with an increasingly demanding federal bureaucracy; the competition of state-supported institutions with much lower tuition costs, and particularly the vastly expanded community college systems; the shrinking student pool from which to draw, as the post World War II baby boom passed out of academia, and student competition for college admission was replaced by college competition to recruit students.

At about the same time, in the early seventies, the Presbyterian Church, U.S., restructured its synod boundaries. King's sponsoring Synod of Appalachia was carved up to form parts of several larger synods. The college now found itself on the northeastern fringe of the new Synod of the Mid-South, stretching from the Gulf of Mexico in the south to the Mississippi River in the west. The new synod inherited several other colleges as well. King continued to draw students from its natural constituency, the fairly homogeneous Appalachian area, but its supporting structures in the region had disintegrated. Its new synod showed little interest.

King struggled. Economies were effected. A new administration was brought in. But debts piled up and the student body melted away. It was no longer a matter of survival as the old King, but of survival in any form. A plan was devised for incorporation into the Tennessee state college system with King becoming a branch of the nearby East Tennessee State University. Southern Presbyterians paid little attention. The plan fell through, and it appeared that King would have no alternative but to close its doors.

At the last minute, in the spring of 1979, rescue came; and it came not from a secular state university system, but from Southern Presbyterians. An ad hoc coalition of five people, three of them ministers of large Presbyterian churches and the other two Presbyterian elders, offered to take over the college. They represented substantial amounts of Presbyterian money. They pledged $900,000 over the first three years, and promised to raise whatever funds would be needed to keep the college solvent.

In return, they required that the Board of Trustees turn the college over to them, proposing to form a new self-perpetuating Board of Trustees with themselves as the nucleus. They would bring in a new president to take charge, and they promised to keep the existing faculty, although without tenure and with one-year contracts only. They proposed to continue King as a Presbyterian college and to maintain a relationship with the Synod of the Mid-South, but they themselves would name the synod's representatives on the board. With no alternative but closure, the Board accepted the proposal. The president resigned to make room for the new president, and all faculty members accepted the offer of one-year contracts with the exception of the three professors in the Bible department who refused, and three others who accepted positions elsewhere.

The denominational power establishment now rose up in arms. The synod, which had made no concerted effort to rescue the college financially in the preceding years, now mounted a major effort to stop the "takeover." Lawyers were retained for court action. All funds currently in the synod's hands, which had been given by the churches and designated for King, were placed in a special account to pay legal fees. Alumni were divided, but those opposing the step were especially vociferous. The three Bible professors became heroes. One of the denomination's leaders in the field of higher education wrote an editorial, which appeared in the denomination's leading unofficial journal, maintaining that it would be preferable to close the college rather than let this new group of Presbyterians assume control.[1]

Why? For what conceivable reason could a denominational power establishment, which had faced with equanimity the prospect of the absorption of one of its church colleges into a secular state university system, make such an uproar over an effort by some of the denomination's own members to rescue the college and keep it Presbyterian? Why should the leadership of a synod which had shown so little earlier concern for support of the college be ready for litigation to keep it out of the hands of some of its own members?

The reason is simple. The new group seeking to assume responsibility and control of the college represented the denomination's evangelicals! The new president they planned to bring in was a vice president of Wheaton College, long known as an educational center of the nation's evangelical Protestants. Although the new board promised the student body that they would initiate no immediate radical changes, they planned to operate it as a "distinctively Christian"—meaning evangelical—college. And the denominational establishment preferred no college at all to a college run by its own evangelicals.

Signs of the Times

The King incident has not been the only sign of the times for mainline Southern Presbyterians. The Covenant Fellowship of Presbyterians, an unofficial organization of evangelicals within the denomination (linked with, but not officially related to the ad hoc group which sought control of King College), had been showing increasing strength and political sophistication. Its most recent undertaking, an effort to defeat a proposal for changes in the constitutional voting provisions—which had the backing of the liberal ecumenical establishment and would presumably have given an advantage to the liberal faction—had been resoundingly successful. Its publication, *The Open Letter*, had acquired a wide readership.

The denominational bureaucracy, dominated by social activists, had long been suffering from fiscal starvation. During the same year that the King episode took place, another ad hoc group of Southern Presbyterian evangelicals had offered fiscal rescue to the establishment. Calling themselves "Advocates for Outreach," they proposed forming a Presbyterian Outreach Foundation to raise large sums of money. They sought the cooperation of the General Assembly Mission Board, offering to channel money into official denominational mission projects—provided they could select the projects and designate the way the money would be spent. The Mission Board had turned down the offer of cooperation, but with enough awareness of the signs of the times to set up a committee to continue to study the matter. When the Foundation was established without the Board's cooperation, it accepted proffered funds.

So King was not the only symbol, but it was perhaps the most dramatic one—a symbol not only for PCUS Presbyterians, but for all mainline Protestants, since all of them face a similar challenge. It was a symbol not only for the denomination's power establishment, but also—and especially—for local congregations and their governing bodies, since it was above all a symbol of a grassroots revolution. Rare is the mainline congregation without its evangelical minority—or majority. The winds of change are everywhere pushing at established patterns. King symbolizes a pressing new agenda for mainliners, and it probably suggests that out of this agenda will come, in the years immediately ahead, significant changes for mainline American Protestantism.

Evangelical Impact

Three factors sum up the impact on mainline churches.

1. The Evangelical Resurgence

The evangelical resurgence was probably the most significant development in American Christianity in the decade of the seventies. Every turn-of-the-decade analysis of the past ten years featured it prominently.[2] Members of the liberal-ecumenical mainline churches were not unaware of the changes taking place. We knew something was happening, but we did not know how seriously to take it. The resurgence began far earlier than the seventies. Its origins probably go back as far as the late forties or early fifties. Not until the late seventies, however, did it become a media event and thus grip our attention. The election of Southern Baptist evangelical Jimmy Carter to the presidency was probably the symbolic event that brought the burgeoning movement to public attention. 1976 was labeled the "Year of the Evangelical." Both Time and Newsweek conferred pop canonization on the movement by running cover stories on the evangelicals.

Mainliners were aware that these things were going on. Billy Graham had stubbornly refused to wither away in the face of establishment scorn. The circulation of Christianity Today (although few of us were reading it) had passed that of Christian Century. A 1979 Gallup survey indicated that it was being read by more than twice as many ministers as our old standby, the Century.[3] In the field of higher education, we were aware that Wheaton and such other avowedly evangelical colleges as Gordon, Trinity, Westmont, and Bethel, were flourishing. But we could hardly take them seriously; some of their students in the sixties had been demonstrating to win the right for girls to wear short-sleeved dresses in the dining hall, while ours had been marching on Washington to protest the Vietnam War. We knew that Fuller and Gordon-Conwell seminaries had won full accreditation from "our" accrediting agency, the Association of Theological Schools. We were strongly aware of the charismatic movement cropping up in nearly every congregation and honey-combing Roman Catholicism as well as mainline Protestantism. It did not quite fit with anything else we were observing, but we certainly knew the evangelicals were around. Jimmy Carter, after all, kept teaching Sunday School in spite of the derision of the Harvard-Georgetown set (a derision which mainline religious establishmentarians could hardly condone, but secretly enjoyed). All three candidates for president in the 1980 election labeled themselves "born again," and Moral Majority claimed credit for Reagan's election.

Yet it has been only a distant awareness. Few of us have read the growing body of evangelical literature coming from the flourishing evangelical publishing houses; it is hard enough for us to keep up with our own. We have continued to lump evangelicals and fundamentalists into one all-embracing "them," clinging to our image of "them" as rigid, anti-intellectual, close-minded, socially uninvolved, and uncooperative. We have been aware of the evangelical resurgence, but as something happening "out there," having little to do with us.

2. Mainline Churches: the Present Focus of the Evangelical Challenge

The King incident symbolizes not only the evangelical resurgence; it also symbolizes the fact that it is no longer something "out there." Wheaton is an independent, non-denominational college, as are most of the evangelical colleges. (The others, for the most part, are affiliated with small, non-mainline sects.) "Wheaton South," however—the label Presbyterian opponents of the King takeover gave to what they perceived to be the college's future—would be a mainline denominational college.

In its early stages the evangelical renascence did indeed take place outside mainline Protestant Christianity. After the Fundamentalist-Modernist controversy of the twenties and thirties, the fundamentalists had clearly lost their bid for control of the mainline denominations. By and large, they had moved into a separatist stance, isolating themselves from the mainstream. Large numbers of conservatives remained within the mainline denominations, true, but the neo-orthodox consensus which dominated the mainline churches through the forties and fifties was sufficiently close to the middle to stay in touch with them—at least at the level of the local congregation. Only outside mainline Protestantism were the fundamentalist remnants in control of the small conservative sects and independent Bible Colleges.

It was outside mainline Protestantism, then, that a new and more vital evangelicalism began to develop in the forties and fifties, rejecting establishment neo-orthodoxy, but seeking to differentiate itself from dispensationalist fundamentalism as well. Reflecting the social environment of a scientifically oriented culture, it was becoming increasingly uncomfortable with the anti-scientism of the extremists. It sought intellectual respectability. Wheaton College, Fuller and Gordon-Conwell Seminaries, and the journal *Christianity Today*—all independent and non-denominational—these were the axes around which the new evangelicalism developed.

But conservative *numerical* strength remained within the mainline churches, and as the neo-orthodox consensus of the middle gave way to the radical theologies of the sixties and the liberation theologies of the seventies, mainline conservatives became restive. Capture of the mainline bureaucracies by social activists committed to sweeping, worldwide economic and social change—sometimes perceived by conservatives as taking Marxist directions—left them uncomfortable about denominational mission undertakings. The gap between the pulpit and pew, and the even greater gap—often outright alienation—between denominational bureaucracies and the pew began to be widely noted. Conservative lay organizations within the various denominations began to be aware of each other—and of the increasing prominence of the non-mainline evangelical movement—and to gain strength.

Mainline church youth programs were moribund, while high school kids—even the pastor's kids—flocked to Young Life. Mainline campus ministries were locked into the marginal world of campus protest, while Inter-Varsity Christian Fellowship and Campus Crusade for Christ flourished among a new generation of non-protesting students. For a while Young Life, Inter-Varsity and Campus Crusade were "out there." Then their products began to show up in the mainline churches. Youth Advisory Delegates to mainline General Assemblies and Conventions had become fashionable in the sixties, when youth demanded a voice—usually a voice calling for radical change—in all establishment structures. None had welcomed the youth delegates more enthusiastically than the mainline denominations, for the radical theology briefly fashionable in the sixties had eagerly baptized the greening of America. Suddenly, however, in the late seventies, the youth delegates began taking positions "somewhere to the right of Ghengis Khan" (in the words of one soured mainline establishmentarian).

The graduates of Fuller and Gordon-Conwell began to fill increasing numbers of "our" pulpits. Faculties of our own seminaries were baffled by student bodies made up of young evangelicals growing increasingly conservative each year. What King and similar events symbolized, then, was not only the evangelical renascence, but the fact that it was no longer "out there." It was here, within mainline American Protestantism. The arena today is the mainline churches.

3. *A Crucial Test for Mainline Pluralism*

King also symbolizes something else: a crucial test for the *pluralism* of the mainline churches in the period ahead. Openness, tolerance, inclusiveness, acceptance of diversity—these have been characteristic of the mainline churches ever since the twenties, when the Scopes Monkey Trial passed into history and fundamentalism lost its bid for mainline control. These are the characteristics of the contemporary American intellectual climate, for that, too, was at stake in Dayton, Tennessee. They characterize the modern, secular-scientific world view out of which our mainline churches operate. They are the basis of the ecumenical movement, long a major preoccupation of mainline Protestantism, which hopes one day to establish an inclusive, tolerant, diverse, accepting, ecumenical church.

Mainline churches are pluralistic by design. They welcome to their membership diversity of faith, style and opinion. While doctrinal standards establish general parameters, they are seldom applied in a way excluding anyone. Even candidates for the clergy, in mainline denominations, are more likely to be rejected for excessive narrowness than for violation of confessional standards. As for the laity, one can hardly conceive a belief, idiosyncrasy, or variance which would disqualify a lay person conscientiously and sincerely seeking membership in a mainline church. In recent years we have cultivated ethnic, cultural, and economic diversity—which most mainline churches have in short supply. We have worked hard to attract Blacks, Hispanics, and other minority groups to our all-too-often lily-white membership. We have come to think of ourselves consciously as pluralistic, describing ourselves with that term. All along, however, our most significant kind of pluralism has been theological and ideological.

Conscious *theological* pluralism is something relatively new to Protestantism. When we disagree, we have preferred historically to divide ourselves up into like-minded groups we call denominations. Such a dynamic is still at work among us. The Episcopal Church; the Lutheran Church, Missouri Synod; and the Presbyterian Church, U.S. have all in recent years seen schismatic groups split off to form new denominations. By and large, however, mainline churches have cultivated the openness, tolerance, and inclusiveness leading to pluralistic membership.

Pluralism implies variety, and theological variety is certainly present in all mainline Protestant denominations. It is a dangerous thing to categorize Protestants too sharply. It is clear, however, that there have been two major groups in Protestantism through much of its history. Certainly throughout this century, beginning with the Modernist-Fundamentalist controversy which marked its early years, two such groups have been identifiable. Modernist versus fundamentalist, liberal versus conservative, activist versus pietist, ecumenical versus evangelical—there have been many ways of labeling the polarization. In the next chapter we shall look in more detail at ways to understand it. But however labeled, and however many variations and shades of opinion may separate the opposite poles, American Protestant pluralism can be seen clearly in terms of two basic orientations. What pluralism really means, then, for mainline Protestants, is that we seek to be churches in which *both* major factions or orientations can be present and reasonably happy.

Since the early part of this century, those at the conservative end of the spectrum have never controlled the mainline denominations, except for the Southern Baptist and the Missouri Synod Lutheran churches, if these be classified as mainline. (They have, of course, controlled the smaller separatist denominations, some of which have been growing rapidly in recent years.) Mainline congregations, on the other hand, have continued to have substantial numbers of conservative Christians within their membership. This kind of pluralism has worked well as long as two conditions have existed.

First, it has worked well as long as church leadership has remained *close enough to the middle of the road* to provide a climate in which all conservatives except extremists could feel reasonably comfortable. This was the situation throughout the neo-orthodox mid-century period. Neo-orthodoxy had developed as a reaction to the liberal extremes and the pre-World War II optimism of the modernist-social gospel era. It was activist on social issues and it took biblical criticism for granted. It did, however, take the Scriptures seriously. It focused attention on the Reformers, and through them on the church fathers. It also took sin and grace seriously. At the popular level, it represented a genuine return to the middle. So as long as it lasted, it held together most of the Protestant spectrum in a broad kind of consensus.

The other condition that made mainline pluralism work was the acquiescense of conservative Protestants in the mainline pews. This acquiescense continued well beyond the breakup of the neo-orthodox consensus. The evangelical renewal was taking place *outside* the mainline denominations, in the independent institutions and small separatist denominations. Conservative leadership, therefore, was outside the mainline. Conservatives inside began in time to turn their attention—and give their money—outside the denominations. As long as they were no threat to liberal power and control of denominational machinery, however, the pluralism continued to be acceptable to the establishment.

What the King incident, and others like it, symbolize is the breakup of these conditions under which mainline pluralism has operated through most of this century. The middle no longer dominates. Its theoretical base was removed by the demise of neo-orthodoxy. As the managerial revolution has increasingly turned denominational leadership over to the bureaucracies, and the bureaucracies have come into the hands of single-minded social activists, any semblance of a leadership of the middle at denominational levels has disappeared.

Further, the conservative minority (or perhaps majority) within the mainline churches is no longer acquiescent. Real challenges to the power and control of the liberal establishment are being mounted. The King incident is only one of many. The participation and apparent influence of conservative Christian political action groups in the 1980 election of President Ronald Reagan and a Republican-controlled Senate may have signaled a new stage in the religious polarization. No longer confined to shadowy ecclesiastical corridors, the confrontation appears once again to be open and public, as it was in the courtroom in Dayton, Tennessee. Pluralism thus faces a crucial test. Can pluralism survive led by one "party" if the other "party" refuses to remain quiet and on the contrary mounts a challenge for power?

Three Choices for Mainline Churches

The answer to that question depends on the direction chosen for the future. At least three choices, and perhaps more, are open to the pluralistic mainline churches in the face of the evangelical challenge. The first is a battle for power and control. "Better no college at all than an evangelical college" as a reaction to the King incident is an expression of this choice.

Church politicans are, in a sense, the most fiercely determined of all politicians because their motives are so noble. They are, after all, fighting on both sides for the health, the purity, and the future of Christ's church. If you are fighting for God and your opponents are perceived as opposing God's will, almost any tactic ("strategies," in the approved ecclesiastical jargon) can be justified, as centuries of holy wars have demonstrated.

Fighting for control was the option chosen once before in this century, when polarization reached a critical point during the fundamentalist-modernist controversy of the twenties and thirties. Battling for control has never completely ceased, of course, and skirmishes between opposing factions have been a standard feature at meetings of congregational governing structures, church courts and conventions. Church people have had plenty of practice at power struggles, and given the natural reluctance of those in power to give it up—together with the almost universal conviction among Christians that God sees things the way they do—this is the option almost sure to be chosen.

There are, however, other possibilities. A second option is a consciously planned pluralism, meaning a pluralism of shared power and policy-making as well as of membership. In theory, the openness, inclusiveness and acceptance of diversity characterizing "liberal" attitudes should point to such planned pluralism. Willingness to accept strongly differing opinions and convictions in the Body of Christ should imply willingness for those with such convictions to promote them, embody them in their church life, and express them in their mission activity. Conservatives should be willing for advocates of social change to seek the destruction of multi-national corporations believed to be exploiting the third world; liberals should be willing for evangelicals to send evangelistic missionaries to convert non-Christians in the third world; and church structures should be available for both forms of outreach. In practice, however, such planned pluralism is hard to achieve, since social change advocates are convinced that those evangelistic missionaries are supporting the dominance of multi-nationals in the third world countries. Evangelicals are equally convinced that the Marxist order they believe would result from destruction of the multi-nationals would be inimical to the spread of the Christian gospel. So out of perceived loyalty to God's claims, neither side can permit the other to operate freely through denominational structures.

In theory, a planned pluralism would lead a liberal establishment, which is clearly in control of and setting the tone for at least seven or eight Southern Presbyterian colleges, to be perfectly willing for evangelicals to control and set the tone for one of them. In practice, however, when one of "ours" is being taken over by a "power play," planned pluralism is not so easy. A church, sufficiently alerted to what is happening and sufficiently determined to avoid blood-letting power struggles like those of the twenties and thirties, might move consciously in the direction of shared power and policy making. An entrenched establishment, however, will not likely move in this direction on its own initiative. Initiative would probably have to come from a sufficiently aroused membership which insisted on it.

The third possible choice is even less likely to be consciously chosen—and perhaps it cannot be, since it will likely come about only by the movement of history under the leadership of the Holy Spirit. This is the restoration of some sort of consensus of the middle under which all members of pluralistic churches except the extremists at either pole could feel reasonably comfortable. Where the ideological and theological foundation for such a consensus might be found is not yet apparent. A modest revival of interest in Barth is evident, but certainly not on a scale promising a return to the neo-orthodoxy underpinning the mid-century consensus of the middle. Neither the liberation theologies of the left nor the conservative theologians of the right appear to be moving in a centrist direction. Some of the so-called "young evangelicals" are certainly moving toward the center in their calls and pronouncements, but they have produced no theologian whose stature is broadly recognized and are not being read by the liberal-ecumenical establishment.

At the practical level, however, a consciously planned pluralism (the second option above) might create a climate in which a consensus of the middle can develop. This hope may be enough to engender the necessary faith—and perhaps ultimately the requisite charity.

chapter 2
the outs move in:
a mainline view of
the evangelical renascence

A mainline Protestant who reads the literature of the "new evangelicals" for the first time is in for some surprises. This literature comes mainly from sources we do not usually notice. Richard Quebedeaux, Donald Bloesch and Bernard Ramm are not familiar names in our circles. Fuller, Gordon-Conwell, and Asbury seminaries have earned a grudging respect, but nevertheless we do not regard them as centers of our kind of scholarship. Eerdmans and Zondervan have been around a long time; Intervarsity Press and Word Books sell well in Bible bookstores, but they are not publishers with whom we are familiar. It is a somewhat foreign world. Mainline familiarity with the evangelical renascence is scanty at best, and it comes through our own filters.

Three main surprises awaited me as I set out to familiarize myself with what the evangelicals are saying about themselves and their movement.[1] First, I was surprised at the insistence and the consistency with which contemporary evangelical writers are separating themselves from fundamentalists. They recognize a common history and ancestry, and doctrinally most of them essentially agree on the character of the "five fundamentals." Almost universally, however, they repudiate the dispensationalism of twentieth century fundamentalism, and they consider themselves to be far removed from the narrowness, closed-mindedness, and hostility of the fundamentalist spirit.

The second surprise was the level of social concern expressed in the writings of the new evangelicals. With increasing insistence they are claiming as their own the nineteenth century heritage of intense evangelical social involvement. Evangelical sociologist David Moberg has set a dominant theme in pointing to the earlier evangelical role in the abolition of slavery, prison reform, humane treatment for the mentally ill, concern with industrial conditions, and pioneering social work. Twentieth century evangelicalism's turn away from such social involvement he has labeled the "great reversal."[2] *Sojourners,* an evangelical magazine, is perhaps the most exciting social action journal in America today.

The final surprise for me was the level of openness I discovered in the literature—the willingness to enter into dialogue with liberals, the acceptance of the reality and even necessity of certain kinds of biblical criticism, and the desire to move beyond the present isolated polarization of Protestant Christianity. I found evangelical writers to be far more familiar with liberal-ecumenical books, ideas, and theology than most of us are with theirs. One cannot easily estimate how influential these new evangelical writers are with the great mass of American religious conservatives (who, I suspect, do not draw as sharp a line between fundamentalism and evangelicalism as the new evangelicals do). This openness, however, is not incompatible with what I have observed in my contacts with evangelicals in my own denomination.

All too often leaders on both sides are guarded, alert for partisan advantage, and suspicious of the concealed dagger in any outstretched hand. I recall an incident at the 1978 General Assembly of my denomination. An agonizing evangelical tried on two successive evenings to get leaders from both camps to come together simply to pray with each other; he was joined both times by the other evangelicals he had invited but found all the liberal-ecumenical leaders "tied up" by previous commitments. I recall his post-Assembly effort by mail to set up a reconciliation meeting, and the stone wall this perhaps naive but well-intentioned gesture met from the liberal-ecumenical power establishment.

My reading of the evangelicals has convinced me that mainline Protestants must venture out of intellectual isolationism and examine with care the evangelical renascence. Considerable evidence suggests it really *is* the significant religious event it has been labeled by the secular media. There is even more compelling evidence that the challenge it now poses for the mainline churches makes it impossible further to ignore it.

Understanding Protestant Polarization

For some time I have thought the most useful way of viewing Protestantism's polarization is Martin Marty's "two-party" analysis of the historic divisions of American Protestantism. The "Private Protestant" party has emphasized individual salvation and personal moral life, while the "Public Protestant" party has emphasized the social order and social destinies of humankind.[3] Sociologist Dean Hoge, in his 1976 book, *Division in the Protestant House,* marshalled impressive research evidence showing how the two parties divide along lines of social concern, with the Christian action of the former group taking private and individualistic forms, and that of the latter group taking forms directed toward changing public policy and economic and social conditions.[4]

The insistence of new evangelicals on social involvement, however—with such expressions as the Lausanne Covenant (the social dimensions of which we will examine later), organizations such as Evangelicals for Social Action, and the downright social radicalism of the Sojourners community and magazine—points to important changes. These signals from the evangelical camp, together with the genuine pietism of some of the most radically involved liberals (particularly those caught up in the charismatic movement), lead one to question whether this particular way of describing the polarization may have outlived its usefulness.

Liberal-conservative terminology has a long and useful history, but it is primarily theological and ideological in connotation. In many parts of the world, "ecumenical" and evangelical are the terms identifying the two parties, but in the United States "ecumenical" has a more limited use. Researchers Dean L. Hoge and David A. Roozen, in an important 1979 book on *Understanding Church Growth and Decline,* have sought to combine the various dimensions. They suggest that American religious groups tend to fall out along a line with two poles; one they label "liberal-pluralistic-culture affirming" and the other "conservative-disciplined-distinct from culture."[5] The dimension of social activism or quietism, which still has some relevance (particularly in identifying mainline leadership), is not included in these labels. It is, however, one of the most useful currently available analyses even though the terms are too cumbersome for frequent repetition. In the absence of any definitive terminology, the term "liberal-ecumenical" will generally be used in this book to identify one group, and "evangelical"—the term of their own choice—to identify the other.

Roots of the Polarization

While the polarization has been a prominent theme in American church history only in the last century, its roots go far deeper. Some evangelical scholars, particularly Bernard Ramm, find the basic dialectic in Puritanism and the Enlightenment, which came together to shape American thought and society at the time of the Revolution.[6] Evangelicalism's spiritual ancestry lay in the Puritan stream—that of classic orthodox biblical Christianity. The Enlightenment challenged the basis of orthodox Christian assumptions, not only in emerging America, but throughout western society. Its scientific explosion, its centering of attention on humanity rather than on divinity, its enthronement of reason, its historical and literary criticism, its skepticism about the irrational in any form, its tolerance and humanitarianism—these not only defined the issues for future religious polarization, but even more basically established the intellectual framework for western thought and scholarship ever since.[7]

Nevertheless, it was not the Enlightenment, but the biblical orthodoxy derived from the Puritan heritage as modified by revivalism which set the tone for American Protestantism during the century after the Revolution. The first Great Awakening, in the 1740s and 50s, had brought a strong Arminian flavoring into New England Calvinism; revivalism and religious determinism somehow became bedfellows. The Enlightenment had given birth to the Unitarian and Universalist movements, had brought a strain of rationalism into the biblical orthodoxy of the Puritan tradition, and had mediated influentially through Jonathan Edwards, John Witherspoon, and others, but it left the basic religious climate established by the first Great Awakening relatively untouched. Rather, the Enlightenment set the tone for *secular* America. The political "doctrine" of separation of church and state made it respectable for religious America and secular America to reflect different assumptions simultaneously accepted by the mainstream.

The second Great Awakening, in the early years of the 19th century, confirmed the evangelical character of American mainstream Christianity. Not only did it set the pattern for the revivalism accompanying the growth of the popular denominations (the future mainline) as the nation moved west; it also provided impetus toward moral reform and generated the pattern of denominational higher education and the voluntary societies which gave birth to the great nineteenth century missionary movement. It established the basic pattern for what historian Sidney Ahlstrom calls "democratic evangelicalism."[8]

The Nineteenth Century Evangelical Consensus

From a late twentieth century perspective we may regard nineteenth century Protestantism as having been far to the conservative right. Yet the evangelical consensus which followed the clash between the Enlightenment and the Puritan heritage was, for its time, the middle ground in American Christianity. Unitarianism, the direct child of the Enlightenment, occupied the liberal left, and for a while its role in American life was prominent. It gradually sank into relative obscurity far to the left of the mainstream. The separatism and absolutism of original New England Puritanism also survived in the more extremist sects on the right, but by and large Puritanism was modified not only by Enlightenment rationalism, but also by the democratic ideals which came from the Enlightenment via the patterns for civil government established by the founding fathers. The democratic evangelicalism of the nineteenth century was in this sense a synthesis of dialectical forces, a middle ground between the extremisms of left and right. With its strong social concern—its abolitionist and prison reform and temperance move-ments—it established the pattern of orthodox biblical theology combined with a vigorous social activism which has been the center in the American religious mainstream.

The nineteenth century evangelical consensus endured until well past the Civil War. It established the character and set the tone for the "Righteous Empire," to use Martin Marty's term for the Protestant experience in America.[9] The antithetical forces which ultimately broke up the consensus began to be strongly felt as the century drew to a close. Some of these forces were clearly secular. Darwinian biology revolutionized the scientific view of humankind. The robber barons of the guilded age transformed American capitalism, while the plight of industrial workers and agrarian populism set up a social polarization. In this context, one of the most important developments of the late nineteenth century was the rise of the Social Gospel movement. The native origins of the movement lay in the abolition of slavery and the other social changes brought into being by nineteenth century evangelicalism. Social concern was nothing new, but the liberal German theologians—espe-cially Ritschl and Harnack, as their influence filtered into America—focused attention on this world rather than the next and provided an optimistic utopianism undergirding the vision of establishing the Kingdom of God on earth. Industrialization and urbanization provided fresh challenges. Marxism was loose in the world. Christian Socialism from Britain had its effect. Ahlstrom labels the late nineteenth century the "golden age of liberal theology."[10] By the end of the century the Social Gospel was a well-established minority movement with theological liberalism undergird-ing its challenge to the still dominant evangelical consensus.

One factor well understood by historians of American higher education and intellectual climate, but sometimes overlooked by church historians, is the transformation of American higher education in the latter part of the nineteenth century. Higher education until that time had been dominated by denominational colleges. State colleges and universities had certainly been present, as had teacher-training institutions and agricultural and vocational schools, but ever since the founding of Harvard College (based on medieval models) by New England Purtians, the dominant pattern had been set by the church-related colleges. The rest were collateral. The opening of the west had been accompanied by the establishment of denominational colleges all across the continent in the train of the pioneers. Their atmosphere was religious, the curriculum Bible-centered, and their intellectual climate not only reflected, but also maintained, the consensus of nineteenth century democratic evangelicalism.

In the latter part of the century, however, the German secular university provided the model for an educational revolution. Importing this model,

Johns Hopkins, the University of Chicago and Harvard forged a new pattern which spread rapidly. In a remarkably short time it came to dominate American higher education. Even in the denominational colleges which continued to flourish—as, of course, most of them did—the secular scientific world view of the German university increasingly challenged the biblical evangelicalism they had fostered. Denominational colleges trained the clergy and nurtured the world view of church people, just as American institutions of higher education generally set the nation's intellectual climate. It is a supportable hypothesis, then, that the revolution in higher education, as much as the Social Gospel movement or any other single factor, set the stage for the breakup of the nineteenth century evangelical consensus.

Early Twentieth Century Polarization

Dialectical forces create their own antitheses. The development of the Social Gospel movement and the establishment of scientific humanism as the dominant intellectual climate were matched by growing identification of conservative Christianity with the "American way" of unrestrained laissez-faire capitalism.[11] This was accompanied by a withdrawal of conservative Christians from the kind of social involvement which had earlier espoused the cause of the industrial masses. The "Princeton theology," expounded for half a century by Charles Hodge, became the mainstay of scholarly conservatism. Benjamin Warfield made it even more rigid as the century drew to a close. Elsewhere, at less scholarly levels, dispensationalist premillennialism was a growing influence.

Several events at the end of the first decade of the twentieth century symbolized the battle lines now drawn in a strongly polarized American Protestanism. Walter Rauschenbusch's *Christianity and the Social Crisis,* published in 1907, marked the apogee of the Social Gospel movement. The establishment of the Federal Council of Churches in 1908, followed shortly by the issuance of the "Social Creed of the Churches" as one of its first acts, revealed the inclination in many of the mainline denominations. 1909, however, brought publication of the first edition of the dispensationalist Scofield Reference Bible—one of the most influential books ever published—which became the study text of generations of fundamentalists. 1910 also brought the initial publication of *The Fundamentals,* ten small volumes originating in the Moody Bible Institute and laying down the fundamentalist gauntlet.

The climax of the fundamentalist-modernist controversy came in the mid-twenties. The Scopes Monkey Trial in Dayton, Tennessee, pitted secular-scientific Clarence Darrow against fundamentalist William Jennings Bryan, providing the prototype media event for a pre-electronic age. The fundamentalists lost far more than the legal point at stake in the trial.

The future for the fundamentalist faction, which had failed in its bid for control of mainline Protestantism, took two directions. One focal point of fundamentalist activity was to be small separatist denominations. The pattern of denominational fragmentation had been set earlier; indeed, it was probably inherent in Protestantism, the Anabaptist sects of the Reformation being the antecedents. The Holiness movement had developed in Methodism in the latter part of the nineteenth century, and by the 1890s rejection by mainline Methodism had made it a separate movement. The beginning of Pentecostalism is usually dated from events at Bethel Bible College in Topeka, Kansas, in 1900 and 1901. Pentecostalism, too, was rejected by mainline Protestantism. The Church of the Nazarene came into existence in 1908 with the uniting of certain pentecostal and holiness groups. The Assemblies of God, formed in 1914, brought together a number of independent Pentecostal churches. More staid and rationalist orthodox extremists also began taking a separatist route. A signal event was the resignation of J. Gresham Machen from the Princeton Seminary faculty in 1929 to found the ultra-orthodox Westminster Theological Seminary. In 1936 he was expelled from the Presbyterian Church, USA, and out of his movement came the separatist Orthodox Presbyterian and Bible Presbyterian Churches. Out of the separatist faction of the Disciples of Christ came the Churches of Christ. The General Association of Regular Baptists broke off from the liberal mainline American Baptist Convention in 1932, and the Conservative Baptist Association broke off in 1947.

A second outcome of the fundamentalist-modernist controversy which provided another focal point for ultra-conservative Christianity was the development of a non-denominational conservative movement, the independent Bible Colleges providing its original base. The impulse behind these colleges had been the interdenominational Sunday School and missionary movements of nineteenth century evangelicalism. The first of them, Nyack Missionary College, had been established to train missionaries. The origins of the Moody Bible Institute had been related to the interdenominational Christian Education work of the Sunday School Union. Many others were founded during the period of the fundamentalist-modernist controversy to train missionaries and evangelists. Dispensational premillennialism provided a common body of theory. It was this educational network, together with the small separatist conservative denominations, which became the locus of fundamentalist leadership. Non-denominational seminaries and a number of independent parachurch organizations gradually followed the Bible colleges and expanded the institutional base of transdenominational (one is tempted to say "ecumenical," but the implication is wrong) fundamentalism.

Of course, large numbers of conservatives remained inside the mainline denominations. Many local congregations were distinctively evangelical, even though denominational leadership was not. After the early part of the twentieth century, following the fundamentalist-modernist controversy, the center of radical evangelicalism had moved *outside* the mainline denominations to the separatist denominations and the non-denominational institutions. Thus isolated, it became increasingly rigid, factious and divisive. With some exceptions (such as the Salvation Army) it turned its back on social concern, regarding the gospel as exclusively "spiritual."

The Neo-Evangelical Movement

The extremes of separatism and dispensationalism, the strident anti-intellectualism, the belligerent defensiveness, and the isolation from the contemporary world, however, began in time to make the more moderate among the conservatives uncomfortable. Some of the small new denominations began to follow the classic sociological route from sect to denomination, from social marginality to respectability. Growth led to organizational sophistication. Seminaries, and even Bible Colleges, needed accreditation to satisfy an upwardly mobile constituency. Inexorably, countervailing forces began to be felt, and the new evangelicals began both to transform and to distinguish themselves from separatist, anti-intellectual, dispensationalist fundamentalism.

Use of the term "evangelical" shows this distinction. Evangelicalism as a self-conscious movement developed very gradually. In 1942, under the leadership of Harold J. Ockenga and others, the National Association of Evangelicals was formed. Approximately 150 delegates, representing 40 denominations, met that year in St. Louis to launch a movement seen as a middle ground between the fundamentalist and separatist American Association of Christian Churches on the right, and the liberal and ecumenical National Council of Churches on the left. Fuller Theological Seminary was founded in 1947 by persons associated with the same movment and was funded by Charles E. Fuller of the radio Old Fashioned Revival Hour. Ockenga became the first president, and under his guidance the seminary quickly moved into a position of leadership in developing evangelicalism. In 1956, *Christianity Today* was established as an evangelical counterpart to the *Christian Century* and became the movement's voice. Carl F. H. Henry, its editor, had called as early as the forties for a commitment to evangelical scholarship and a recovery of evangelical social concern. Evangelical scholarship began to dispel the anti-intellectual image, and seminaries such as Fuller and Gordon-Conwell, together with colleges like Wheaton, Gordon and Westmont, acquired full accreditation. By the mid-seventies a group of "young evangelicals" was deeply involved in social change activism. *Sojourners* magazine became one of their voices, while *The Other Side* and *The Reformed Journal* were also increasingly influential.

The line between evangelicals and fundamentalists is not as clear to mainline Protestants as it is to the new evangelicals themselves. Indeed, many of the sweeping claims from evangelical sources concerning the numerical strength of the movement certainly include fundamentalists within the reported totals. The term "Born Again Christians," a popularized code word for the contemporary movement—sometimes shortend to "B.A." among initiates—clearly includes both categories. [12] Evangelicalism is a wide-ranging and diverse movement; one prominent spokesman identified three major sub-groups: the fundamentalists, the charismatics, and the neo-evangelicals. [13]

Yet this distinction, at least in terms of a significantly changed emphasis, is real. Doctrinally most evangelicals probably adhere to the so-called "five fundamentals": verbal inspiration of Scripture as the Word of God; the virgin birth of Christ; substitutionary atonement; the bodily resurrection of Christ; and the second coming. There is, however, a difference of spirit; the doctrinal "fundamentals" are not generally the center of concern for new evangelicals. Their central concern, says Richard Quebedeaux, a leading commentator on evangelicals, is for a common goal of evangelizing the world for Christ, rooted in historic biblical orthodoxy. [14] Another evangelical writer, Robert Johnston, has expressed the same thing in terms of two central principles: "(1) the need for a personal relationship with God through faith in the atoning work of Jesus Christ, and (2) the sole and binding authority of the Bible as God's revelation." [15] Arthur Carl Piepkorn, in his discussion of the evangelical movement in the final volume of his major work, *Profiles in Belief,* suggests that evangelicals are united on three principles: the complete reliability and final authority of the Bible as the Word of God, the necessity of a personal faith in Jesus Christ as Savior, and the urgency of reaching out to evangelize the world for Christ. [16]

As the evangelical movement has grown, both numerically and in religious importance, divisions and controversies have arisen within it. The most important, perhaps, is the controversy over the nature of biblical authority and inspiration. [17] It retains, however, its identity and coherence as the most significant current movement in American Christianity. Its contemporary spokespersons are not the old fundamentalists, but the new evangelicals.

Characteristics of the New Evangelicalism

Presumptuous as it may be for a mainline observer to attempt to delineate the movement, there are certain themes common to the writings of most of today's new evangelicals distinguishing them from the separatist fundamentalists. From a mainline perspective, the following would seem to be the major characteristics of the new evangelicals.

1. The principle of the reliability and final authority of the Scriptures in matters of faith and practice is central for evangelicals. They are not, however,

agreed on the nature of biblical inspiration, and their differences may be critical for the movement's future. Some prefer to avoid the term "plenary." Historical criticism is accepted to some extent by many of them. There is, however, a difference in tone between the liberal and evangelical approaches to criticism. The liberal tends to approach the task from the scientific side; criticism is a given, and the liberal looks for the religious values still to be found in the Bible despite its human and historic conditioning. The evangelical approaches from the biblical side; the authority of the Scripture is given, and the question is how criticism can help to understand it.

2. Evangelicals are united in giving a central place in their concept of Christianity to personal faith in Jesus Christ as savior from sin, and to commitment to him. There is, therefore, a strong emphasis on the urgency of the conversion of sinners. "Evangelizing the world for Christ" tends to be the primary goal, and this is what the word "evangelical" means. They continue to have a strong interest in overseas mission work aimed at evangelizing those who are unreached. The Lausanne Covenant is an important statement for them.

3. They believe in sanctification conceived as a distinctively Christian life following rebirth. They are, however, less likely than fundamentalists to define that Christian life in terms of prohibitions against such things as drinking and dancing, or in terms of a traditionalist sexual code.[18]

4. Many, though not all, are deeply involved in social concerns. This is especially true of those known as the "young evangelicals."[19] Some who are not so young—and who may be quite fundamentalist in theology—see commitment to social action as the single most important difference between evangelicals and fundamentalists. Evangelicals want to combine evangelism with social action and insist on both.

5. Evangelicalism is marked by friendliness to science, which is no longer seen as the enemy. One prominent spokesman distinguishes between fundamentalism and evangelicalism in terms of the rejection by the former of the modern scientific-historical world view derived from the Enlightenment, and acceptance by the latter.[20]

6. Evangelicals insist on a rational faith and reject the anti-intellectualism of some fundamentalists. They have sought academic respectability for their version of Christianity through fostering of sound scholarship and full accreditation of colleges and seminaries. They have studied the classic liberal and neo-orthodox theologians and have found much to affirm in the writings of the latter, particularly of Barth. They have been influenced by French evangelical sociologist Jacques Ellul—who is not a biblical literalist—by Dietrich Bonhoeffer, and particularly by C. S. Lewis. They have called for evangelical attendance at seminaries like Yale, Harvard, Union and Chicago for academic prestige.[21]

7. While their attitude toward ecumenism is ambivalent, it is not the unqualified rejection of fundamentalists. Some use the term "ecumenical" as a label designating their opponents within Christianity.[22] Others seem to be drawing closer to liberals, and most are willing to enter into dialogue with them. They are not primarily interested in conciliar ecumenism, and they stress the importance of doctrinal unity for organic unions. They do, however, talk about and practice a functional ecumenism and are often deeply involved in non-institutional ecumenical undertakings.

8. New evangelicals tend to reject dispensational premillennialism, particularly the dispensationalism associated with the Scofield Reference Bible, even though Dallas and Trinity Seminaries are still influential. They do not reject the second coming of Christ.

9. Perhaps the greatest difference between evangelicals and fundamentalists is tone, style, or spirit. Evangelicals reject the narrowness, defensiveness, and extremism of fundamentalism. They reject its anti-cultural, world-denying characteristics.[23] They reflect a more open, listening, and reconciling spirit than do their fellow conservatives of the extreme right.

If the hypothesis of this book is correct—that the arena of mainline-evangelical confrontation and interaction is now the mainline churches themselves, rather than the independent colleges and seminaries and small separatist denominations "out there"—then it is important that mainliners begin to understand this new major force in Protestantism and what it bodes for the future.

chapter 3

the target:
mainline churches

On a visit to Brazil in 1977, I was startled to hear Brazilian Methodists, Presbyterians, Lutherans and Episcopalians refer to themselves as the "mainline churches." Brazil is an overwhelmingly Roman Catholic country. Even within the small Protestant minority, these groups are greatly outnumbered by Pentecostals, Baptists and Independents. They are a minority within a minority, but their self-concept reflects that of the North American denominations to which they are related by birth and tradition.

Even in the United States, "mainline" is a somewhat presumptuous and self-confident title, implying that other groups are branch lines, or less important lines. It has come into widespread use only recently, in a period when Protestantism no longer has the dominance it once enjoyed in American life, and when organized religion itself is regarded by many as a social institution of declining importance. Yet "mainline" is today the standard way of referring to a particular group of American Protestant churches. Why?

What Does "Mainline" Mean?

In the context of today's Protestantism, "mainline" means "liberal." The mainline churches are identified by distinguishing them from the conservative churches. Evangelicals who consider themselves in the mainstream of Christianity may object to this use of the term "mainline" by the liberals, just as mainliners who consider themselves evangelical may object to the use of the term "evangelical" by the conservatives. Such objections, however, do not change the fact that the term "mainline" refers today to the liberal wing of Christianity.

Mainline today also means "ecumenical." In general, mainline denominations are those that belong to the National Council of Churches, and those that make up the American membership of the World Council of Churches. Many of them are the products of unions between denominations—the *United* Presbyterian Church, the *United* Methodist Church, and the *United* Church of Christ, for instance. Some are currently engaged in negotiations or preliminary discussions about possible organic union: the United Presbyterian Church with the Presbyterian Church, U. S.; the United Church of Christ with the Disciples of Christ; the Lutheran Church in America with the American Lutheran Church. Most of them belong to the Consultation on Church Union (COCU), which looks forward to one Uniting Church at some future date. In addition to the denominations already mentioned, COCU includes the Episcopal Church, the American Baptist Churches, the Reformed Church in America, and three black Methodist churches (African Methodist Episcopal, African Methodist Episcopal Zion, and Christian Methodist Episcopal). The two Lutheran churches mentioned above are not members but are definitely mainline. The ecumenical stance is so characteristic of mainline churches that in many instances (particularly in Protestantism outside the United States) "ecumenical" is the term used by evangelical Protestants to identify "the other side."

Social activism is another way of identifying mainline churches today. Earlier we discussed Martin Marty's analysis of American Protestantism in terms of two parties, the Private Protestants and the Public Protestants. Many have found this delineation useful. Mainline churches have by and large exemplified the public party, emphasizing social change more than personal piety at least as regards visible leadership and pronouncements. Church historian James H. Smylie suggests that to discuss mainline Christianity in terms of social activism is to oversimplify. Following the decline of white Anglo-Saxon Protestant dominance and the emergence of a pluralistic society, he says, mainline Protestant bodies have been engaged in a quest for identity. As part of this process they have taken up an identity as transformers of culture.[1]

The dynamics of mainline social activism have indeed been complex. Further, the identification with mainline churches is less decisive than in the past. We have already noted that the new evangelicals and even fundamentalists are increasingly interested in social and political action, and that the "public-private" delineation previously distinguishing social activist from individualistic Christians is no longer generally applicable. Yet in terms of positions taken by *church governing bodies* and *official* pronouncements, the distinction is still useful. Social concern on the part of evangelicals still tends to be an individual or likeminded group position rather than an organizational position.

All these ways of identifying mainline churches—liberal, ecumenical, and social activist—must be used with care. Certainly the ecclesiastical machinery is largely in the control of leaders fitting this description, and this is even more true of the bureaucracies running denominational agencies. Yet the membership of the mainline churches today is not consistently liberal, ecumenical, social or activist in orientation. Quite the contrary. The membership covers the entire spectrum, and this points to another characteristic of mainline churches, perhaps the most distinctive one: their pluralism. They tend to be inclusive churches, made up of persons representing a broad range of positions—socially and economically, liturgically, and theologically.

Whether the liberal-ecumenical-social activist position of the denominational power establishment is a reflection of the views of a majority or a minority of the membership is difficult to estimate. Certainly it reflects positions taken officially by denominational governing bodies—conventions, conferences, synods, and general assemblies. The power establishment itself perceives these actions as mandates based on majority votes of representative bodies over many years. Evangelicals are likely to claim that these represent parliamentary victories brought about by the political control of the ruling establishment. In any event, at least sizeable minorities in the mainline denominations, if not the majorities the evangelicals claim, are conservative and do not sympathize with the liberal-ecumenical-social activist power establishments. This explains the well-known gap between denominational bureaucracies and the people in the pew.

Identification of the mainline churches in terms of the liberalism, the ecumenical stance, and the social concern characterizing official denominational positions, and even in terms of the pluralism of their membership, is a relatively new development. The term "mainline" suggests identification with the historical mainstream of American Protestantism. It implies something about size; the term refers to *major* denominations. It points to those denominations with roots deep in American history. The Episcopal Church, with colonial roots in the Church of England; the Presbyterian and Reformed churches, derived from Dutch and Scottish colonists; the Congregationalist and Baptist families, tracing their roots to the Independents and Puritans of the colonial period; the Methodists, of English ancestry and of frontier America; the Lutherans, tracing their ancestry to the German and Scandinavian immigrations—this is the historical mainstream. Mainstream does, however, imply more than "large" and "historical" in contemporary American Christianity. The Southern Baptist Convention; the Lutheran Church, Missouri Synod; and some of the major black Baptist groups, are certainly large denominations with deep roots in American history, but they would be omitted from many "mainline" lists. Why? Because they are strongly conservative and are not part of the ecumenical movement.

Some of the smaller denominations derived from mainline families—the Orthodox and Bible Presbyterians, the Free and Wesleyan Methodists, and numerous Baptist groups—would probably not be included in the "mainline" because of their separatism as well as their conservatism.

Clearly no conclusive definition of mainline is possible. Any denomination can include itself. A working definition of mainline, however, as the term is usually used today, would refer to the *large historical denominations having memberships reflecting great diversity, but leadership and official positions putting them generally in the liberal, ecumenically inclined and socially concerned wing of Christianity.*

Mainline as the Center Stream

The American mainline in Protestantism, like the political and social mainstream, has historically stayed reasonably close to the middle. Just as the Democrats and the Republicans are both basically centrist parties, almost indistinguishable in some respects and leaning only slightly to the left and right, so also have the mainline denominations clustered in the religious center.

As the modernist-fundamentalist controversy of the first third of the twentieth century came to an end, with the fundamentalist extremists withdrawing into small separatist denominations and independent institutions, the liberals were clearly in control in the mainline. Large numbers of conservatives, however, remained in the membership. Mainline leadership did not long remain far to the left. Reaction against the extremes of theological liberalism and the optimism of the Social Gospel took shape in Europe after the First World War, its strong theological voice being given in the work of Karl Barth and Emil Brunner. The trauma of the Second World War killed the expectation that human beings would soon establish the Kingdom of God on earth. Neo-orthodoxy became the theological undergirding of mainline Protestantism in the forties. The Niebuhr brothers, Richard and Reinhold, were perhaps most instrumental in formulating the American neo-orthodox consensus.

With its direct rejection of biblical literalism and its strong—even radical—insistence on the social as well as individual dimension of Christianity, neo-orthodoxy was no more acceptable to the fundamentalist extremists than modernism had been. For the rank and file, however, at the operative level of mainstream Protestantism, neo-orthodoxy represented a genuine return to the middle. Its biblical focus spoke to the mainline conservative, and its serious grappling with sin and salvation was at the heart of the evangelical concern. For millions of fairly orthodox Christians, the prefix "neo" was a small price to pay for being brought back into the mainstream. Lay people who were themselves biblical literalists found common ground with not-so-literalist clergy who nevertheless spoke to their basic concerns. From the perspective of the history of evangelicals and the mainstream, the significance of the neo-orthodox consensus of the forties and fifties was that it kept the majority of the evangelicals in mainline churches. They were to the right of center, true, and controversies and tensions persisted, but the center had moved close enough to them to offer a resting place.

But not for long. The neo-orthodox consensus of the middle began to break up in the sixties. Though the "death of God" in theology was taken seriously only by a few extremists, as a media event it attracted as much attention as had the Scopes Monkey trial. Denominational agency restructuring in the late sixties and early seventies gave control of denominational bureaucracies to single-minded social activists, so by the mid-seventies the consensus of the middle was a thing of the past.

A number of contemporary writers—among them Dean Hoge and Martin Marty—have said that the "collapse of the middle" is characteristic of the present American religious climate. Marty has suggested that this disappearance of the middle has particularly serious consequences in a pluralistic culture;[2] and in such a climate, the moderate evangelicals of the mainline have become increasingly restive—indeed angry.

The decidedly liberal-ecumenical character of mainline church leadership today may mean one of two things. The center for American Protestant Christianity may have moved permanently in a more liberal direction. The other possibility is that today's liberal stance is a temporary swing of the theological pendulum, and that a swing back toward the center is likely in the future. The outcome of the growing evangelical challenge to the liberal domination of mainline Protestantism may well determine which of these two possibilities is the direction of the future.

Historically, the mainline middle has been considerably more conservative theologically than is today's mainline. The nineteenth century mainline consensus was an evangelical consensus. Diversity was certainly present in nineteenth century Protestantism, but the differences were more likely to be found *between* than *within* denominations. The pattern of denominationalism has been American Protestantism's way of handling pluralism. Every mainline denomination was at one time a breakaway group founded as an expression of religious diversity. In the classic pattern, each of these denominations was relatively homogeneous internally. Denominational mainline Protestantism as a whole was pluralistic, but each of the denominations was internally a consensus group. They recognized the legitimacy of the others, cooperated to some extent, and got along reasonably well with each other; but each insisted on its own distinctiveness.

The differences between the denominations reflected not only national origins, but also the various Arminian, Calvinistic, Lutheran, or Anabaptist traditions. They reflected a wide range of liturgical preferences as well as class and educational differences (although all the mainline denominations tended to exhibit middle class status by the end of the nineteenth century), but few of them strayed far from the classic mainstream of orthodox Protestant theology. The so-called "five fundamentals" of the early twentieth century fundamentalist controversy would not even have been debated in most of mainline Protestantism prior to the late nineteenth century; they were taken for granted. In spite of the traditional, liturgical, educational, and social class pluralism—expressed in differences between denominations—enough common ground existed for revivalist movements, the foreign mission movement, and the Sunday School movement to sweep through all of them on a non-denominational basis.

Late Twentieth Century Developments

Some internal pluralism has always been part of each denomination in the Protestant pattern, as evidenced by the long history of controversies, splits and reunions. Overall, however, an internal denominational consensus was the normative pattern until this century. The change from pluralism *between* denominations to an acceptance of pluralism *within* denominations may have been a product of the accelerated pace of trends and changes characterizing the twentieth century. The rapidity with which major change takes place—the "collapse of time"—has become a truism of twentieth century social analysis. The neo-orthodoxy of mid-century, representing a return to the middle for mainline Protestantism after the polarlization of the early decades, lasted a scant quarter-century. The radical theologies of the sixties came and went with bewildering rapidity. None of the liberation theologies of the seventies appears likely to last long. They have, however, become symbols of the radical polarization which has returned to nearly all the mainline denominations.

Another twentieth century movement which has deeply affected the mainline churches is the managerial revolution. The effect of this pervasive and far-reaching change in church organizations is only now beginning to be analyzed.[3] The managerial revolution has in various ways affected all churches, liberal and conservative, ecumenical and separatist, large and small. The effect on the pluralistic mainline churches, however, has in certain respects been quite different from that on consensus churches, which (whether large or small) reflect general agreement among the membership.

The most obvious effect of the managerial revolution is bureaucratization. This, of course, is true not only of churches but of all social institutions. In a technological society, institutions are bureaucratically organized, and professional experts—who have mastered the various mechanical, scientific, and cybernetic technologies of the age—are in charge. The class of professional experts who have mastered the most critical technology of all—the technology of handling other people and thus running the organizations of the society—are the managers, the new elites. The managers are professional experts in the exercise of power and control. In an earlier age, power and control were the haphazard result of instinct, ambition, competitiveness, common sense, and good luck. In a technological society, power and control have become a science—"behavioral science"—and this science provides the basis for management.

This combination of bureaucratic organization and managerial expertise has entered the churches gradually, its effects being felt most strongly in the post-World War II period. The wave of organizational restructuring which swept through the mainline denominations in the late sixties and early seventies probably marked the final triumph of the managerial revolution in church organizational structures. Present church agency organizations are made to order for managers.

The significance of this for our present purposes—in the context of the mainline-evangelical confrontation—lies in the opportunity it has given the liberal-ecumenical faction in the mainline churches to acquire and maintain control over church organizational structures. There has been nothing sinister about it. Battles for control are not new, and growing bureaucratic organization has probably been inevitable. The tools of behavioral science have been available to anyone who acquired the expertise to master them, but the liberal-ecumenicals—perhaps because they are by inclination more alert to the new, open to the secular world, and inclined to respect science in any form—have become the skilled process managers, strategy planners, and agents of change. This is no doubt only one of many reasons they are now the power establishment in mainline church organizations, but it *is* probably *one* reason.

A second effect of the managerial revolution comes from the organizational studies accompanying and informing it. Churches, whatever else they may be, are clearly organizations. As such, they have sought to understand themselves as organizations and to seek the help of organizational experts in dealing with a multitude of organizational problems. Contemporary experts all start from one basic assumption: organizations are social units or human groupings created to achieve particular goals.[4] So universal is the goal-seeking paradigm that it is not even questioned in organizational studies. The result is that managers and their consultants focus on organizational goals and how to achieve them.

Well and good. Churches, however, are unique organizations, and have not historically been associated with goal-seeking. They have been perceived as *being* the people of God—as being a response to God's action rather than goal oriented. They can be explained partly in terms of human dynamics, but must also be explained in terms of the unique and extraordinary presence of the Holy Spirit.

One can no doubt think of churches as goal oriented, and these days we usually do. The simultaneous subtle change in frame of reference, however, may once again be significant for our present concern—the current mainline-evangelical confrontation. The application of the organizational, goal-seeking paradigm to our thinking about the church has tended to make us associate the church with its social goals. If its effect on society is worthwhile, the church is worthwhile; if not, the church is not.

This kind of thinking is far more in accord with the social activism of the liberal-ecumenical frame of reference than that of the evangelicals. It encourages us to approach the church in terms of social goals. Social goals are not uniquely liberal. We have noted earlier that social concern had a prominent place in nineteenth century evangelicalism. The social activism of Christians in earlier periods, however, has been an activism of individual Christians responding to the claims of the gospel upon them. When individual Christians have banded themselves together to achieve social goals, they have formed special organizations. Whether inside (as in the case of Roman Catholic religious orders) or outside the church (as in the case of nineteenth century abolitionist societies), these organizations have been distinct from the official organization of the churches themselves.

The managerial revolution has led us to think of church structures in terms of goal-achievement. The capture of these church organizational structures by the liberal-ecumenical faction for the purpose of achieving particular social goals has been its legacy. The managerial revolution has helped this faction consolidate and maintain its power.

The Present Disarray

Mainline Protestantism today is in a serious state of disarray. These large, historic American denominations—liberal, ecumenical, and socially concerned, with their pluralistic membership and activist power establishments—are clearly in trouble. Almost without exception they have been declining in membership. This was the case all through the decade of the seventies, and it is still the case today. Their declining rolls were preceded by even more radical declines in church school enrollment, baptisms, and professions of faith. Virtually all are trying to cope with massive funding changes. Contributions from the membership for denominational programs have declined so radically that they have been forced—many of them repeatedly—to cut back, reduce their commitments, and slash the size of their bureaucracies. They have been faced with a loss of interest in denominational affairs and with growing localism and regionalism diverting not only money, but also attention. The "connectionalism" holding them together appears to be disintegrating.

There are many reasons for these trends, and some of them, certainly, are entirely beyond church control. They reflect trends and changes in the entire society. Hoge and Roozen, in their research on denominational membership changes, have found that at least half the mainline numerical decline—and perhaps as much as ninety percent—is a result of "contextual factors": demographic changes, socio-economic conditions, social trends.[5] Fiscal starvation of denominational agencies is at least partially a product of localism. Healthy involvement of congregations in local mission consumes a larger share of congregational benevolences than before. Declining trust and interest in denominational programs is at least partially related to a parallel decline in trust and interest in major social institutions in secular and political life.

Yet we cannot blame it all on society. Neither can we—in the short run at least—do much to change the contextual factors. We must simply live with them. We must look at factors within the churches themselves for solutions. From that perspective, this book suggests that in important respects the mainline crisis today can best be understood in terms of the challenge of a renascent evangelicalism.

In the next section we shall examine from this perspective a series of "crisis points." One is the swing to evangelicalism of mainline young people. Another is the striking growth of evangelical parachurch organizations both inside and outside mainline churches. A third is the crisis in the overseas misson movement. A fourth is the charismatic movement inside and outside mainline churches. Another is the membership crisis reflected in the evangelism controversy and the Church Growth movement. Finally we shall look at the deterioration of denominational cohesiveness. Each of these directs our attention to the impact of the evangelical renascence on the mainline churches—both as a source and as an outcome of the crisis. In the final section we shall look at the options before mainline Protestant churches as they face the future and at practical ways in which mainline congregations can cope with the evangelical challenge.

part two

contemporary mainline crisis points

chapter 4

where have all
the young folks gone?
the mainline youth vacuum

The dinner party included the cream of the liberal establishment of a mainline Protestant denomination. Present were two professors from a nearby seminary, three denominational executives, and the president of a church-related liberal arts college, all with spouses. Most were Democrats. They were appropriately committed to massive governmental programs to solve social problems, and to church involvement in the process. They were concerned about world hunger. They shared an intellectual commitment to a simpler lifestyle ("live simply that others may simply live") and had somewhat guilty consciences about their own affluence. They deplored the exploitation of third world countries by multinational corporations and generally approved various liberation theologies. They staunchly supported the ecumenical Christian Education literature ("Christian Education: Shared Approaches") for which one of the executives had a considerable measure of responsibility, and were appalled by the findings of a recent survey that nearly half the churches in the denomination were rejecting it, preferring David C. Cook or Gospel Light. They were scornful of the neanderthals in the denomination who accused the World Council of Churches of fostering Marxist movements. They deplored the narrowness of the group of evangelicals now in control of the Student Christian Association on the college president's campus, and the lack of interest in religion on the part of the majority of students. They shared the frustration of the seminary professors at having to cope with the increasing conservatism of each incoming class, and laughed as one of them jested that they seemed to be training the future leadership of the Orthodox Presbyterians and the Conservative Baptists.

Then the hostess got a telephone call from her teenage son, who was attending a meeting of Young Life. The conversation turned to Young Life and the fine young man who headed up the program in the local high school. The host couple had two children involved, and they were delighted with what was happening. Another couple—one of the seminary professors and his wife—reported that their two sons were also deeply involved in Young Life in another high school in the city. They, too, were pleased with it; the wife wondered with pardonable pride how many mothers had sent two sons off to summer football camp with their Bibles packed on top of their sleeping bags.

One of the denominational executives began to talk about the lack of content at the parish youth fellowship his children attended; it seemed largely recreational. Another deplored his inability to get his children to participate in his congregation's youth program at all, although he admitted it was so inconsequential and poorly attended that he couldn't blame them. He recalled the significance of his own church youth group experience, the familiarity with the Bible that came out of his Sunday School attendance, and the spiritual intensity of his adolescent religious experience. He frankly—and sadly—saw nothing in his family's parish that could provide anything similar for his own children. And he wished his kids would join Young Life!

What Has Happened to Mainline Youth Programs? The Sixties Roots

These were leading liberal establishmentarians. Nothing could more vividly portray the youth dilemma in the mainline denominations than their conversation. Where have all the young folks gone? Primarily to Young Life or to Youth for Christ; to Campus Crusade, Inter-Varsity Christian Fellowship, or to the Sunday evening program of a nearby Southern Baptist church. Or nowhere. Mainline Protestant parish youth programs—with some notable exceptions—are moribund. Mainline campus ministries play to empty halls. Mainline denominational youth ministry bureaucrats, by and large, are still hooked on the greening of America.

This is our heritage from the sixties. Nowhere in American society did the youth counterculture values of that decade receive a more sympathetic hearing than in mainline churches. And for understandable reasons. The idealism, the activist involvement, the commitment to radical change—all these the mainline applauded. Along with *The Graduate,* thoughtful avant-garde Christians in those days were rejecting the "Mrs. Robinsons" they found in their own institution. We marched alongside the counterculture in the civil rights movement and the anti-Vietnam War movement. We had a common cause. Draft card burnings nearly always featured a William Sloane Coffin or a Dan Berrigan right up in front of the TV cameras. The rising young liberal-ecumenical leadership of the period espoused protest and rejected "establishment values." Youth was the "cutting edge." Countless religious retreats plumbed the theological profundity of Beatles songs (especially *Sgt. Pepper's Lonely Hearts Club Band,* the tunes of which can still bring on an attack of acute nostalgia for anyone who, like myself, was working with young adults during that period!) Countless church youth groups listened to or performed "Jesus Christ, Superstar." A lingering image of the sixties is the middle-aged clergyman with long graying hair, guitar, and denim jacket, striving desperately to "relate" to youth.

Many of today's mainline denominational executives cut their teeth on the counterculture. Radical protest was the norm of their formative years. Today they find a newer generation of young people—success-oriented, non-protesting, with traditional values—baffling and unsettling. Many associate pastors and youth ministers in charge of youth programs in local churches are themselves products of the high schools, colleges, and seminaries of that period.

Another major influence on their own spiritual formation was the human relations movement, which also reached its peak in the sixties and early seventies. Its groupiness, its "touchy-feely" games, its self-discovery and affirmation, its simulation and trust-building exercises—these were the "methodologies" of the period. The fact that they were all methodology and no theology seemed irrelevant at the time. It was a compliment in human relations circles to be called "process oriented," an insult to be called "content oriented."

Mainline Youth Work Today

The above picture may be overdrawn, but it is accurate enough in many respects to describe current youth work in mainline denominations. The counterculture is dead—except as the context for denominational youth programs. Campus ministry in particular has provided a last bastion. Mainline campus ministries, often isolated from parish life and accountable only to ecumenical bureaucracies far removed from and independent of either university administration or the people in the pew, are still trying to fan the embers of radical protest. Local church youth groups are too often still playing trust games or engaging in "value clarification."

Mainline denominational constituencies are deeply concerned. They know the youth vacuum is there. Statistical studies of their membership losses show the biggest factor to be the decline in the number of young people.[1] So dramatic has been the decline in youthful members that the United Church of Christ, for example, now has an average membership age of 57 and a median age of 50.[2] One self-described "middle-aged, (upper) middle-class, white, liberal, Protestant parent," writing about the college students her generation of "genteel Christians" has produced, put it this way:

> They had participated little in any organization which might have demanded loyalty or submission of one's own agenda for the achievement of a whole greater than the sum of its parts. . . . A few had had some competitive team-sports background; even fewer had had a vital church youth-group experience. Mostly their earlier lives had consisted of school, a few family rituals (Christmas, Easter and birthdays) and television.[3]

Church members, by and large, do not understand what is wrong with youth programs in their congregations and are not sure what should be done to fill the vacuum. They know, however, that the vacuum is there, and they want something done about it. My own denomination provides an illustration. The Presbyterian Church, U. S., like all mainline churches, has been going through a period of budget-cutting and belt-tightening by its national boards and agencies as contributions to denominational programs have declined. The Office of Review and Evaluation, which I head, has been directed by our General Assembly to review all programs on a continuing basis and to make recommendations as to which of them might be cut back or discontinued. One criterion we have used is that of duplication with work done at regional and local levels. On this basis we made such a recommendation a few years ago concerning denominational youth programs. We pointed out that youth work was near the top of membership priorities in every constituency survey we had conducted, but we concluded that the priority should be expressed locally. We noted that youth work is necessarily done in the local church, that most presbyteries provide youth work resources and coordination, that plenty of materials are available from a wide range of publishers and bookstores, and that the denominational youth office was not doing much anyway; so we recommended that youth work be phased down nationally and left largely to the presbyteries.

Even before the General Assembly met to act on our recommendation, we began to realize we had opened up a hornet's nest. People who had never heard of the Office of Review and Evaluation were up in arms at the idea of the denomination deemphasizing youth work. When the Assembly met, it soundly rapped our knuckles, letting us know that whatever else might be dropped in the funding crisis, youth work would not be.

We got the message, and in the next year's program evaluation we sought to act accordingly. Constituency surveys had indicated that while church members ranked the denominational youth program high in importance, they ranked it quite low in effectiveness. What could be done to make it more effective? A new survey sought to pin down the kind of youth work Presbyterians wanted. Did they want a standardized program across the denomination? Did they want something like Youth for Christ or Campus

Crusade? No clear guidance emerged. The people in the pew really did not know the answer; they just knew they wanted a strong denominational youth program, and they wanted it badly.[4]

Fortunately, the Holy Spirit often has answers when evaluators and planners do not. The early eighties saw a spontaneous movement among many mainliners recalling an earlier pattern: the reemergence of Youth Councils, Youth Rallies in local areas, and a growing call for denominational resources and for Christian content—not just methodology—in such resources. Whether this will prompt a genuine recovery of mainline youth programs remains to be seen, but early signs are hopeful.

Whatever the answer for mainline churches may be, many young people have waited neither for their parents, for the young associate ministers who run the programs in their parishes, nor for their denominational bureaucracies. They have found their own answer outside the mainline churches. One dimension of the youth counterculture of the sixties and seventies which received a great deal of attention in the press but very little in the mainline churches was the "Jesus People." Jesus freaks, they sometimes called themselves; and to mainliners, freaks they were. Considering, however, the inclination of today's religious young people, the Jesus people won. The secular counterculture is dead, but the Jesus movement is alive and well in the evangelical, non-denominational youth movements.

Evangelical Youth Movements

Most of the major evangelical youth movements predate the sixties, but their greatest impact on mainline young people has come since then. Bible study is their stock-in-trade. They work through young, attractive, dedicated, full-time staff workers who are often required to raise their own salaries. In contrast to moribund mainline denominational youth programs, they are flourishing.

Youth for Christ

At the high school level, the largest of the evangelical movements is Youth for Christ. Founded in 1944, this movement has been associated with Billy Graham, who was its first full-time worker. A worldwide organization, it has branches in thirty-nine countries, operates campus-oriented evangelistic teen clubs at well over a thousand American high schools, publishes *Campus Life*—a slick, attractive evangelical magazine for teenagers—and also provides programs for delinquents and troubled urban teenagers through its "Youth Guidance" operation. Its more than one thousand full-time staff workers have all completed college as well as a one year training program.

Young Life

Even older is Young Life, founded by a Presbyterian minister in Texas in 1941, and now headquartered in Colorado Springs. Like Youth for Christ, it is a high school (and sometimes junior high) movement, with about eleven hundred clubs that "come together for fun, fellowship, singing and a talk by the leader in comfortable everyday language about Jesus Christ and His reality in today's struggles." Its nearly 500 full-time field staffers are college graduates trained in Young Life's own Leadership Institute. Jeb Magruder, who like Chuck Colson had been converted to evangelical Christianity following Watergate and his prison experiences, joined its national administrative staff. In addition to its high school clubs, Young Life operates weekend and summer camps at centers throughout the United States. It has recently added an Urban Young Life operation for inner city teenagers—mostly blacks—with emphasis on justice and jobs as well as its usual spiritual concerns.

Campus Crusade for Christ

Campus Crusade is by far the largest and most aggressive of the evangelical youth organizations. Probably the most conspicuous Christian organization on college and university campuses, it has branched out into several other specialized youth and young adult ministries such as its high school branch—which operates both in schools and in local churches, an extensive ministry to young adults in the American armed forces all over the world and an organization of Christian athletes. It provides a ministry to international students in the United States and trains nationals from other countries to work among their own people. Its Agape movement is a two-year Christian peace corps.

In addition to these extensive youth activities, Campus Crusade has broadened its area of concern in recent years. Its intercultural ministry, which trains minority persons to reach their own people with the Gospel, is actively concerned with social justice issues. Its prison ministry not only works with persons in penal institutions, but also assists parolees and their families with readjustment. It has a special outreach to persons in positions of leadership, and its "Christian Embassy" in Washington is a link to governmental leaders. Aggressive evangelism is the heart of all its activity. Its best known and most controversial attempt at mass evangelism was the "I Found It!" campaign— "Here's Life, America!"—which began in 1975. Huge numbers of Americans were exposed to this campaign, and millions of telephone and personal contacts were made. The campaign brought Campus Crusade into closer cooperation with local churches than is its usual style, and although statistical studies suggest that the "I Found It" effort was not particularly effective in terms of actual church membership increase,[5] the vigor and impact of the organization are undeniable.

Campus Crusade for Christ was founded in 1951 by Bill Bright, an ex-businessman who, with his wife, Vonette, still directs its extensive activities from its multi-million dollar headquarters in Arrowhead Springs,

California. Begun as a student ministry at the University of California in Los Angeles, its backbone is still work with students and young people. It has sixty-four hundred staff members (including those in foreign affiliated ministries) working in 84 countries. Most of them are young and they must raise their own support. The evangelistic approach is highly standardized and, from a mainline perspective, somewhat simplistic. It focuses on the "Four Spiritual Laws," with the Bible as reference, and encouragement to "receive Christ" immediately. The convert is enrolled in a follow-up program of Bible study and encouraged to join a church.

Inter-Varsity Christian Fellowship

Inter-Varsity Christian Fellowship is far older than Campus Crusade, being an outgrowth of Inter-Varsity Fellowship (now Universities and Colleges Christian Fellowship) in England, which dates back to the nineteenth century. Its chapters meet weekly for Bible Study, prayer and fellowship on over 800 American campuses. Although student-controlled, IVCF does have staffers, who—like those of Campus Crusade—must support themselves. Its style of evangelism is lower key than that of Campus Crusade and considerably less aggressive. Its lifestyle expectations are less legalistic, and it leans more to the evangelical left (particularly as regards social concerns) than Campus Crusade, which tends to be identified with the more conservative views of Bill Bright. It publishes *His* magazine; and the InterVarsity Press in Downers Grove, Illinois is a major publisher of both popular and scholarly evangelical books. Related to Inter-Varsity is the Theological Students Fellowship, which has provided a support system for evangelicals in liberal interdenominational or denominational seminaries.

Inter-Varsity is well known for its triennial Urbanna (University of Illinois) missionary conventions. Top evangelical leaders from all over the world are brought to Urbanna as speakers, and the focus is on encouraging students to consider mission work as a vocation. All of the more than 18,300 spaces for attendance at Urbanna '79 were filled two months before the convention began. Speakers included Billy Graham, British leader John R. W. Stott, and others. Inter-Varsity committed itself at Urbanna '79 to motivate at least one thousand young persons a year to enter overseas missionary service for the next five years. The majority of attendants were from mainline churches, the largest single group being United Presbyterians with 1,104 delegates.[6]

Inter-Varsity Christian Fellowship is less rigid and standardized than Campus Crusade, and its chapters vary considerably, both culturally and theologically, on different campuses and in different regions.

The Navigators

Another predominatly youth-oriented organization is The Navigators, which originated as a movement among enlisted men in the Navy during the

Second World War. In the postwar period, when the peacetime draft and large military establishment of the Cold War era brought millions of young people into the armed forces on a continuing basis, it spread to the other American military services and to bases all over the world. We sometimes forget how many young people in our times, even with a reduced military, still find their formative experience in the armed services. Only the colleges have a larger number of alumni.

My own experience with the Navigators as a Navy chaplain for nearly thirty years was quite positive. I seldom went aboard a ship or station without finding a small group of sailors meeting regularly for Bible Study and mutual support. Both Navigator groups and staff members showed eagerness to support and work with chaplains of all denominations when possible (although their cooperation was not always welcomed by non-evangelical chaplains).

In recent years, Navigators has expanded its ministry beyond the armed forces to other young adult communities, primarily college campuses. Its full-time staff, in 1979, was about fourteen hundred. Staff members, mostly former service personnel who have received intensive training, are required to secure their own support from individuals and churches, and a portion of that income goes to cover the expenses of the Colorado Springs headquarters operation. A monthly magazine, *Navalog*, is published. The stationing of American military personnel around the world in the period since World War II accounts for the rapid global spread of the Navigators ministry.

Fellowship of Christian Athletes

The Fellowship of Christian Athletes bands athletes and coaches together to influence young people. With a staff of about 120, it sponsors high school "Huddles" and college "Fellowships." Coaches' clinics, rallies and banquets are all widely used in a ministry aimed basically at personal evangelism. A monthly magazine, *The Christian Athlete*, is published for the approximately fifty thousand members, ranging from junior high school through professional sports. In 1979 there were 169 Junior High Huddles, 1,538 Senior High Huddles, and 222 College Fellowships. Other activities include work with disadvantaged young people and a witness to military personnel. While I was touring Army bases in Europe for a special project in 1975, my itinerary happened to overlap at several points with that of a well-known professional football player representing the Fellowship of Christian Athletes. His tour had been arranged by the Army chaplaincy. I attended and observed some of his meetings with young soldiers and was strongly impressed both by the appeal of a well-known athlete to the young men and by the positive impact of his witness.[7]

Others

Although these are the best known, they are by no means the only evangelical youth and young adult movements. The evangelical counterpart of Navigators for officers is the Officer Christian Union, which has members of all ages but appeals especially to young officers. It conducts particularly active programs on the campuses of the military and naval academies.

Youth Specialties trains and provides resources for youth workers. Its bi-monthly magazine expressing evangelical social concerns, the *Wittenburg Door,* has a wide circulation.

The Maranatha Christian Fellowship, an aggressive evangelistic group, is an outgrowth of a youth revival held in Paducah, Kentucky, in 1972. It focuses primarily (though not exclusively) on college students. Organized into local "churches," it verges on the cultic.

Teen Challenge, established in the sixties by Pentecostal Dave Wilkerson following publication of his successful book, *The Cross and the Switchblade,* works with teenage drug addicts. Collectively, the independent evangelical youth organizations are the most significant and influential Christian youth movement in contemporary American society.

Christian Academies and Colleges

Influence of the evangelical youth organizations is reinforced from other sources. My young teenage daughter reported recently that she "can't stand" one girl in her Sunday School class whose one-upsmanship consists of frequent reminders in class discussions that, "Of course, *I* go to a Christian school." The Christian Academies found in most cities are almost without exception evangelical, frequently representing the fundamentalist wing of evangelicalism. They are sometimes operated by conservative congregations and are sometimes independent. Throughout the South, many of them originated as thinly-veiled segregation academies during the upheavals following the Supreme Court public school desegregation decisions. Governmental pressure—largely financial—has since moderated this dimension, and few now explicitly exclude racial minorities; indeed many actively recruit them.

The more recent proliferation of Christian academies, beginning in the late seventies and still continuing, has not been racially motivated. Some upwardly mobile black families find them the only available alternative to substandard public schools. At the end of the seventies, between seven and eight hundred new private Christian elementary or high schools were being launched each year. More than five-and-a-half million students are currently enrolled in private elementary and secondary schools, two-thirds of them in Christian schools.[8]

Many have sought alternatives because of what is widely perceived as a decline in the public school system: the emphasis on social goals; the "professionalization" of the educational establishment; the succession of educational fads—"progressive schools," "whole-child" and "child-centered" emphases, "existential" education, "open classrooms"; the demise of discipline; and the widely-documented decline in standard achievement scores. The traditional upper class private schools are largely for the rich. The Christian academies, which do frequently have higher academic standards than public schools, have provided the only real alternative for the not-so-rich, including many liberal mainliners. As Lyle Schaller has pointed out, the Christian schools pose a dilemma for mainline churches. "Will the Methodist, Presbyterian, United Church of Christ, Christian (Disciples of Christ), Episcopal, Brethren, Southern Baptist, Nazarene, American Baptist, Moravian and Mennonite denominational leaders come out in support of Christian day schools in their denominations," he asks, "or will they leave that alternative to a relatively small number of denominations representing the more conservative end of the theological spectrum?" [9]

The evangelical colleges continue the same educational influences at a higher level. Schaller suggests (on the basis of research) that for Christians interested in influencing the development of future adults, the best investment of scarce financial resources is in elementary and secondary schools rather than colleges. Yet the colleges are numerous and flourishing. Wheaton and Gordon have been the best known of the non-denominational evangelical colleges, but there are many others as well. Unlike the Christian academies, to which many children are sent for reasons unrelated to the evangelical orientation—discipline and academic emphasis—the evangelical colleges are usually chosen explicitly for their religious stance. Distrust in the secular scientific world view and the absence of constraint in the student environment of secular universities and liberal mainline denominational colleges have led parents to choose them. Young people of evangelical convictions have chosen them for themselves.

In 1977, on an evaluation tour of my denomination's mission involvements in Latin America, I was struck by the large number of Presbyterian missionaries I visited whose children were attending these colleges and the small number enrolled in church-related colleges. So strong was the impression that when I returned from the trip I conducted a survey to determine the actual numbers. I found that 56 percent of the Presbyterian missionary children from that area then in college were at evangelical institutions; only 22 percent were in colleges related to the denomination even though the missionary parents, with few exceptions, were themselves products of these denominational institutions. [10]

Studies of Attitudes and Trends Among Young People

The prominence of the non-denominational evangelical youth organizations like Young Life and Campus Crusade, and the growing influence of Christian academies and evangelical colleges, are not the only sources of data showing what is happening to young people of mainline churches. The

Princeton Religious Research Center, which bases its reports of religious trends on polls conducted by the Gallup organization, reports that the evangelical movement is strong among the nation's youth. Evangelical gains—"often at the expense of mainline churches," according to the Center—are evidenced by the high percentage of teenagers who say they have had a "born again" experience: 46 percent of those identifying themselves Protestants, and 22 percent of the Catholics.[11]

Similar evidence came from a Religious News Service end-of-the-decade report on increasing interest in religion among college students in the second half of the seventies. Pointing to such indicators as the growing popularity of religion courses and the addition of such courses and of departments of religion by responsive administrations, increasing attendance at religious assemblies, growing willingness to voice religious opinions in class, and experiments in Bible-based community living, the RNS survey saw the trend as a conservative one; increasing numbers of students were going into conservative or fundamentalist groups.[12]

The report noted the popularity of informal Bible-reading or study groups in dormitories. Military chaplains have also observed a striking increase in such Bible study groups in barracks, camps and ships, among young service men and women. The Princeton Religious Research Center reported that 33 percent of Protestant teenagers and 20 percent of the Catholics say they are involved in Bible study groups.[13]

The involvement of young people in "fringe" religious sects, movements, or practices such as the Unification Church of the Reverend Sun Myung Moon or eastern religions, has been a widely-noted phenomenon. The Princeton study, however, indicated that the most popular of these fringe involvements are those associated with certain evangelical groups: speaking in tongues (experienced by 7 percent of the Protestant teenagers) and inner or spiritual healing (8 percent). Five percent reported themselves involved in Yoga, 4 percent in Transcendental Meditation, 3 percent in eastern religions, and 1 percent in Hare Krishna. Although more than half were aware of Rev. Moon's Unification Church, only 1 percent had a favorable opinion of it. The general picture seems to be one of some experimentation with extremes (probably considerably less than in the sixties and early seventies), but more often a searching youth reaching in the direction of orthodox religious expressions. Indeed, the Princeton Center sees one of the characteristics of youth in the dawning eighties to be a return to traditional values. Except for marked differences on certain social issues (acceptance of marijuana usage and sexual freedom), the study found remarkably little difference between the attitudes of teenagers and college students and those of older Americans in a marked swing toward traditional values.[14]

These findings were further confirmed by a 1979-80 survey of students listed in *Who's Who Among American High School Students*. It identified a decidedly conservative trend among high school leaders. Though religion has always played a significant role in the lives of this particular group, a striking 86 percent said they belonged to organized religion, up sharply from 70 percent in the 1969-70 poll ten years earlier. Three quarters said religion was an important part of their lives, and 67 percent claimed to have chosen their religious beliefs after independent personal investigation. [15]

Youth's Search for Meaning

The interest of American youth in both evangelical Christianity and fringe religions suggests a search for meaning in life. Martin E. Marty, in one of his *Context* newsletters, quotes Dr. Gerald L. Klernan, the nation's highest ranking mental health officer:

> The church—organized religion—has (in the past) played two important roles as a social support system. It attempted to provide cognitive meaning to life, and consolation during periods of despair, particularly those associated with death and other mysteries of existence. Second, the church was until recently the main system for the delivery of social services. We have now secularized the process with social service agencies, child-guidance clinics, family service, and so on. For most Americans, the church no longer provides cognitive meaning or a support system. However, the fact that many of today's youths are seeking alternative religious groups indicates that there are limits to which people in general, and the young in particular, can exist without some kind of social support. [16]

Dean Kelley, in his book, *Why Conservative Churches Are Growing* (a book, incidentally, which has played an important part in the awakening of mainline churches) also points to the basic need for a meaning support system. Kelley suggests that the secret of the growth of the conservative churches may not be so much their conservatism as their focus on the historically essential role of religion, that of providing a meaning structure for life. [17]

What are young people seeking? The liberal mainline establishment too often envisions them seeking channels for idealism, for protest, for action aimed at bringing about social change. The youth counterculture of the sixties and early seventies, Christian and secular, was indeed seeking such channels. It is questionable, however, if even then a significant number of young people were seeking such channels to express either a distinctively *Christian* idealism or social change as expressions of Christian meaning structure. Today's social activists in the mainline church establishment, on the other hand, are by and large responding to a Christian dynamic. Their meaning structure is a deep faith often acquired in a more conservative church environment in their youth. The generation they have produced in mainline churches with their attention fixed on social change, however, lacks that rooting in a deep faith. Members of this generation are finding a meaning structure in the evangelical youth movements, the evangelical colleges, and in a turn toward traditional values and conservative religion.

What Does It Mean for the Mainline Churches?

Significance is generally ascribed to trends among young people in terms of what they foreshadow for the adults of tomorrow. The Princeton Religious Research Center report on the strength of evangelicalism among the young is part of a report labeled "A Look Toward the Future: The Shape of the 1980s." A fairly clear picture emerges. Many of our youth have left us. They no longer see the church as a meaningful part of their lives. A significant part of those still with us, however, are young evangelicals. In 1979 the General Assembly of the Presbyterian Church, U. S., began for the first time to record the results of a straw vote among the Youth Advisory Participants alongside the official action of the commissioners. On a surprisingly large number of those issues with an identifiable "conservative" and "liberal" side, the youth vote has been more conservative than that of the adults. Some of these evangelical young people are being shaped in our own congregations, particularly those congregations making up the evangelical wing of the mainline denominations. Many, however, are finding their meaning structure elsewhere. Young Life, Youth for Christ, Campus Crusade, Inter-Varsity Christian Fellowship, Christian academies, non-denominational evangelical colleges—all these are now playing a part in shaping the new generation in the mainline churches.

This influence is even more pronounced at the college level. Asked about student Christian groups at a major Ivy League campus in early 1980, the chaplain of the university replied, "Well, of course, the Student Christian Fellowship is affiliated with Inter-Varsity. Then Campus Crusade came in, feeling that Inter-Varsity was too liberal. So now we have two." This evangelical sweep of the campuses does not necessarily mean a loss of interest in social action and an exclusive concentration on evangelism. The most socially concerned evangelicals call themselves the *young* evangelicals. Inter-Varsity strongly reflects their viewpoint, and even Campus Crusade has seen fit to add minority work with a strong concern for justice. It does, however, reflect what can probably be interpreted as a resounding vote of no confidence from young people themselves in the kind of diet, left over from the sixties, which mainline establishment youth and campus workers have been offering them.

Nowhere is the future leadership of the church more clearly foreshadowed than in the seminaries. The seminaries of the fifties, sixties, and seventies nourished today's leaders on a diet that ranged from Barth to Bonhoeffer to Bishop Robinson and Harvey Cox to Gustavo Gutiérrez. If denominational seminaries seemed too confining to earlier generations, the more adventurous went off to interdenominational Yale, Harvard, Union, Chicago, or Berkeley. Now the more adventurous are forsaking denominational seminaries—but in the opposite direction. They are going to Fuller and Gordon-Conwell. The largest Presbyterian seminary in the world (in terms of the number of Presbyterian candidates for the ministry enrolled) is Princeton. But the second largest is Fuller, and the third Gordon-Conwell.

Further, evidence suggests that students in the mainline denominational seminaries are coming from conservative sources. We have already noted that numbers of them are graduates of Youth for Christ or Inter-Varsity. Says Richard Lovelace of this trend:

> The remarkable thing which is occurring is that the Evangelicalism which apparently cannot touch these young men and women in their home churches is reaching them through campus missionaries and then thrusting them back into their home denominations via the seminaries to renew the leadership of the mainline churches.[18]

Those seminarians whose sense of calling has been nourished in their home churches are coming from the evangelically-oriented mainline congregations. A 1979 study of candidates for the ministry within my own denomination, the Presbyterian Church, U. S., showed that 44 percent of all candidates came from just 82 congregations—2 percent of the PCUS congregations, with 10 percent of the membership—and that most of these were known as conservative congregations.[19] Establishment liberals teaching in denominational seminaries are baffled as each entering class is more conservative than the last. The seminary professor quoted at the beginning of this chapter as saying his seminary was training the future leadership of the Orthodox Presbyterians and Conservative Baptists was dead wrong—it is training the future evangelical leadership of his own mainline denomination. A "reformed liberal" faculty member in one Methodist seminary calls it "postmodern orthodoxy."

> The sons and daughters of modernity are rediscovering the neglected beauty of classical Christian teaching. . . . They have had a bellyful of the hyped claims of modern therapies and political messianism to make things right. They are fascinated—and often passionately moved—by the primitive language of the apostolic tradition and the church fathers, undiluted by our contemporary efforts to soften it. . . . Finally my students got through to me. They do not want to hear a watered-down modern reinterpretation. They want nothing less than the substance of the faith of the apostles and martyrs.[20]

The results of these now well-established trends are already apparent. A 1980 study of the American clergy conducted by the Gallup organization found that ministers are generally more conservative than the usual image (of a liberal clergy serving a conservative laity) would imply. Over half—53 percent—identify themselves as evangelicals. One third say they are "traditional confessional." Over 20 percent call themselves fundamentalists. Only 15 percent characterize themselves as liberals, and 8 percent as neo-orthodox (more than one category could be selected, so the totals add up to more than 100 percent). An even more striking finding, however, is that throughout the study and in almost every category of response, *young persons in the clergy (under 30) are now more traditional and theologically conservative than their older colleagues*. Furthermore, when ministers were asked which of their programs they regard as most successful, the largest number selected worship services. *Among those who identify themselves as evangelical, however, youth ministries top the list*.[21]

The wave of the future is already upon us. Where have all the young folks gone? The evangelicals appear to have the answer.

parachurch organizations: second home for mainline evangelicals

If any person in America could be labeled "Mr. Evangelical" it is Billy Graham. For more than thirty years—coinciding with the period of the rise of contemporary evangelicalism—he has been the best known religious leader in America. A moderate among evangelicals, he has been a reconciling and binding force bringing disparate elements of the movement together again and again. He was instrumental in the founding of *Christianity Today*, the preeminent evangelical journal. His was the original idea for the landmark 1974 Lausanne Congress on World Evangelism. His weekly "Hour of Decision" radio broadcasts; his television specials; his monthly magazine, *Decision*, with a circulation of millions, show a mastery of the media. Year after year his name has shown up on the list of "Most Admired Americans." He has been on terms of intimate friendship with nearly all our recent presidents—the only one who did not invite him frequently to be a guest in the White House was fellow Southern Baptist evangelical Jimmy Carter. (Graham was an overnight guest of the Carters, but not nearly as frequently as with Johnson, Nixon, and Ford.) To the chagrin of those who keep saying he is past his peak and no longer has his former appeal, his crusades continue to draw hundreds of thousands. This has been done, moreover, almost entirely outside the normal mode of American church life—the denominations!

Certainly Graham has cooperated with denominations and their local congregations. He is an ordained minister of the Southern Baptist church. His brother-in-law and heir apparent, Leighton Ford, is a Presbyterian minister. Every crusade is sponsored by a broad coalition of churches in the target city.

Every maker of a decision for Christ is channeled to a local church and urged to affiliate. The Billy Graham Evangelistic Association, however, headquartered in Minneapolis (though Graham himself lives in North Carolina), has since 1950 been an independent organization with its own Board of Directors and unaffiliated with any particular denomination. If Billy Graham is Mr. Evangelical, the independent and non-denominational pattern of his association is also a model of evangelicalism. The parachurch organization has become the second spiritual home for mainline evangelicals.

Today's evangelicals have found the ideal vehicle for mounting their challenge to the mainline in such organizations, though this vehicle is by no means a new one. Parachurch organizations have existed alongside and within the official church organizations from Christianity's early days. They are nothing more than voluntary associations of Christians for particular purposes. The prefix "para," which comes from the Greek, means "beside" or "alongside of" or "near." It has become popular in recent years as a designation for groups which are not only alongside, but also supportive of more basic institutions. Paramedics work alongside and extend the ministrations of medical professionals. Paralegal workers do the same for lawyers. Parachurch organizations have traditionally been in an analagous relationship to official church governing structures. They have operated alongside and have served to extend the influence of the official churches.

Dr. Ralph D. Winter, a former missionary and professor at Fuller Theological Seminary, now Director of the United States Center for World Mission in Pasadena, California, has written extensively on the historical relationship between parachurch groups and official church organizations. He uses the terms "sodality" and "modality" to designate the two. "Sodality" is a term borrowed from Roman Catholicism and derives from a Latin word for "brotherhood." Dr. Arthur F. Glasser of Fuller Seminary, who also employs the terms, defines a sodality as "a society with religious or charitable objects."[1] Winter adopts the term "modality" to refer to the official governing structures of denominations. Both kinds of organizations, he says, have existed throughout Christian history.[2]

Historically, Roman Catholic sodalities have had a recognized place *within* the official church. The various priestly and lay religious orders have been the classic form and have served a wide range of purposes: contemplative, missionary, educational, charitable. They are essentially voluntary associations, self-governing internally, and operate with the official approval and under the general supervision of the hierarchy (the modality). The normal mode of church life for Roman Catholicism throughout most of its history was the universal church, perceived as a basic social structure to which everyone belonged by birthright. The parachurch organizations functioned as internal agencies for special interest groups and as the normative mode for carrying out various mission activities. Within limits, they also functioned as acceptable channels for diversity and even dissent. Only heresy and rejection of ecclesiastical authority were beyond the acceptable limits. It is an arguable proposition that its hospitality to internal parachurch organizations made the Roman Catholic "universal church" model possible.

Parachurch Roots of American Philanthropy

In Protestantism, the characteristic form of parachurch organization has been found *outside*, and generally across, denominational lines. Until this century, such parachurch organizations provided the normative channel for religiously-inspired missionary, educational, charitable and philanthropic activity. William G. McLoughlin has traced the history of Protestant philanthropy in the United States. In the early years the American population was so overwhelmingly Protestant and the climate of thought so religious in tone, he suggests, that Protestant and public philanthropic efforts were undifferentiated. Interdenominational charitable societies, often founded by the clergy but soon dominated by the laity, provided the normal mode of public philanthropy from the colonial period.[3] Such parachurch organizations continued as the standard Protestant pattern for Christian humanitarianism through most of American history. The pattern received its strongest thrust, say Jeremy Rifkin and Ted Howard in their account of American evangelicalism, from the revival wave in the nineteenth century. "By the Civil War," they say, "the concept of the volunteer association had broken out from the narrow confines of the church and had entered the secular realm as a major force in the social and cultural life of the nation."[4]

Patterns of Protestant Mission Organization

Most of the "churchly" mission concerns in American Protestant history followed a pattern similar to that of philanthropy. The golden era of interdenominational parachurch mission organizations was the period following the Second Great Awakening, which began in the 1790s and continued through the early years of the nineteenth century. Sidney Ahlstrom calls the "new kind of religious institution, the voluntary association of private individuals for missionary, reformatory or benevolent purposes" the most basic outgrowth of the evangelical enthusiasm aroused by that Awakening.[5]

None of these interdenominational parachurch organizations was more influential than the American Board of Commissioners for Foreign Mission, formed in 1810 as an outgrowth of the famous "Haystack Prayer Meeting." The modern missionary movement in Protestantism is usually dated from these events.

The American Bible Society was founded in 1816 and in less than four years had distributed nearly a hundred thousand Bibles. The New England

Tract Society came into being in 1814. By 1823 it had become the American Tract Society; in 1825, when it merged with another New York society with the same name and a similar history, it became genuinely national. The interdenominational American Home Missionary Society was formed in 1826. For two generations, says Ahlstrom, "its missionaries were a major force in the development of the west, not only as apostles and revivalists, but as educators, civic leaders, and exponents of eastern culture."[6]

The American Sunday School movement also received its major impetus from the Second Great Awakening. The American Sunday School Union, organized in 1824 as an interdenominational parachurch organization, was the foremost channel in its development. Interdenominational voluntary associations were formed for a wide range of causes during this period—anti-dueling, temperance, Sabbath-keeping, and other worthy objectives. The parachurch model of Christian activity continued to be common for many years. The YMCA and YWCA (in those days explicitly Christian in purpose) were founded in mid-century. In 1881 the Christian Endeavor Society was organized, and within six years there were more than seven thousand self-managed local societies with half a million members.[7]

Throughout this period, the trans-denominational parachurch organization was the normative mode of expression for mission in Protestantism. Denominations—modalities—had never been totally unconcerned about mission. Despite Presbyterian involvement in both the American Board of Commissioners for Foreign Mission and the American Home Missionary Society, for instance, the General Assembly had begun home mission work of its own in 1802. Insistence on this approach by the Old School faction of that denomination had divided the denomination in 1837. By and large, however, official denominational structures had in the earlier years concerned themselves primarily with church government and discipline, content to leave mission concerns to the voluntary associations. In the second half of the century new forms of denominational self-awareness began to change the Protestant climate.[8] More and more denominations formed their own boards or committees not only for foreign and home missions, but also for publications and Christian education.

The new denominational agencies were formed to make mission the business of the church itself and were intended to enlist the support of all members. They were subordinate to church governing structures. In practice, however, they tended to take the form of internal sodalities or parachurch groups and were generally semi-autonomous, self-governing associations. With denominational consent and cooperation, they cultivated their own constituencies, raised their own funds, and carried out the kind of mission or activity supported by the consensus groups they represented. Not until the mid-twentieth century did these agencies become the central concerns of denominational governing bodies. The full integration of denominational mission agencies into the organizational governing structures of mainline denominations was not achieved until the wave of restructuring that swept through all the mainline churches in the late 1960s and early 70s.[9]

Mainliners in Contemporary Independent Parachurch Organizations

We noted earlier that after fundamentalists lost their battle with the modernists in the first quarter of the twentieth century, the center of Protestant conservatism moved out of the mainline churches. The small separatist denominations became one locus of conservative church life; the other, however, was a non-denominational conservative movement. Along with the independent Bible institutes and the non-denominational evangelical colleges and seminaries which provided the intellectual and theological underpinnings, the evangelical parachurch organizations have provided the major organizational pattern and have formed the institutional base of the evangelical renewal.

These organizations are not made up of free-floating, unaffiliated evangelicals. *The mainline evangelicals themselves are the backbone of the massive parachurch organizations dominating much of American Christianity today.* The mainline liberal establishment should not delude itself on this point. Campus Crusade was founded and is still run by a layman who was and remains active in a United Presbyterian congregation. Oral Roberts is a Methodist. Young Life was begun by a Presbyterian minister. It may be that only a minority of the *leaders and directors* of parachurch organizations worship in mainline pews. A number, like Billy Graham, are Baptists, Baptist freedom and individualism being a comfortable environment. Many leaders belong to the small conservative denominations. But the rank and file support and contributions clearly come from the mainline. The millions, perhaps billions, of dollars which flow each year into parachurch coffers are not coming from Bible Presbyterians, or even Southern Baptists, since they are by and large quite satisfied with their own denominational programs and support them generously. The parachurch dollars are coming from mainline pockets.

Mainline circles are well aware of this outflow. A 1979 stewardship appeal addressed by a General Presbyter to churches in his area of responsibility listed eight parachurch organizations with a combined income of $293 million, compared with a relatively modest denominational request. It concluded, "Your local church, related to the Presbytery, Synod and General Assembly, is the place to give your money if you want to witness effectively for Jesus Christ through His church."[10] Largely for financial reasons, perhaps, and certainly in part because they represent the "other side" in today's polarized Protestantism, the mainline liberal-ecumenical establishment tends to regard the parachurch organizations with distaste.

Yet they represent a long-established and, until recently, normative pattern for Protestant Christian life. Christianity has seldom been without the characteristic cross-hatch of sodality and modality. Voluntary consensus groups, organized to express a particular interest or engage in a particular form of mission, have nearly always been present. For most of Christian history they have been approved and encouraged by church governing structures. Even today, at the local church level, they are present and taken for granted by congregations and pastors. Women's organizations, youth groups, organized Bible classes or prayer groups, organizations formed to conduct particular forms of local mission, are nothing more than local parachurch organizations.

Interdenominational parachurch organizations follow an equally long-established pattern. The fact that the evangelical renewal has developed, grown powerful, and now is increasingly mounting a challenge to the mainline establishment through parachurch organizations should be understood in this light. These organizations have provided for mainline evangelicals a channel for dissent and alternative activity not available to them through official channels. Now, with their strength, power, and wealth, they provide a ready vehicle for the evangelical challenge to the liberal-ecumenical establishment both outside and increasingly inside the mainline churches.

Panorama of Evangelical Parachurch Organizations

The number, range, and vitality of these organizations is astounding to the mainline Christian who begins to explore the field. Frequently they are organized around one central person, as with the Billy Graham Evangelistic Association. When the founder dies or moves out of the central role, they sometimes disintegrate, but many of them become permanently established. We can identify four major areas in which they operate.

1. *The Youth-Oriented Organizations*

We noted in the last chapter the importance of parachurch organizations in the present mainline youth crisis. While denominational youth programs are moribund, and establishment leaders search frantically for answers to the insistent call from their constituencies to "do something about youth work," Young Life, Campus Crusade, Youth for Christ, and Inter-Varsity Christian Fellowship are flourishing, indeed flourishing generally with mainline young people. Their alumni are becoming the young officers and leaders of mainline congregations and are filling the mainline seminaries. More clearly, perhaps, than in any other single area, the parachurch youth organizations have not only challenged the mainline for the right to develop tomorrow's Christian leadership; to a considerable extent they have carried the day.

2. *The Overseas Mission Organizations*

A second area in which parachurch organizations have had enormous success is overseas mission. Here the challenge to the mainline is not so apparent, since most mainline denominations do maintain large (though truncated and still declining) international mission agencies. Mainline missionary decline has, however, been more than matched by the increase in the number of overseas workers sponsored by parachurch organizations. Of the 620 North American overseas agencies listed in the current (eleventh) edition of the *Mission Handbook,* the vast majority are in the parachurch category. Agencies like World Vision International and the Wycliffe Bible Translators exceed all but the largest mainline mission agencies both in funds raised and in the number of workers overseas. This aspect of the parachurch phenomenon will be examined in greater detail in the following chapter on the crisis in overseas mission.

3. *The Electronic Church*

Perhap the most striking and the most influential of all categories of parachurch organizations are those directly associated with modern technology, the Christian broadcasters. An estimated billion dollars a year flows into these agencies. More than thirteen hundred radio stations and at least twenty-five television stations concentrate almost exclusively on religious broadcasting. New religious radio stations are opening up at the rate of one a week, TV stations about one a month,[11] and a Christian television network is even in operation. Hundreds of commercial stations also carry the well-known programs.

Since the broadcast organizations generally focus on one radio or television personality, since their mode is that of "programming" and "audiences," the parachurch label may seem questionable. Certainly for many listeners or viewers who do not become actively involved they represent nothing more than a form of "spiritual entertainment." For many who identify strongly, sign up as "members," and commit themselves to contribute money regularly, however, they represent far more. The central organizations, tightly structured, well-funded, and strongly institutionalized, show all the classic signs of such organizations, and their role in contemporary American evangelicalism is an enormously important one.

The Christian Broadcasting Network and the 700 Club. Potentially if not actually, the largest and most influential of the TV parachurch organizations is the Christian Broadcasting Network (CBN) with headquarters in Virginia Beach, Virginia. Its founder and president is Marion G. "Pat" Robertson, son of a long-time U.S. Senator, who began his TV ministry in 1960 with assets of less than seventy dollars. He established the nation's first Christian television station (WYAH, Channel 27, in Portsmouth, Virginia) in 1961. The best-known CBN program is the 700 Club with more than half a million contributing "members." This program is the heart of the CBN operation, raising most of the money that keeps it going. A Johnny Carson style variety-talk show, the 700 Club began in 1963 with a telethon asking for 700 contributors. It is broadcast by almost two hundred TV stations and one hundred fifty radio stations in the United States alone. CBN now owns four television and six radio stations. With WYAH as its base, it has grown into a $50 million a year operation, with programs beamed by satellite across the nation and into twenty-two foreign countries.

But this is only the beginning. Robertson's vision for the future is expansive, and he is well on his way toward achieving it. He is establishing nothing less than a fourth nationwide television network with a full range of family viewing—news, sports, movies, drama, and even a soap opera, "The Light Inside." Its $50 million headquarters complex was opened at Virginia Beach in the fall of 1979. A commercial affiliate, the Continential Broadcasting Network, has been formed to handle commercial business and types of broadcasting not permitted by CBN's religious, non-profit status. Robertson expects to claim a ten percent share of the total TV audience with this new network. Part of the headquarters operation is a graduate School of Communications which is attracting large numbers of students. Studios, production equipment, and expert technicians are the best available. The potential appears almost unlimited.[12]

The PTL Club. Jim Bakker, earlier an associate of Robertson on the 700 Club, left the CBN organization in 1972 to found the Charlotte, North Carolina based PTL (for "Praise the Lord" or "People that Love") Club. Following a variety-talk show format similar to that of the 700 Club, the PTL Club is the 4th largest purchaser of air time in the United States and is seen on 179 television stations. Approximately half a million PTL "members" contribute $25 million a year to finance the operation. A single telethon in 1979 brought in one million dollars. The $3 million studio in Charlotte is among the best equipped in the world.

Like Robertson, Bakker has moved into network operations. The PTL Television Network has its own satellite and beams religious programming worldwide, twenty-four hours a day, featuring programs such as those of Oral Roberts, Robert Schuller, and Jerry Falwell as well as its own. PTL has also branched out in other directions. "Heritage, U.S.A." is a fourteen hundred acre complex across the South Carolina border from Charlotte. It includes a recreational mecca for members; lakeside chalets, tent and camper hookups, swimming, tennis, hiking, and a two thousand seat auditorium where summer TV programs are taped, are available. Financial difficulties have plagued

Bakker in connection with these ambitious projects, but his television following has been loyal and generous. [13]

Both the 700 Club and the PTL Club have used a pioneering form of two-way communication to move beyond passive viewing toward active involvement. Each has a large corps of trained volunteer counselors staffing regional telephone centers around the country. Viewers are urged to call toll-free numbers throughout the program to discuss their personal or spiritual problems. Many decisions for Christ are made through such calls, and spiritual healing has a prominent role in the ministry of each. The operators have computerized forms on which they record the calls, and each caller becomes a "member" who has moved beyond passive watching to some kind of response. Sophisticated computer technology enables the TV minister to send highly individualized letters to those who call in. Each of the clubs receives well over a million calls a year.

Other Forms of the Electronic Church. In moving beyond the mode of programming for audiences into two-way communication and other forms of active response, evangelical religious broadcasting has made unique use of the electronic media and earned the label "parachurch organization." Some broadcast organizations, indeed, are not even "para"; they have become modalities rather than sodalities. In the early days of radio, R. R. Brown was perhaps the first evangelical broadcaster to see his audience as a new form of church and to issue membership cards to those who joined his "World Radio Congregation." In the mid-thirties, Herbert W. Armstrong founded the more durable Radio Church of God, which has since been re-named the Worldwide Church of God. Despite a somewhat turbulent history centering around widely-publicized charges of misconduct, excommunications, and mutual recriminations among Armstrong, his son, Garner Ted, and other church leaders, it has become a well-established denomination with its own Ambassador College. Its "World Tomorrow" TV show is the major support vehicle for the college and other denominational operations headquartered in Pasadena, California. Robert M. Liebert, professor of psychology and psychiatry at the State University of New York, predicted at a 1980 National Council of Churches sponsored conference on the electronic church, that the eighties will see a rise in such electronic church denominations. [14]

Some major electronic media personalities use radio or television as an extension of church ministries related to existing denominations. Robert Schuller's "Hour of Power" is an extension of his Garden Grove, California, church affiliated with the mainline Reformed Church in America. Jerry Falwell's "Old-Time Gospel Hour" is based in the sixteen thousand member Thomas Road Baptist Church in Lynchburg, Virginia. The ability to elicit a sense of identification and response from viewers, however—impressive monetary response and, in the case of Falwell, political action in behalf of far right causes—make the parachurch label still appropriate. More than two million persons were on record as active donors to Falwell's broadcasts in 1979. We are talking here about sodalities related to modalities rather than independent sodalities operating across denominational lines. Overall, the media organizations occupy an extremely important corner of the "second home" mainline evangelicals have found in parachurch organizations.

4. *Social and Political Activist Organizations*

No evangelical parachurch organizations reveal a more striking change of climate than those devoted to political and social change. As recently as the mid-seventies, Sociologist Dean Hoge—building on the work of Martin Marty, who had classified the two on-going "parties" in American Protestantism as "Public Protestants" and "Private Protestants"—found the major difference between the two parties in the area of social action. The public Protestants were generally social activists. The private Protestants emphasized evangelism and were only marginally interested in—and often directly opposed to—social action as a form of Christian mission.[15]

As noted earlier, the late seventies brought a major change in this pattern. The "young evangelicals" generally express a religiously conservative interest in the same kinds of social change as those sought by liberal social activists (social justice for women and minorities, alleviation of world hunger, a changed economic order, world peace, and environmental issues). They are perhaps best represented by Sojourners, a Washington, D. C., based koinonia group which publishes the widely-read social action magazine *Sojourners*.

Evangelicals for Social Action is an organization of new evangelicals headed by Ron Sider, an Eastern Baptist Seminary professor best known for his book *Rich Christians in an Age of Hunger*.[16] It has a forty-member board of directors including some leading new evangelical figures. The organization publishes tracts on justice issues and sponsors workshops to train local pastors for social justice ministries. Leighton Ford, Billy Graham's associate, has also taken an active leadership role in evangelical social action causes.

Right wing political action by evangelical groups—the newest entry into the parachurch field—reflects a different set of concerns. Said Richard A. Viguerie, publisher of *Conservative Digest* and a key figure in the so-called "new right," "During the 25 years that I've been active in politics, the major religious leaders in America have been liberals who were in bed politically with the Democratic party. But most are now over the hill. And it appears that the future belongs to people like the Rev. Jerry Falwell, the Rev. Pat Robertson, the Rev. James Robison."[17]

An array of right wing evangelical organizations took an active role in the 1980 election campaign, supporting conservative congressional candidates—

regardless of party—and a range of conservative political causes. Two of these, "Christian Voice" and "Moral Majority," registered as non-profit, non-exempt corporations. Contributions to them are not tax-exempt, and they can therefore lobby extensively and engage in campaign activities without the restrictions limiting the political activities of most religious organizations. The press credited right-wing evangelical organizations with major influence on the platform adopted by the Republican National Convention for the 1980 election.[18] The extent to which they can claim credit for the Republican victory in that election has been hotly debated.

Christian Voice was founded early in 1979 by a group of Californians headed by Robert Gordon Grant, a travel agent who is a graduate of Fuller Theological Seminary. Earlier he had founded "American Christian Cause" to combat gay activism. Author-lecturer Hal Lindsey *(The Late Great Planet Earth)* is a member of the policy committee. By the end of 1979, sixteen members of Congress had been recruited for the congressional advisory committee of Christian Voice. Three million dollars was budgeted for the 1980 political campaign, with a blitz of spot announcements for Christian television viewers. Activities included political commentary, a monthly legislative bulletin for clergy, and an annual rating of congressional members on a "morality scale."

Moral Majority was organized in 1979 by Jerry Falwell of the "Old-Time Gospel Hour" as a political arm for his television ministry. More than one-third of its first year budget of $1 million was raised in the first month of activity, and the group entered actively into the 1980 campaign.

The late seventies also saw an increase in the number of evangelical parachurch organizations dealing with specific social problems. The Prison Fellowship formed by Charles Colson of Watergate fame has been well-funded and active in penal reform and prisoner rehabilitation programs. Tom Skinner Associates has carried on a ministry focused on social problems in the black community. As noted earlier, both Campus Crusade and Inter-Varsity Christian Fellowship have established branches dealing with minority group social concerns. Looser coalitions of evangelicals have formed around the homosexuality and abortion issues.

While many evangelicals are obviously still individualistic in their faith, emphasizing conversion and personal pietism, the striking proliferation of conservative parachurch organizations devoted to social and political activism at the end of the seventies and beginning of the eighties does appear to be a significant change. It may be a particularly important change for the mainline denominations which in the past have seen themselves as the social activist wing of American Christianity.

The radical difference between the social priorities of the new evangelicals and those of the right wing political activists who first gained public prominence in the 1980 political campaign, may drive a wedge into the evangelical movement. The "new" evangelicals tend to focus their concern on environmental and lifestyle issues, on economic, social, and racial justice, and on peace issues—generally the same cluster of concerns addressed by mainliners. The new activists of the Christian right tend to be concerned with preservation of traditional family values (expressed in opposition to homosexuality, abortion, and the Equal Rights Amendment), anti-communism, and a strong national defense. Although the right wing activists refer to themselves as evangelicals, their leaders tend to represent the fundamentalist wing of evangelicalism. They have tapped into a much broader wave of renascent patriotism and concern about deterioration of the traditional family, and their following probably includes large numbers of non-fundamentalist evangelicals. Many of the "new" evangelicals, however, find themselves in sharp and increasingly public opposition to them.

5. *Sampler of Other Parachurch Groups*

Besides the four major categories we have examined—those focused on youth, overseas mission, electronic media, and social or political action—a wide variety of others remains. *Jews for Jesus,* headed by Moise Rosen, is devoted to personal evangelism among ethnic Jews. Incorporated in California, the group had a salaried staff of eighty in 1979. The *Full Gospel Business Men's Fellowship,* also California based, is a charismatic organization which has achieved some notoriety as the sponsor of Prayer Breakfasts attended by prominent political figures. It has approximately five hundred thousand dues-paying members meeting in chapters which conduct weekly prayer meetings and monthly public gatherings, and now functions in several other countries as well as the U. S. Its women's counterpart is the *Aglow Fellowship.* The *Bible Study Fellowship,* made up primarily of women, had eighty thousand regular attenders in 1979 meeting weekly for two and one-half hours of lectures on Bible passages and discussion of homework assignments, all prepared by Miss A. Wetherell Johnson, who was formerly a missionary under an independent agency, the China Inland Mission. In 1979 there were five hundred teaching leaders, and the demand for trained and approved leaders far exceeds the supply.[19]

Certainly not all the supporters and contributors to the independent parachurch organizations are mainline church members. Indeed, one relatively new conservative denomination, the Presbyterian Church in America, made an official decision in establishing its overseas mission to limit its own denominational work to one field (urban mission in rapidly growing cities) and to carry on its remaining mission through parachurch groups. It now has thirty missionaries with Wycliffe Bible Translators, and smaller numbers with several other agencies.[20] Other evangelicals also give to parachurch groups. For the most part, however, the small separatist denominations and the larger conservative denominations both have consensus group constituencies strongly committed to their own denominational programs and financially supportive of them. By and large, mainline evangelicals are the ones looking outside their denominations for channels of financial support. In a general sense, then, *the massive independent parachurch movement is a phenomenon of divided mainline American Protestantism.*

Parachurch Organizations Within Mainline Denominations

As noted, parachurch organizations generally have flourished outside the mainline denominations. This has been true of the evangelical movement itself which has developed since the 1920s outside the mainline. Perhaps the most significant change in the decade of the seventies, however, was the rapid growth in both numbers and influence of evangelical parachurch organizations *within* the major mainline denominations. These represent a direct challenge to denominational establishments, their immediate goal being a stronger voice and greater influence for evangelicals in denominational affairs. Ultimately they expect evangelicals to move into the majority position and assume control.

Many of the denominational evangelical organizations emerged in the mid-sixties. Presbyterians United for Biblical Concerns (PUBC), which operates in the United Presbyterian Church, was organized in 1965 to oppose the confessional reformulation which ultimately resulted in the adoption of the liberal "Confession of 1967." Although PUBC did not succeed in defeating the Confession, many of its suggestions were incorporated into the final draft so that it did succeed in modifying the document. Whereas, PUBC is an organization of both clergy and laity, the Presbyterian Lay Committee—another parachurch organization within the same denomination—is entirely lay controlled. Organized in 1964 by a group of seven Presbyterian corporation executives, it grew rapidly and in 1968 began founding local chapters throughout the denomination. It publishes the widely circulated and influential *Presbyterian Layman*. While originally more conservative than PUBC, it has tended to moderate its positions somewhat, and the two organizations now work closely together.

The Fellowship of Witness in the Episcopal Church was also organized in 1965 and is part of the larger worldwide Evangelical Fellowship of the Anglican Communion. It publishes the magazine *Kerygma* and its support was an important element in the establishment of Trinity Episcopal School for the Ministry in Pittsburgh in 1971. The 1977 schism in the Episcopal Church, which resulted in the formation of the Anglican Church of North America, bled off some of its most conservative support, but it remains a strong evangelical voice within the denomination and is staunchly supported by evangelicalism within the Church of England.

The Good News Movement within the United Methodist Church began in 1966 and has grown rapidly. It has an able spokesman in Paul Mickey, a professor at Duke University Divinity School who has served as chairman of its board of directors. It has a small salaried staff, and like most of its counterpart organizations it publishes a magazine, *Good News*. The Good News movement has focused considerable attention on financial issues, advocating designated giving to causes supported by evangelicals as a way for church members to "vote with their dollars." In 1979 its board of directors announced for the first time a policy that would publicly encourage United Methodists to support and advocate non-Methodist mission agencies and causes, but was unsuccessful in its efforts to persuade the 1980 General Conference to approve a designated giving policy. In general, however, Good News was pleased with its impact on that General Conference.[21]

The Covenant Fellowship of Presbyterians in the Presbyterian Church, U. S., like its counterpart in the United Presbyterian Church, has opposed confessional modernization. Largely because of a requirement for approval by three-fourths of the denomination's presbyteries, the PCUS conservative voice succeeded in defeating the denomination's "New Confession" despite nearly universal support by denominational leadership. Much of its energies over the years has been devoted to opposing various plans for union with the United Presbyterian Church, long a major goal of liberal ecumenicals. At the end of the seventies, however, while confronting the issue of ordination of homosexuals in the two denominations, the Covenant Fellowship began to explore with its counterpart organization in the UP church the strength that might lie in evangelical unity. As a result, an apparent change of strategy has led to the appointment of conservatives from both denominations to the Joint Committee on Union in the hope they might produce a Plan of Union which the evangelicals in both denominations will be willing to support.

In addition to these evangelical organizations, most of the mainline denominations also have internal charismatic fellowships. We shall examine those in a later chapter.

Significance of the Parachurch Organizations for Mainline Protestantism

Why are there so few liberal parachurch organizations? The answer, obviously, is that they are not needed. The liberals have the modalities. The counterpart of the "political maneuvering" of evangelical parachurch groups within the denominations is to be found in the "strategies" of the governing establishments. The establishment has no need of parachurch structures; it controls the official structures. It has no need to "divert" money through "unofficial channels." It controls the official money through the official channels.

Generally speaking, "coalitions" of liberal Christians (usually for the sake of social action) have not become parachurch organizations because they have not needed to raise money directly from members, though there are exceptions. The Witherspoon Society was formed by liberals in the United Presbyterian Church (which has constitutional provisions for official recognition of internal parachurch organizations) in the early seventies to counter the influence of the Lay Committee and Presbyterians United for Biblical Concerns. A Methodist Federation for Social Action has existed for some time as a counter-force to Good News, and a liberal Coalition for the Whole Gospel was formed in that denomination shortly before the 1980 General Conference in order to counter efforts of Good News to influence that Conference. In general, however, liberal organizations within the denominations have been less effective and less durable than those of the evangelicals. There has been little need for them, since the official organizations have been in liberal hands.

Liberal versions of the huge non-denominational parachurch organizations have been almost non-existent for essentially the same reason. The denominational youth work departments and networks are the liberal counterparts of Young Life, Youth for Christ, and Campus Crusade. Mainline denominational overseas mission agencies are the liberal counterparts of World Vision and Africa Inland Mission. The structures of the National Council and World Council of Churches form the transdenominational organizations through which liberals work together, and since they are officially funded by the denominations, no need has arisen for direct fund-raising among the liberal constituency. The parachurch organizations have become the second home for mainline evangelicals precisely *because* the official organizations are the channels used and controlled by the liberal-ecumenical groups within the denominations.

It is somewhat paradoxical that rank and file mainline evangelicals, feeling excluded from the decision-making processes and unable to affect policy in their own denominations, have channeled their support to parachurch groups over which they have far less control. Without exception, every mainline denomination offers channels for democratic participation by grassroots members. Delegates to denominational conventions—locally, regionally, and nationally—are generally elected through processes that begin at the congregational level. In every case, policy domination by liberal-ecumenical establishments would have been impossible without the approval—generally reaffirmed year after year—of such representative bodies.

In contrast, few if any of the parachurch groups offer any significant opportunity for democratic participation in their governance by rank and file supporters. Many are "one-man" operations ruled with an iron hand by the charismatic founder of the movement, and their books are sometimes closed to outside inspection. They often follow a highly corporate style of operation much closer to the "big business" management model than is possible for any traditional denomination. In contrast to denominations, which seek to touch every aspect of the believer's life, many neither ask nor expect anything of the rank and file except financial contributions. Their appeal lies in their "product"—their specific form of mission or service—and this is far more to the liking of many mainline evangelicals than that of their own denominations. In supporting them, rank and file Christians are not finding more opportunities for personal participation, but often far less.

Despite this, their support is enormous, and their role in the evangelical renewal is a major one. What does the ubiquity, the success, and the influence of the evangelical parachurch organizations portend for the mainline churches? In a sense, their presence need not alarm mainliners. A careful reading of church history will show that such groups have always been present in Christianity in one form or another, and a study of organizational dynamics will suggest that they are probably inevitable in a movement as large and diverse as Christianity. As Lon Fuller has demonstrated with regard to voluntary organizations generally, only small consensus groups based on fully shared commitment of all members to a particular cause find internal subgroupings harmful. Larger organizations, in which legal principles have replaced fully shared commitment as the binding force, *require* internal consensus groupings.[22] Christian history has illustrated this again and again—particularly in Protestant denominationalism. A newly formed sect, insistent on doctrinal, ethical, and missional purity and established to maintain it, can remain "pure" only for a short while. As soon as it grows in size and develops diversity, it finds itself with its own internal groupings which must be accommodated in some fashion.

A recent experience of mainline denominations is instructive: the deemphasis of women's organizations on the basis of the impeccable theory that women ought to be fully integrated into the governing and missional organs of the whole church and not relegated to second class status in their own parachurch organizations. Women's organizations have simply refused to wither away, and though full integration has not proceeded as rapidly as we would have wished, clearly this is not the only reason. Many women have a *need* for their own sodality groups. Similarly, youth groups and even men's organizations are making a comeback as groups join to express shared interests. Larger consensus groups, based on common interest or a shared sense of calling to a particular form of activity rather than common sex or age, have an equally insistent history in the church. The *presence* of parachurch organizations should not disturb mainline churches.

But the form they have taken, together with their rapid growth, influence, and effect on church funding, does have a message for the mainline. The major function of most of these contemporary parachurch organizations has been to provide a channel for *dissent* and for *alternative activity*.

In my own Presbyterian Church, U. S., the internal parachurch groups have begun to fill for evangelicals within the denomination many needs once filled by official agencies and programs. Denomination-wide conferences (some at the church's official conference center) for adults and young people; a congregational renewal program available to any local church; alternate channels of overseas mission outreach through a private denominational foundation—these and other services are available. Along with Sunday School curricular materials and leadership training activities from independent sources (often more readily available than from the denomination itself), they constitute a *fairly broad range of alternate structures, already in being*. An evangelical congregation choosing to utilize them can enjoy a fairly full and by no means isolated denominational life. And many do.

Outside parachurch groups provide an even broader range of activities and outlets. All of them have grown and flourished as the mainline has declined. They have become the second home for mainline evangelicals. And they can no longer be ignored or simply deplored.

The future is not clear. Martin Marty has suggested that movements rather than denominations are the true center of loyalty today, and has predicted that the "1980s will continue to be a time of movements and not denominations."[23] This would suggest that the parachurch organizations embodying non- or trans-denominational movements may be around for a long time. One senses that as long as the present situation within the mainline continues, the parachurch organizations will not wither and die. Perhaps they will become the denominations of the future, since such organizations have been one source of denominations throughout history. Some parachurch groups have already taken this route. The electronic church groups noted above are the most prominent, but not the only examples. A group of Campus Crusade staff members resigned in 1974 to form the "New Covenant Apostolic Order," charging that Campus Crusade was assuming many of the functions of a church without assuming the responsibilities. In 1979, according to a news report, the group established itself as the Evangelical Orthodox Church, reporting fifty congregations with a total of twenty-five hundred members.[24] The Maranatha Christian Fellowship, a strongly evangelistic group operating primarily (though not exclusively) with young adults, is organized into local "churches" ruled by "elders" trained by Bob Weiner, the founder and director of the organization.[25] Parachurch organizations are not likely to disband of their own accord regardless of what course the mainline takes in the future. Organizations seldom lack a tendency toward institutional self-preservation even when their usefulness is past.

The passing of their *usefulness*, however, may be the most significant possibility for the mainline to contemplate. At present, they *meet needs that mainline evangelicals do not find met in their own denominational structures*. Though the liberal-ecumenical establishment finds the idea of a pocketbook vote distasteful, the massive pocketbook vote which has poured millions into the Billy Graham organization, Campus Crusade, World Vision, and the 700 Club—while denominational mission funding melts away—must be saying something. To continue to tell evangelicals that if they are loyal Methodists or Episcopalians they *must* give their money to fight multinational corporations in developing countries and institutional racism at home, and that they must do this because majorities of General Conferences have voted to support such activities, is futile. The outflow of money into parachurch organizations supporting evangelical causes is not slowing down. By every sign it is accelerating.

Historically, however, the mainline has been the mainline because its centrist positions and activities have met the needs of a wide range of people. Reestablishment of a consensus of the middle would gradually make the parachurch channels peripheral to—and congruent with—mainline church life as in the past. Such organizations will become less important to the extent that a viable middle is restored and evangelicals become more comfortable in the mainline churches.

Such a change cannot be brought about overnight. Whether it could ever be brought about by intentional planning and strategies is doubtful, since the present establishmentarians who control the mainline denominations fervently believe they are right. They believe the programs they design and support are "God's agenda"—the proper response to God's claims on the church, and they are not likely voluntarily to surrender control of church structures which they fought so hard to achieve, to turn it over to or even share it with a group they believe to be at best misguided and at worst subverting God's will for the church.

Perhaps the most that can be hoped for in the immediate future is for the pluralistic mainline churches to become more consciously pluralistic, to allow parallel structures for evangelical outreach within them, and to allow some measure of legitimacy and acceptance to the evangelical parachurch organizations. Parachurch organizations historically have been, and still may be, useful devices for handling pluralism despite the challenge they are presently mounting.

chapter 6

crisis in overseas mission: shall we leave it to the independents?

In no area of church life is the confrontation between the mainline establishment and resurgent evangelicalism more troublesome than in overseas mission. South African missiologist David J. Bosch, writing about this confrontation from a non-American perspective, suggests that the international mission movement today is in "a crisis more radical and extensive than anything the Church has ever faced in her history." He analyzes it in terms of "fundamental differences" between the "ecumenical" and "evangelical" understandings of mission.[1] In one sense the confrontation is a tragedy of miscommunication. The situation is seen so differently from the mainline and the evangelical perspectives that in their disputes they are seldom talking about the same thing. Even the words have different meanings for the two groups.

The basic facts are incontrovertible. From 1969 to 1975, the period summarized in the most recent issue (eleventh edition, 1976) of the authoritative *Mission Handbook*, the number of missionaries serving overseas under the auspices of denominations comprising the Department of Overseas Mission (DOM) of the National Council of Churches—generally the mainline—decreased from about eight thousand to five thousand. This was a decline of almost one-third (31 percent) in a six-year period and continued a trend that had begun long before 1969. Dean Kelley, in his book *Why Conservative Churches Are Growing*, reported that in the fourteen years between 1958 and 1971 the number of missionaries sent abroad by the six major Protestant denominations making up the heart of the mainline declined from 4548 to 3160—a 31 percent drop in that period.[2] It is a trend that has continued since the 1975 terminal date for *Mission Handbook* statistics.

To mainline evangelicals, the missionary decline is a dismal picture and one they blame on the denominational power structures. They see the establishment bureaucrats deemphasizing overseas mission generally and seeking to shift funds to activities in the United States. This is a focal point of their "lack of trust" in the way the bureaucracy uses benevolence contributions. By designating funds for particular causes rather than contributing to central budgets, overseas mission causes are central in their efforts to thwart the bureaucrats.

Further, they suspect the mainline establishment of trying to change the character of the remaining overseas involvements. Denominational leaders, they charge, are interested only in bringing about social, political, and economic change overseas, and they often perceive the changes toward which liberal social activists are working as influenced by, or allied with, Marxist movements. They feel that mainline bureaucrats are not interested in evangelism overseas and charge that missionaries are being downgraded in the total overseas program. The decline in the number of missionaries sent abroad has become for them a symbolic focal point in their concern about the entire denominational involvement overseas.

The liberal-ecumenical perception of the situation is quite different. Mainline leaders see the overseas mission-oriented evangelicals as unwilling or unable to accept a radically changed situation. They see them as clinging to an "old style" of mission activity closely associated with the now discredited imperialism of an earlier period. They believe this "old style" is paternalistic and that it has been rejected by the churches of the third world. They believe evangelicals attach an exaggerated importance to missionaries in whatever role remains for western churches overseas. Those evangelical "old style" missionaries who are still serving overseas under the auspices of their boards are perceived by the liberal-ecumenicals as supporting repressive economic and political systems in developing countries in order to achieve the "stability" which will enable them to gain admittance to those countries and be left free to evangelize. They believe evangelicals at home are using overseas generosity as an "easy out," a way of salving their consciences to avoid facing social problems and the need for change at home.

In such a situation, no wonder the two sides shout past each other, neither really understanding the other. They start from such radically different assumptions, and they perceive the problems—and each other—so differently, that within the mainline churches there has been little or no progress toward resolving the issue. The resolution has been coming *outside the mainline* in the form of a massive shift of evangelical money, personnel, and emphasis from denominational overseas programs to independent parachurch agencies.

The Dropping of the "s" from Missions

One root of the problem is a change in the definition of the word "mission." In 1969 the *International Review of Missions,* long the preeminent interdenominational journal in the field of overseas mission, dropped the "s" from the last word of its title, becoming the *International Review of Mission*. An editorial in the issue inaugurating the change explained that it made the term more palatable to non-western church leaders.[3] Behind the dropping of the "s," however, lay far more than a transition from plural to singular.

Throughout most of Christian history, the term "mission" meant what believers were "sent out" to do. What they were sent out to do was clear to most; it was to propagate Christianity by making converts and establishing churches. The mission text was the "great commission," "Go therefore and make disciples of all nations, baptizing them in the name of the Father and of the Son and of the Holy Spirit" (Matt. 28:29). The plural form of the word, "missions," referred to the specific undertakings by which this was carried out. There were "home missions" in this country and "foreign missions" overseas. In the so-called "great century" of the expansion of Christianity, the nineteenth century, and continuing through the first half of the twentieth, foreign missions became so central in the outreach of evangelical Christianity that the term "missions" was generally understood to mean foreign missions. A glance at the works listed under this term in the card catalog of any seminary library will make that reality abundantly clear.

Somewhere around the middle of the present century, however, a change began to take place. Mission, or "the mission of the church," began to be used in a much broader sense to refer to the whole range of what the church seeks to do. Reasons for the change were complex, and a theological reformulation was clearly involved. Mission came to be understood in terms of the church's total involvement with the world. The famous dictum of the Uppsala Assembly of the World Council of Churches (1968), "the world provides the agenda," was indicative of the liberal-ecumenical perspective. One factor in the mainline establishment's understanding of mission may have been the military connotations of the term widely popularized during the Second World War and picked up by business and government agencies in the managerial revolution which followed.[4] Undoubtedly the change also reflected the search for integration and "holism" which has been a prominent theme in the period. Whatever the sources, the effect has been significant. Anglican Bishop Lesslie Newbigin, long a leader in the international mission movement (as Director of the International Mission Council from 1958 to 1963 when it was merged with the World Council of Churches, and then as Director of the WCC Commission/Division of World Mission and Evangelism until 1973) sought to clarify the changing usage in 1960.

We have to begin making some verbal distinctions if we are going to have our thinking clear. The first is between *mission* and *missions*. When we speak of the *mission of the Church* we mean everything the Church is sent into the world to do—preaching the gospel, healing the sick, caring for the poor, teaching the children, improving international and interracial relations, attacking injustice—all of this and more can rightly be included in the phrase the *Mission of the Church*. But within this totality there is a narrower concern which we usually speak of as *missions*. Let us, without being too refined, describe this narrower concern by saying: it is the concern that in the places where there are no Christians there should be Christians. And let us narrow the concern down still further and say that within the concept of missions there is the still narrower concern which we call—or used to call—*Foreign Missions*, which is the concern that Jesus should be acknowledged as Lord by the whole earth. (italics added)[5]

The evolution of "mission" has now moved beyond Newbigin's definition. The mission of the church is now understood by most mainline liberal-ecumenicals in terms of the whole range of the church's service and witness to society and the world. It includes not only everything the church is "sent out" to do—its outreach—but *everything it does, including all its own internal and maintenance activities*. Distinctions between "expenses" and "benevolences" have been wiped out in "mission budgets." Paying the pastor, repainting the church kitchen, utilizing a management consultant to improve internal communication processes for the church staff, as well as providing a church school, a local ministry to the poor or aged, and contributions to regional and national denominational program—all these are included in the concept of "mission of the church."

In examining the significance of this changed understanding for the evangelical confrontation with the mainline churches, we must remember that *evangelicals define themselves in terms of evangelism*. This, quite simply, is the derivation of the label. Whatever else may be held in common throughout this increasingly diverse movement, the unity of evangelicals is in their "common goal of evangelizing the world for Christ." [6] Newbigin's second category—missions as "the concern that in all places where there are no Christians there should be Christians"—is a foundation of evangelicalism. It is not a "negotiable issue," but rather the starting point. Most mainline evangelicals have accepted the fact that "mission of the church" is now used in a much broader sense than this. They are willing to go as far as Newbigin's definition, although they may be somewhat uncomfortable with the further broadened managerial use of the term which embraces everything the church does.

But for them—and this distinction is crucial—"mission of the church" has not *replaced* "missions." Missions remains central and is perceived as the most important aspect of the mission of the church.

For mainline liberal-ecumenicals, "mission of the church" has *replaced* "missions" in their understanding of the church's goals.[7] When they speak of overseas mission or international mission, they do not mean at all the same thing as evangelicals who use these terms. They mean rather that dimension of the one "mission of the church" in all its inclusiveness which takes place overseas. They will likely avoid even making a geographical distinction between home and overseas and seek rather to conceptualize mission as the same inside or outside the United States. Thus the Board of Global Ministries of the United Methodist Church encompasses ministries in America as well as overseas. It does have National and World Divisions within that Board. The Program Agency of the United Presbyterian Church does not even make this distinction, although it has Area Liaison desks for various regions of the world.

The terms "overseas mission" or "world mission" or "international mission" mean for evangelicals exactly the same thing "foreign missions" used to mean for them—spreading the gospel to the unreached. They have always included social dimensions in this definition. Healing the sick, caring for the poor, teaching the children, alleviating suffering—these have traditionally been part of the evangelical concern. Newer evangelicals are frequently willing, even insistent, that this concern be widened to include social change: attacking injustice, improving the social and economic order, but always with the goal "that Jesus should be acknowledged as Lord by the whole earth."

No wonder, then, that debates between mainliners and evangelicals about "overseas mission" are so often circular, fruitless, and frustrating to all concerned. The two sides are not talking about the same thing.

The Changed Situation in the Third World

The semantic problems over "missions" and "mission of the church" have developed against the background of a radically changed situation in that area of the world which has historically been the site of "foreign missions." The contemporary term "third world" distinguishes it from the first world of western democratic government and capitalist economic systems, and the second world of communist countries. Until the Second World War, most of Africa consisted of dependencies of the western colonial powers, whether officially known as colonies, as mandated or trust territories, or as independent nations "associated" with a colonialist power. The situation was similar in southern and southeastern Asia and in much of the Middle East. Most of the Latin American nations were independent, but they were unstable, underdeveloped, and economically dependent.

The two decades following the Second World War brought what was probably the most sweeping worldwide change in governmental systems since the fall of the Roman Empire. This vast region—practically the entire southern hemisphere—gained its political independence and set out in pursuit of "development": the industrialization, technology, and affluence of the first and second worlds.

A largely unrecognized and unappreciated dimension of this revolutionary change was the contribution made by a century of "foreign missions." One of the legacies of the foreign mission movement was educational. Nearly all the colonial powers had provided some elementary-level educational opportunities for indigenous populations and the more enlightened administrators had provided higher education and technological training for a limited number of indigenous elites. Nearly everywhere, however, the mission schools were an extremely important element—in some areas the dominant element—providing at least a nucleus of educated indigenous leadership ready to assume responsibility when independence came. Throughout Africa, in country after country, today's leadership is the product of yesterday's mission school system. A second major legacy was a social welfare infrastructure. Hospitals in particular were mission products, as were a wide range of health care and social service institutions. In many—perhaps most—of the developing nations the missions provided the base on which national programs of social welfare have been built.

The most important legacy of the foreign mission movement, at least from the Christian perspective, was the network of churches in every region, every culture, every new nation. Mission agencies had sometimes been church-based and sometimes independent, sometimes denominational and sometimes interdenominational, but the goal in the mission field had always been the formation of churches. No matter how tenuous had been the relationship with institutional churches at home, the church was to be the institutional form in the new region. Even though in many instances denominational structures had not been formed when independence came, a network of local congregations was invariably ready to become a denomination.

The independence and autonomy of national churches is now the third world reality with which western mission agencies deal. In some instances this independence resulted from government action, requiring mission property and church control to be turned over to the indigenous church. In others, it was simply a cultural necessity in the new situation of national independence and self-consciousness. In general, the mainline mission agencies were quicker to relinquish control and to place their missionaries under the authority of the national churches than were the conservative and independent missions. Tim Stafford, a Youth For Christ magazine editor in Kenya, illustrated this difference:

> In the Anglican Church . . . which in Kenya is basically evangelical in belief, national leaders govern not only the church, but also the missionaries who come to help. Africa Inland Mission, an evangelical interdenominational mission with 350 missionaries in Kenya, is somewhere in the middle: the church [Africa

Inland Church] runs the church, but the mission still runs the missionaries; they are working now to change that. With other missions, it is no secret that the missionaries still run virtually everything.[8]

Foot-dragging, however, as Stafford goes on to suggest, can be counterproductive. "A young well-educated Kenyan knows quite well which churches are likely to offer him chances at leadership." The transition is being made across the board—mainline church and independent mission, with or without governmental pressure. The new pattern is recognized and accepted by liberal-ecumenicals and evangelicals alike.

The now autonomous churches have provided one of the most significant elements in the new third world equation. "Foreign missions" did its work well; so well, in fact, that numerically the balance of worldwide Christianity has shifted to the southern hemisphere, and Christians in the developing world below the equator now outnumber those in the western nations. They are the church of the future.[9] Despite the dependency engendered by mission structures, the tendency of missionaries in the old order to hold the reins of power, and the paternalism inherent in the old system, the new churches have become strong and autonomous with remarkable speed. They are among the best-organized, best-led, and most stable institutional structures in the new nations, and their role in national development has thus been an important one.

In this climate, a number of indigenous denominations have become a major force, denominations unrelated to western mission agencies or missionaries and entirely independent in origins—such as the Kimbanguists in central Africa, other African Independent Churches in southern and East Africa, and a number of Pentecostal denominations in Latin America. As we shall see in a later chapter, the new churches of the third world are having a significant effect on the older western churches, and they may play a particularly important role in the solution to the confrontation between evangelicals and the mainline denominations.

The self-consciousness of the developing nations has meant affirmation of their own cultural traditions and identity. It has meant rejection of imperialism, of paternalism, and of all vestiges of the old order. For obvious reasons, though, they have seldom really rejected, and have often eagerly sought, those aspects of westernization associated with material prosperity. In some instances it has meant a closing of the door to missionaries who have been associated with the old order. More often, however, mission agencies and missionaries have continued to be welcomed as contributors to national development.

I remember vividly the customs official in Zaire as I left Kinshasa for Kananga, who, on learning that my visit had to do with the missionaries in Kananga, placed the necessary stamp on my baggage with some reluctance and the accusatory question, "Why do you not send missionaries to my region?

We need them just as much as Kananga!" As long as they have respected the authority and institutions of the new nation, most missions have continued to be welcome.

The national churches in the developing world have readily recognized their common identity with worldwide Christianity and have made common cause with western Christians. This does not mean they have all joined the World Council of Churches (though many have, including some of the independent indigenous churches without western missionary roots.) They tend, by and large, to be more conservative than the mainline denominations of the United States. They are, however, well—and ably—represented in international consultations and conversations, whether or not they are part of the liberally-oriented conciliar ecumenical movement.

How Mainliners and Evangelicals See the Change

The radically changed context in the third world is obviously of major importance for the overseas mission enterprise, but the perception of the mainline power structure is quite different from that of the evangelicals. Mainliners tend to think evangelicals are not aware of, or are unwilling to accept the reality of, the changes. They accuse them of still operating as if the world were divided into colonial powers and colonies, of paternalism toward "natives," and of trying to foist their own western values and goals on societies in which these are inappropriate.

Certainly remnants of the old attitudes remain, though they are undoubtedly more prominent in long-term evangelical missionaries who date back to pre-independence days than in the younger liberal-ecumenical community development workers overseas. It must be said in fairness, however, that paternalism is as inherent in the liberal's insistence on "appropriate technology" in the face of a new nation's determination to have its own steel plants, as in the conservative's insistence on monogamous marriage in the face of tribal insistence on polygamy. The mainline perception that evangelicals have not adapted to the changed situation is, by and large, inaccurate. Both groups are quite aware of the changes, both know and respect the young churches in the developing countries, and both want to work in partnership with them. The difference lies in the *ends* of that partnership—the commitment to "missions" and to "mission."

Mainliners tend to define overseas mission exclusively in terms of *partnership* with overseas churches (or ecumenical agencies). They seek to make it a two-way partnership even to the extent of occasionally footing the bill for a reverse missionary from a third world nation to work in this country. Since the realities of resources and needs are mainly in one direction, however, overseas mission does tend to become *interchurch aid* to third world churches. The mainliners try to let the receiving churches define the kind of aid they want, "responding" to "requests" from the churches (although they often plant or shape the requests to which they respond). To third world ambivalence about missionaries they respond either by playing down the role of missionaries or by moving from "old style" (evangelistic) to "new style" (social change or institutional support of the church) missionaries.

Evangelicals, too, work in partnership with younger churches in the radically changed third world.[10] The voice of third world Christians was probably just as strong at the International Congress on Evangelization in Lausanne in 1974 as at the World Council of Churches in Nairobi in 1976. The basic difference is the *goal* of that partnership. For evangelicals, "mission of the church" has not replaced "missions," but has only placed missions in a broader context. They do not regard missions—understood as reaching the unreached—as "old style," but as the unchanged central element in the "mission of the church." They carry on this activity in partnership with like-minded third world churches, and in areas where churches (or churches of a similar perspective) do not yet exist. They engage, as they always have, in works of mercy and compassion and are increasingly willing to participate with partner churches in ministries of social change as well. Many of them understand and support the concern of young church leaders for liberation from oppressive social systems as well as from personal sin and do not challenge the right of third world churches to work for such liberation. The ultimate purpose of their partnership as evangelicals, however, is always "evangelizing the world for Christ."

In passing we should note that a divergence between evangelicals and liberal-ecumenicals similar to that found in mainline American denominations also exists in the third world (where liberals are often known simply as "ecumenicals"). In Africa, which I visited on behalf of my denomination in the spring of 1979 to evaluate overseas mission involvements, the denominations which are offspring of mainline American churches are generally more conservative than the parent churches. They are evangelical, have been growing quite rapidly, and are continuing to grow. Both rank and file members and pastors are preoccupied with spreading the gospel, assimilating new members and new congregations, and with a multitude of internal problems common to all vigorous young institutions.

Church leaders, as part of the intelligentsia of the developing nations, are much concerned with liberation issues, particularly as they relate to white South Africa and the remaining countries in southern Africa where majority rule has not yet been achieved. They tend to identify with black guerilla movements and to oppose repressive regimes, black as well as white. They are intensely concerned with the development of their countries, particularly in the fields related to social welfare. They are concerned about economic exploitation and about the affirmation of their own indigenous culture and traditions. In all these areas, their attitudes are generally congruent with those of the western mainline churches who cooperate with them through the national councils of churches and the various African ecumenical organizations (which are generally funded from American and European sources).

Yet one finds very little of the kind of polarization between socially concerned church leaders and the evangelical rank and file which one finds between the liberal-ecumenicals and the evangelicals in the United States. Except for a few who have been co-opted into the international organizations in staff positions and who reflect the liberalism of their western colleagues, these leaders share the evangelical theological orientation of their churches. Many are probably closer in spirit to the socially involved "new evangelicals" in America than to American mainline leadership. A "moratorium" on the sending of missionaries, earlier proposed by some indigenous church leaders, is not much of an issue with them. Generally they welcome missionaries and are happy to work in partnership with evangelicals in the task of reaching the unreached in their nations. They also welcome the institutional support and the social change ministries which American mainline leadership prefers to send. Offered a choice, some of the leaders prefer and request missionaries of the latter kind, though not, as mainliners like to tell themselves, because they consider evangelistic missionaries "old style" and paternalistic or have disavowed evangelism by westerners, but rather because they can provide evangelization themselves. Social change technologies and sophisticated institutional management techniques—which the American mainline leadership can provide—are in short supply. One finds remarkably little polarization between evangelism and social change in African Protestantism on the whole because they are combined in these vigorous young churches.

In Latin America, which I visited on a similar mission evaluation tour in 1977, the situation is different. Here evangelicals and "ecumenicals" are highly polarized. Protestant churches, generally, are extremely conservative, and those with roots in North American mainline churches especially so. Few of them are related to the World Council of Churches or to the network of western-sponsored "ecumenical" committees and action groups throughout the region. The leadership of the Roman Catholic Church in Latin America is closest in spirit to mainline North American church leadership.

In the Far East one also finds a pattern of daughter churches tending to be far more conservative than the mainline American denominations to which they are related. This is not universally the case. Within the Kyodan in Japan (the product of a union between Protestants of many denominational backgrounds), the same kind of internal polarization between liberals and evangelicals exists as in the American mainline.

One other important factor for the evangelical perception of mission is the minority status of the Protestant churches in most of the third world. In Latin

America, the majority is Roman Catholic. The maintenance of evangelistic mission activities aimed at converting Christians (albeit nominal Christians without a vital faith) from Roman Catholicism is hard to justify, even for the highly sectarian. For mainline evangelicals it is still harder. In the rest of the non-western world, however, where the great non-Christian religions— Islam, Buddhism, Hinduism—have their strongholds and where large numbers of primitive animists remain, the evangelicals still see a major task. The two-thirds of the world's population as yet unreached for Christ remains for them the basic challenge.

The point of difference between the mainline establishment and the evangelicals is not the failure of the latter to recognize and understand the changes that have taken place in the third world. It is their response to these changes. The mainline establishment sees a third world where churches are already established, and no longer a "mission field" in the classic sense. The planting of churches throughout the world has now been achieved. Overseas mission now becomes partnership with and aid to these churches in their broadly defined mission. The relativism and tolerance of a liberal world view now demand a kind of respect for non-Christian religions which precludes overt attempts to evangelize among them. Evangelism as such is a low liberal priority in any case. So the mainline establishment, while permitting some "old style" remnants to continue, seeks partnership with those denominations, leaders, and ecumenical organizations sharing the goals to which it is committed: institutional support and maintenance and social change.

Evangelicals see the established and autonomous denominations in the newly independent countries of the third world as an unfinished task. They seek the partnership of these churches in *completing* the task of reaching the unreached and tend to be more comfortable with the denominational rank and file in these areas than are establishment representatives; their evangelical viewpoint is probably more common at the grass roots than that of the mainliners, which is limited to a relatively small leadership class. They are willing to engage in joint evangelization efforts with the indigenous churches in reaching their own people, or to focus through cross-cultural evangelism on areas not yet reached by the national churches (these churches tend to be concentrated in particular areas). Finally, they continue to support the kind of medical and social welfare ministries to which they have historically been committed as forms of Christian witness. But their basic goal continues to be reaching the unreached.

Both mainliners and evangelicals, then, are fully aware of the radically changed context in overseas mission, but their *responses* to it are quite different.

The Shift from Mainline to Parachurch Dominance

The structures through which mainliners and evangelicals respond are also quite different. Since the liberal establishment controls the mainline denominations—particularly the bureaucracies of the mission agencies—the liberal-ecumenical view prevails in the official denominational structures. What takes place overseas is not "missions" but "mission"—the whole mission of the church. It takes place through a variety of channels by no means limited to missionaries; indeed the sending of missionaries has long been deemphasized. Among those still being sent overseas, those engaged directly in evangelization are a small minority. Most are either in support roles for the national churches or in social ministries. When I visited Zaire—my own denomination's largest mission engagement in Africa—in 1979, I found that although many of the missionaries are themselves evangelicals and although they regard their work (largely medical) as evangelical, only three of the thirty-four were assigned as evangelists.

Yet overseas mission remains in a special way the "cause" of the evangelicals. They are committed to it, and they provide the bulk of its financial support. Hence the conflict.

The evolution from "missions" to "mission" in mainline overseas involvements has been neither simple nor direct. It has taken place slowly and with mixed results, and is certainly not yet completed. Until the restructuring of the mainline denominational bureaucracies in the 1960s and 70s, control of the foreign mission agencies (which to a considerable extent operated as semi-autonomous internal parachurch agencies) had remained largely in the hands of the evangelicals of the denominations. After the changes brought by restructuring, evangelicals in the pew continue to identify overseas mission and missionaries with their own evangelical goals. Although puzzled and often angry and frustrated with the trend they perceive, they continue to trust and support denominational overseas mission activities more than other aspects of denominational programs. In a climate of growing suspicion and awareness of change, however, they have been increasingly aggressive in two ways. One is to seek restrictions on the way the money they give to the denomination can be used. Evangelicals regard overseas mission as "their" cause, and they have increasingly been designating their gifts to support it. In my own Presbyterian Church, U. S., donor-designated and specialized giving now exceed contributions to the regular budget of the General Assembly Mission Board, and by far the largest portion of it is restricted for overseas use. More recently, as awareness has grown that not all overseas work is in accord with their intentions, the trend has been to designate the *way* money can be used overseas.

More significant in the long run, however, may be the second way evangelicals have been reacting, through the support of non-denominational parachurch organizations engaged in overseas mission. We noted at the beginning of this chapter the declining number of missionaries serving overseas under the auspices of denominations affiliated with the Department of Overseas Mission (DOM) of the generally mainline National Council of Churches. In the six year period from 1969 to 1975, the total dropped by about one-third, from 8,000 to 5,010. There are, however, two other groupings of missionary-sending agencies: the Evangelical Foreign Mission Association (EFMA), representing thirty-seven conservative denominational agencies and thirty-five independent agencies; and the Independent Foreign Mission Association (IFMA), with forty-four independent groups. (Some overlapping occurs, since a few agencies belong to two associations.) During that same six-year period, the number of missionaries serving overseas under EFMA agency sponsorship *increased* by 15 percent, from 6,500 to 7,500, and the number serving under IFMA increased from 6,000 to 6,500 (8 percent).[11]

Financial comparisons are even more striking. While overseas mission funds contributed through NCC-DOM decreased in that period from $145 million to $125 million (down 13 percent), funds contributed through the other two associations, EFMA and IFMA, *increased* by 136 percent, from $95 million to $225 million. When the agencies not affiliated with either EFMA or IFMA are taken into consideration, total overseas mission income, when adjusted for inflation, increased in this six year period from $317 million to $404 million.[12] The number of missionaries increased from 34,460 to 36,950. The "decline in overseas mission," then, is not a decline at all, but is rather a *shift* from mainline dominance to evangelical and parachurch dominance.

Parachurch Overseas Mission Agencies

The largest of the independent evangelical parachurch agencies devoted to overseas mission is Wycliffe Bible Translators. In fact, in the number of personnel overseas it was in 1975 (the last year for which comparative figures were available) the largest of *all* agencies, denominational or independent, having passed the previous leader, the Southern Baptist Foreign Mission Board, in the preceding three-year period.[13] With a reported income of $19.1 million in that year, it was also one of the largest agencies in terms of funds received, exceeded only by overseas agencies of the Southern Baptists, the Seventh Day Adventists, the Church World Service agency of the National Council of Churches, the Assemblies of God, and the United Methodist Church.

The primary emphasis of the Wycliffe organization is linguistic analysis and Bible translation as a tool for evangelism. Organized in 1935, it has been a major force in the movement toward making Scriptures available in ever increasing numbers of languages and dialects. Affiliated with it is the Summer Institute of Linguistics (SIL), which often contracts with third world governments to carry on linguistic studies, and which plays a primary role in

Wycliffe's linguistic work. Headquartered in Huntington Beach, California (with several branch offices), the Wycliffe organization has a staff of around three thousand. It is involved in aviation, literacy aid, and medical missions as well as Scripture translation and publishes a monthly periodical, *In Other Words.*

Wycliffe Bible Translators received a great deal of publicity in 1956 when five of its missionaries were massacred by the Auca Indian tribe in a remote area of Ecuador. Wycliffe continued its work with the Aucas (now known as the Waorani tribe); the wife of one of the slain missionaries, who returned to continue the work after her husband's death, completed the translation of the first portion of the Bible (the Gospel of Mark) into the Waorani language. As a result of the Wycliffe work, about one-third of the tribe is now Christian.[14]

Equally large in terms of income is World Vision International with a reported income of $19.1 million in 1975. A younger agency than Wycliffe (established in 1950), World Vision sends few Americans overseas but carries on an extensive program of emergency relief, child care, and evangelism in thirty-six countries. As a relief agency it has become, in effect, the evangelical counterpart of the mainline Church World Service (related to the National Council). It serves both missions and national churches, and it has conducted more than a hundred pastors' conferences in over thirty countries. It publishes the monthly *World Vision* magazine.

An important subsidiary of World Vision International is the Missions Advanced Research and Communication Center (MARC), located at the home office in Monrovia, California. MARC, providing both research on evangelism as well as management training and consultation, functions as an information center on church and mission activities overseas. It published (jointly with the Division of Overseas Mission of the NCC) the current (eleventh) edition of the *Mission Handbook*, the source of most of the information in this section.

The Evangelical Alliance Mission (TEAM) is one of the oldest and best known independent evangelical agencies engaged in the traditional evangelism and church planting endeavors. Its overseas corps of 892 missionaries placed it, in 1975, within the top ten agencies. TEAM was established in 1890 as the Scandinavian Alliance Mission, the present name being adopted in 1949. In addition to traditional evangelistic activities, it is also involved in education, literature, linguistics, medicine, radio, and other specialized services. It operates in twenty-one countries from a home office in Wheaton, Illinois.

The New Tribes Mission, established in 1942 to evangelize and establish churches among unreached tribal people, is also in the top ten agencies in number of personnel overseas. Its 864 missionaries work in sixteen countries, usually in remote areas.

Many of the independent parachurch agencies, such as the Africa Inland

Mission or the Brazil Gospel Fellowship Mission, focus on one region or country. Others provide highly specialized services. The Mission Aviation Fellowship, for example, supplies aviation, radio, and purchasing services to mission agencies and churches in fifteen countries. The World Radio Mission Fellowship broadcasts over shortwave in fifteen languages from the famed "Voice of the Andes" radio station, HCJB, in Quito, Ecuador. Some, like "Youth with a Mission" (with a thousand young people serving one-year terms overseas) and Teen Missions (sending teenagers on summer work programs and evangelistic teams), offer mission opportunities to a specialized American constituency. Others, such as Campus Crusade and Navigators, extend specialized services first developed in the United States to other countries throughout the world and are now numbered among the major overseas agencies.

The role of Inter-Varsity Christian Fellowship, which like Campus Crusade and Navigators is one of the major youth-oriented parachurch organizations in recruiting for overseas mission service (see chapter 4), should not be overlooked. The triennial Urbana conventions, attended by tens of thousands of young people, are focused almost entirely on presenting the missionary challenge. At Urbana '79, Inter-Varsity committed itself to motivating at least one thousand persons a year for the next five years to enter missionary service.[15]

Most of the parachurch overseas mission agencies are quite small. Of the 620 agencies (denominational and independent) listed in the eleventh edition of the *Mission Handbook*, 346 reported a specified number of overseas personnel. One half of these (mostly independent) had seventeen people or less serving overseas. As we have seen, however, the parachurch agencies represent cumulatively an enormous expenditure of funds and dedicated effort. As we noted at the beginning of this section, by far the largest share of American overseas mission work is now evangelical rather than mainline, and of that evangelical work, the larger share is under the independent agencies. The "decline of overseas mission" has not been a decline at all, but rather a massive shift from mainline to evangelical, from church-sponsored to parachurch overseas mission. The data show that we are indeed "leaving it to the independents."

Two Symbols: The World Council of Churches and the Lausanne Committee

The World Council of Churches has played a particularly significant role in defining overseas mission for the mainline liberal establishment. A longtime symbol of church unity—one of the most enduring of the liberal Christian goals—the World Council is viewed by mainline liberal-ecumenicals as the most important overseas engagement and, with its wide-ranging social concerns, the centerpiece of overseas mission. Its church conciliar model is congruent with the church partnership mode of mainline relationships. Its Geneva bureaucracy is the mecca to which mainline bureaucrats go and come, many of them serving in its agencies for a period and then returning to their own churches.

Because the Assemblies and Committees of the World Council are staffed by denominational power elites, there is a minimum of the kind of influence from grassroots evangelical minorities which tends to moderate the positions and actions of the denominations themselves. The World Council, therefore, is probably the place where the liberal-ecumenical vision of world Christianity is purest, where the devotion to social change is most fully realized. It has symbolic significance, therefore, not only for mainline supporters, but also for evangelical dissenters, as evidenced by the title of a recent book, *The World Council of Churches and the Demise of Evangelism*.[16] During the late seventies, grants from a WCC agency to Zimbabwean guerila groups became a focal point for much of this symbolism.

Throughout the third world there is a network of ecumenical agencies which are generally related to the World Council. They receive their financial support largely from the World Council and from WCC-related denominations in the west. Their activities tend to focus on social change, and their base of support in the indigenous churches tends to be small, although if they are organized as Councils of Churches (as is frequently the case) their Assemblies and committees are made up of indigenous church leaders. Their bureaucracies, however, tend to be funded almost entirely from foreign sources, and this gives them an important measure of independence in their work for social change. So clear is the identification and so great the symbolic significance that throughout much of the third world, as we have noted earlier, "ecumenical" is the term used to label liberal-social activist Christians.

A symbol on the evangelical side corresponding to the World Council and its network of ecumenical agencies may be the 1974 International Congress on World Evangelization, held at Lausanne, Switzerland, with the resulting Lausanne Covenant and Lausanne Committee. Whether the Lausanne Committee will develop into a permanently staffed evangelical counterpart to the World Council of Churches remains to be seen, though such a development does not appear likely. The "spirit of Lausanne" itself, however, remains active. Follow-up national congresses have been held in a number of countries (a major one in the United States took place in 1981 in Kansas City), but the Committee lacks the conciliar base of the World Council, and ecumenism (as an end in itself rather than a means to other ends) does not have the priority for evangelicals that it does for liberal-ecumenicals.

Nonetheless, the worldwide movement launched by the Lausanne Congress continues to gather strength. "Mission 80," the Second Missionary Conference for European Youth held in Lausanne in the last five days of 1979, was planned for three thousand young people (twenty-five hundred attended the first one in December 1975). It was swamped by an attendance of more than seven thousand from over twenty countries.[17]

Perhaps the greatest impact of the Lausanne Congress has been its symbolic importance to the evangelical community. In its first three articles on the purpose of God, the authority and power of the Bible, and the uniqueness and universality of Christ, the Lausanne Covenant provided what is probably the best and most widely-accepted statement of the evangelical concept of mission. It affirmed the centrality of evangelism in this concept. In its fourth clause, beginning with the words, "to evangelize is to spread the good news," it provided an authoritative (for evangelicals) definition of evangelism: "the proclamation of the historical, biblical Christ as Saviour and Lord, with a view to persuading people to come to him personally and so be reconciled to God."

From the mainline perspective, however, probably the most significant thing about the Lausanne Congress and Covenant is the seriousness with which Christian social responsibility has been taken. Not only is the fifth clause of the Covenant devoted to this theme, but the relationship between social concern and evangelism was one of the intensely discussed issues at the Congress. The Covenant says, "we express penitence both for our neglect and for having sometimes regarded evangelism and social concern as mutually exclusive." The Christian judgment on "every form of alienation, oppression and discrimination," the denunciation of injustice, and the call for Christian socio-political involvement are clear and explicit.[18]

The Lausanne combination of evangelicalism and social responsibility is probably much closer to the spirit of third world Christianity generally than is mainline American Christianity. The relativistic scientific world view which underlies mainline liberalism finds it hard to be completely comfortable with the exclusive character of the evangelical claim. Because of its respect for other religions, it is at best ambivalent about evangelization of non-Christians. Its witness is necessarily unaggressive, and it is far more comfortable with social witness. Third world Christianity, however, combines an uncomplicated evangelicalism with an intense social concern based on the experience of oppression.

Lausanne may also be a harbinger of the direction in which American Christianity is moving, with a renewed and growing evangelicalism recovering the historic social concern of its earlier tradition. It may point toward the kind of center position which could once again engage the commitment of the mainstream.

Too much can be read into the symbolism of the World Council of Churches, representing the liberal-ecumenical vision of world mission, and the Lausanne Committee on World Evangelization, representing the evangelical vision. Yet the differences are real and clearly perceived. In 1980, both agencies sponsored world evangelism conferences. The Commission on World Mission and Evangelism of the World Council met in Melbourne, Australia, in May. The Lausanne Committee sponsored a Consultation on World Evangelization in Pattaya, Thailand, in June. The theme of the World Council's Melbourne conference was "Your Kingdom Come," and its emphasis was on the identification of Christianity with the poor and marginalized of the world in their struggle for liberation and justice. The Lausanne Committee's Thailand conference theme was "How Shall They Hear?" and it focused on the worldwide evangelization task in terms of specific strategies for reaching tribes, cultures, communities, and groups as yet unaware of the gospel.

The contrast in themes, constituencies, and goals—and the symbolism of the two consultations—are inescapable. Arthur F. Glasser, editor of the journal, *Missiology*, expressed in a pre-conference editorial his concern that the outcome would be further polarization. He pointed, however, to the strongly scriptural orientation of the materials for both conferences—the pre-Easter words of Jesus from the Gospels, on which the Melbourne conference focused, and the post-Easter commission and texts from the Epistles of Pattaya. He pointed to the potential for unity in a gospel which included both the call for the Kingdom and the task of evangelization. The proclamation of a balanced gospel giving full rein to both emphases may be the compelling challenge for the international mission enterprise today.[19]

chapter 7

the charismatic
renewal:
bridge or shoal?

"Charismatic" is a scare word to many mainline ministers. Some congregations have been split—and others renewed—by the movement. Some pastors have been fired—and others revitalized—because of it. Church members caught up in the movement have been seen as divisive fanatics—or Spirit-filled healers. Once regarded as oddballs or scornfully dismissed as "holy rollers," charismatics in growing numbers are now vestry members and Sunday School teachers in mainline churches. They are our sons, daughters, and spouses, and they frighten us.

An examination of the charismatic movement and its implications for mainline churches would probably best begin with a brief look at the term "charismatic." [1] It is used here to refer to a particular kind of religious experience, to persons who have had the experience, and to a loose network or movement, organized and unorganized, of such persons throughout the churches. The term "pentecostal" is often used to mean roughly the same thing, although the latter word, for many, has institutional associations with the pentecostal denominations.

At the heart of either term is an *experience* of the Holy Spirit; this is the first important aspect of the meaning of the term "charismatic." An early meeting of Catholic charismatics in Rome (1970) described it as "the personal and direct awareness and experiencing of the indwelling of the Holy Spirit." Theological discussions tend to center on the "baptism of the Holy Spirit" or "second baptism." Our concern is not with this dimension, but with the experience itself.

Second, it is regarded as of the same order as the experience of the original disciples at Pentecost, and the experience discussed at some length in the Pauline epistles (most prominently in the treatment of spiritual gifts in chapters 12, 13 and 14 of 1 Corinthians). The word "charismatic," of course, is directly derived from the New Testament Greek word, "charism" or "charisma," usually rendered as "spiritual gift." The "charis" or grace of God is manifested in "charismata," gifts of grace.

Finally, the experience to which we are referring is prominently manifested in "glossalalia" or "speaking in tongues," although many who do not speak in tongues consider themselves charismatics.[2] Glossalalia is only one of the spiritual gifts listed and discussed in the New Testament. Along with spiritual healing, however, it is a distinctive mark of the charismatic movement in this century. Today's charismatics, says Richard Quebedeaux, "usually feel that the ability to 'speak in tongues' as a prayer language is the best evidence of Spirit baptism."[3] We are talking, then, about an intense personal experience of the Holy Spirit in the tradition of the experience of the disciples at Pentecost and often accompanied or expressed by speaking in tongues.

World Pentecostalism

When I visited churches and church leaders in Latin America in 1977, I saw at first hand what many observers have pointed out, namely, that Protestantism in Latin America is predominantly pentecostal. Mainline churches there, products of North American missionary activity, are small and isolated compared to the large and growing indigenous pentecostal churches. Apart from Cardinal Ernesto Arns and Dom Helder Camara of the Roman Catholic Church, the most impressive religious leader I met in Latin America was Manoel de Mello, head of a large Brazilian pentecostal denomination.

The impression of pentecostal vitality was further reinforced for me on a 1979 visit to churches and church leaders in Africa, the Middle East, and Europe. I found that by far the largest Protestant denomination in Zaire (and one of the largest in Africa) is the Kimbanguist Church (the Church of Jesus Christ on Earth through the Prophet Simon Kimbangu), mentioned in the last chapter as a major indigenous African denomination without missionary roots. Whether it can be called a pentecostal church in the popular sense is debatable, since it does not strongly emphasize speaking in tongues. Certainly, however, it belongs to the pentecostal family; the experience of the Holy Spirit is central and spiritual healing is a prominent element. In Israel, on the same trip, I encountered by chance a Pentecostal minister from Kansas en route back to the United States from a visit in the Soviet Union. The purpose of his trip had been the smuggling of funds to underground Russian pentecostals, and he told me that two pentecostal congregations had recently been established in Leningrad and Kiev with official approval—a breakthrough. But this, he said, is only the tiny tip of the huge iceberg which is the underground church. I asked him how large the Soviet underground pentecostal movement is. About five million, he told me. Even allowing for the natural enthusiasm of one as dedicated to the cause as he, and for an expansive definition of pentecostalism, that is an enormous movement! In Brussels my wife attended an ecumenical meeting of women. By chance she sat next to a Catholic charismatic from Ann Arbor, Michigan. This woman and her husband, because of their charismatic involvement, had been invited to Brussels by the cardinal to help revitalize the Belgian church. Under the leadership of Cardinal Suenens, Brussels has become something of an unofficial headquarters for the worldwide Catholic charismatic movement.

Henry Pitney Van Dusen, in the late 1950s, after discovering Latin American pentecostalism during a Caribbean vacation, labeled the pentecostal denominations a "third force" in world Christianity alongside Protestantism and Roman Catholicism.[4] We provincial Americans are often unaware of just how major a force it has become on the rest of the globe. The twelve thousand delegates to the twelfth Pentecostal World Conference, held in Vancouver, B. C., in 1979, were told that there are now more than fifty million pentecostals in eighty nations.[5]

American mainliners in the past were distantly aware of the American pentecostal denominations. We thought of them as one group of the small separatist fundamentalist denominations "out there" on the periphery of mainstream American Christianity. In the last decade, however, with the flowering of the neo-evangelical movement, pentecostalism has made itself forcefully felt in our own country. Jeremy Rifkin and Ted Howard, in their book *The Emerging Order,* see the charismatic movement as a major element in the evangelical renewal which they expect will modify substantively the world view of western humankind faced with an age of scarcity and the collapse of the Enlightenment-Calvinist faith in economic expansionism. They are ambiguous as to whether they regard the charismatic movement as *part* of renascent evangelicalism or as a parallel development.[6] It may be regarded as a parallel movement since its numbers include some liberal-ecumenicals as well as evangelicals. One writer sees the two movements as "overlapping circles: many evangelicals define themselves as charismatics; many charismatics define themselves as evangelicals."[7] However delineated, contemporary pentecostalism is clearly a major movement related to the evangelical renewal, with worldwide manifestations and with special implications for mainline American Protestantism.

Theological Context

The theological context of the contemporary charismatic movement is a significant revival of interest in the Holy Spirit. William G. McLoughlin, in his book on *Revivals, Awakenings and Reform,* suggests that a "Fourth Great

Awakening" may have been under way in the United States since the 1960s. The awakening entered all three of America's faith groups, he says, "as a new concern over direct personal encounters with God's Spirit." He sees the revival of orthodoxy and rising interest in Hasidism as pentecostal and charismatic counterparts in Judaism.[8]

The theological journal *Interpretation* devoted its entire issue for the first quarter of 1979 to the Holy Spirit. Hans Küng—whose writings have been almost as influential with Protestants as with his own Catholic Church—in his monumental work, *The Church*, makes it a central theme that the church is what it is through the presence and power of the Holy Spirit. Jürgen Moltmann, an extremely influential Protestant theologian, called a recently translated work *The Church in the Power of the Spirit*.[9] These two books deal with the doctrine of the church; charismatics, however, have very little interest in "doctrine of the church." The significant thing is that non-charismatics, theologians, and ecclesiologists with a strong concern for the institutional church are also focusing attention in quite a different way on the Holy Spirit. This popular, personal, experience-oriented movement, based on the presence of the Spirit in the lives of people, is part of a larger recovery of the sense of the presence of the Spirit in theology and institutions.

Even in such a prosaic and sociologically oriented field as church organizational studies, the Spirit movement is being felt. As we have already noted, mainline churches since mid-century have been participating enthusiastically in the managerial revolution which has changed the character of our whole society. Many of our organizational and managerial assumptions, derived from management science and the human relations movement, led us to seek organizational, structural and managerial solutions to the church's problems. The wave of restructuring in the late sixties and early seventies and the infatuation with goal-setting and Management by Objective (MBO) in the late seventies were illustrations. Now we, too, are waking up to a renewed appreciation of the uniqueness of the church. My own book, *Wheel Within the Wheel: Confronting the Management Crisis of the Pluralistic Church*, reflects the trend. The "wheel within the wheel"—that metaphoric title from the old spiritual—is the Holy Spirit, the power source within the organizational wheel. "The key," says my introduction to that book, "is the uniqueness of the church, which is centered in the active presence of the Holy Spirit. If we take that Presence seriously, the organizational and managerial implications are truly awesome." [10] The theological context, then, is a far broader renewal of interest in the Holy Spirit.

Historical Roots

The contemporary charismatic movement is a fairly new phenomenon, though church history has been filled with Spirit-filled renewal movements.

Although glossalalia had not been prominent in Christianity from the end of the apostolic age until the beginning of this century, continuity of other aspects of pentecostalism with earlier Spirit-filled renewal movements is apparent. Pentecostal historians find the roots of the recent resurgence in the eighteenth and nineteenth century holiness movements which gave birth to Methodism, to "quietism" in Roman Catholicism, and "pietism" in Protestantism. Spirit baptism, sanctification, and the "second blessing" were parts of the holiness experience, and we find a few references to speaking in tongues in the nineteenth century revivalist surges. Several prominent American church historians are examining the present charismatic movement in the context of the First and Second Great Awakenings, the previous major outbreaks of the experience of the Holy Spirit in American church history. James Smylie does this in the 1979 issue of the theological journal *Interpretation* referred to above, as does the Methodist ecumenist Albert Outler.[11] Speaking in tongues played a very minor role in the previous two Great Awakenings (mainly in the Shaker movement), but other manifestations of the Spirit were prominent.

The pentecostal churches usually date the beginning of the modern movement from events at Bethel Bible College in Topeka, Kansas, at the turn of the century. A student Bible study group had been formed in 1900, and on January 1, 1901, in a prayer session, a young woman student began to speak in tongues. Within a few days the whole community had received what it regarded as the baptism of the Holy Spirit, and the modern pentecostal movement was born. The experience was largely rejected by mainline Protestantism, but it spread rapidly to Texas, Los Angeles (in 1906, where it grew substantially), Chicago, and New York. It had appeared in England and Scandinavia by 1915. In 1914 the first American pentecostal denomination, the Assemblies of God (still the largest) was incorporated. By the middle of the century a number of other denominations had been formed, and there are now about thirty-five such denominations.[12] Though pentecostalism had little effect on mainline churches until mid-century, it became recognized as an element in the American religious scene.

Neo-Pentecostalism

The charismatic movement began to make headlines with the development called neo-pentecostalism, which has permeated the mainline denominations since mid-century. Among the mainline groups it began in the Episcopal Church, where in 1958 it first attracted attention in California and Illinois. The Episcopal hierarchy quickly became concerned and appointed investigative committees. The reports of those committees in the early 1960s resulted in a statement issued by Bishop James A. Pike in 1963 strongly discouraging the use of glossalalia, the laying on of hands, and unofficial exorcism. Nevertheless, the movement spread quickly to other denominational groups, involving both Lutherans and Presbyterians in the early sixties. An American Lutheran report in 1962 focused primarily on the problems and dangers associated with pentecostalism. The United Presbyterian Church took official cognizance of its charismatics in 1968, by appointing a special study committee. Its report, presented to the 1970 General Assembly, adopted what it called "a position of 'openness' regarding the Neo-Pentecostal movement within our denomination."

Internal denominational parachurch organizations have given the mainline movement some cohesion and organization. The Presbyterian Charismatic Communion, uniting charismatics in both the United Presbyterian Church and the Presbyterian Church, U. S. (Southern), was organized in 1966 and is thus one of the oldest mainline Protestant parachurch organizations for charismatics. It presently has a headquarters staff of nine and publishes a bi-monthly magazine, *Renewal News*. The first Lutheran Conference on the Holy Spirit was held in 1972. Lutheran Charismatic Renewal Services brings into fellowship representatives of the Lutheran Church in America, the American Lutheran Church, and the Lutheran Church, Missouri Synod. (The Missouri Synod is one of the denominations, along with the Southern Baptist Convention, which has strongly opposed the charismatic movement.) An Episcopal Charismatic Fellowship was begun in 1973, giving organizational form to one of the oldest and strongest of the denominational movements. Its name was recently changed to Episcopal Renewal Services. In 1979 its chairman reported that more than 2,000 Episcopal priests—nearly a quarter of the total—are charismatics.[13] A United Church of Christ Charismatic Fellowship was organized in 1977.

The charismatic movement has also become a major force in Roman Catholicism. It began early in 1967 at Duquesne University in Pittsburgh among a group of faculty members who had for some months been studying the baptism of the Holy Spirit. It spread quickly to Notre Dame and then to other Catholic universities and into American Catholicism in general, the Cursillo movement having done much to foster it. (Interestingly, David Wilkerson's book, *The Cross and the Switchblade*, is mentioned in several accounts of the beginnings of the Catholic movement as having been influential.) An extremely important feature of the Catholic movement has been the absence of anti-institutionalism or separatism. Said an editorial in the Catholic magazine, *America*, late in 1979:

> All along, in the midst of its Bible enthusiasm, participants insisted on the importance of the sacraments. That is mainstream Catholicism. From its inception in 1967, charismatics have shown a straightforward attachment to priests and bishops. One of the best measures of the movement's acceptance is the fact that hundreds of priests show up at summer conferences, scores of

bishops endorse and take part in them. Many dioceses now have liaison officers, and the bishops' conference has an established committee on renewal activities.[14]

National conventions, publications, periodicals, and directories are all well established. The last of many regional meetings in the summer of 1979 drew thirteen thousand Catholic charismatics to New York's Yankee Stadium in September of that year.

The first International Conference on Charismatic Renewal in Christian Churches, an ecumenical gathering, was held in Kansas City in 1977, bringing together more than fifty thousand participants. The largest group was Roman Catholic and the second largest unaffiliated Protestants. Other major groups were Episcopal, Lutheran, Baptist, Methodist, Presbyterian, and Mennonite. The conference also brought in for the first time representation from the traditional Pentecostal denominations. Although some are suggesting that the movement peaked with the 1977 convention, no real evidence suggests that it is declining. Another major rally, "Jesus '79" was held in 1979.

Sociological Context

The significance of the charismatic renewal for the mainline churches emerges against the background of mainline emphasis on the rational and the formal in religion. Another important factor is mainline loyalty to the secular scientific world view of the contemporary university with its rejection of the irrational, the supernatural, and at times even the transcendent. Finally, the background includes mainline Protestantism's recent infatuation with managerial modes of thought and techniques, leading to attempts at renewal of the church through such organizational techniques as goal-setting.

The sociological context may be understood in terms of a concept developed back in the early part of this century by pioneer sociologist Max Weber, called "the routinization of charisma." It applies not only to Christianity, but to the dynamics of religious organizations generally. Weber uses the term "charisma" not to denote speaking in tongues, but in the sociological sense of personal magnetism having its source in an immediate experience of Divine Spirit. Social movements, he said, begin under the leadership of charismatic persons. Jesus Christ, of course, is the most obvious example. From the Christian perspective, his charisma is incarnational, the Word made flesh, the immediacy of the divine presence. Weber applies the term to other movements and leaders as well.

As long as the charismatic leader of a movement is present, said Weber, people are stirred and motivated to respond, and the movement is held together and propelled by the personal force of the charisma. Formal organization is not needed. Once the leader is no longer physically present, however, if the movement is to become permanent, the charisma—the spiritual motivation—must be institutionalized and the group organized. Large numbers of people working together require rules, order, and standardized procedures. Such routinization is, of course, deadening to charisma. Members of the institution inevitably become less spirit-filled, more routinized.

Again and again charismatic movements (in Weber's sense) have arisen in religious history in opposition to a deadening, institutionalized church. Each charismatic renewal calls forth church members to a rebirth of commitment, enthusiasm, and immediacy of Christian experience. However, each such movement in turn either becomes institutionalized as a new group or subgroup within the church, and the experience it celebrated becomes "routinized," or it dies. The "Jesus movements" of the late sixties are an example. Those that survived, as we have seen, are now institutionalized as parachurch organizations. The others are long gone. The hostility toward "organized religion" and the "institutional church"—also part of the counterculture of the late sixties and early seventies—was another and related outcropping of this recurrent theme in religion. Then as always it was based on an accurate perception: "organized religion" *is* deadening to the immediacy of experience and ethusiasm.

Christian history has known a long series of Spirit-filled movements that have sought to eliminate, or at least minimize, church organization. Such movements have generally emphasized the Christian's personal experience and have therefore been individually oriented. The experience of community is not foreign to them—indeed the closeness of the group sharing the immediacy of the Spirit is a major element. The group must, however, remain small and informal. Organization and routine are the enemies of ecstacy and enthusiasm. A spiritual fellowship should need no organized forms according to this view. Yet organization and routinization inevitably follow as functions of size. As soon as the new Spirit-filled movement grows beyond a very small group, it must organize. Religious history has unfolded in this tension and dialectic between charisma and routine, enthusiasm and organization, inspiration and institution, Spirit and letter (to use Paul's terms).

Uniqueness of the Contemporary Charismatic Movement

This time, however, there is a difference. There is enormous hope for the whole church in the present charismatic movement, and it grows out of an extremely important characteristic of *this particular* movement. Unlike many previous spirit-centered movements which have followed the classic Weber paradigm, this movement is not essentially anti-institutional, but is rather making a conscious and generally successful effort to remain within the existing churches. A remarkably high percentage of individual charismatics and charismatic groups are making a determined effort to support, remain loyal to, and work within the existing structures of their own congregations. They are often the most loyal, most enthusiastic, and most active workers and supporters. A great many non-charismatic ministers would be startled to learn how many of those they regard as pillars of the establishment speak in tongues in their private and small group devotions.

Writing in the newsletter of the Presbyterian Charismatic Communion, a Lutheran charismatic leader (one of the founders of Lutheran Charismatic Renewal Services), put it this way:

> I consistently counsel renewed people to remain in their congregations and be a positive influence. The tensions may be a tool which the Lord uses to deal with their old nature. Even a few renewed persons can make a major impact on a church. On the other hand, I strongly counsel pastors to feed their flock. Through spiritual experience some sheep develop a much greater appetite for the Word of God. Charismatics can create tension by exhibiting a bad attitude or an impression of super-spirituality. . . . Is it inevitable for the charismatic renewal to create another denomintion as some contend? It is my conviction that this does not have to happen.[15]

The contemporary charismatic movement owes this extremely important characteristic—the desire to remain in the traditional churches—in considerable measure to the prominence of Roman Catholic charismatics in the overall movement. As we have seen, Catholic charismatics, with few exceptions, do not think the gifts of the Spirit separate them from the church. They regard themselves as faithful Catholics and generally see no conflict between charismatic experience and loyalty to the church. In the early stages of the movement, the hierarchy showed some ambivalence and concern; the pentecostal Protestant models were, after all, highly sectarian and far removed from mainstream Catholic experience. The Catholic propensity for incorporating diversity, however, won out, and the hierarchy in general welcomed the renewal. Because of the practical ecumenism of the charismatic movement—a widely shared sense of commonality transcends denominational lines among charismatics, and both local groups and national or international gatherings are likely to be trans-denominational—and because of the large number of Catholics involved, this attitude has influenced Protestant charismatics. This movement, far more than most similar movements in church history, has been willing to cooperate, remain in, and support existing institutional structures, and has been willing to reach out in brotherhood to non-charismatics.

As we have seen, the cooperation-minded South American Protestant denominations belonging to the World Council of Churches are generally the indigenous Pentecostal denominations rather than the so-called mainline denominations. Mainline churches there are the small, inward-turning offspring of a century of mainline missions in Latin America. Openness is a pentecostal characteristic.

At a far more personal level, I sat in an adult Sunday School class recently when a study of 1 Corinthians 15 turned into a discussion of speaking in tongues. A member of the class said quietly, "I have had this experience." It turned out a little later that her husband was also a charismatic. A third member, although she herself did not speak in tongues, reported that her most meaningful prayer experiences are with an interdenominational group of charismatics. All three were long-time members of the class, and among the most loyal, active members of the congregation. The class, which had begun the discussion of speaking in tongues as if it were a strange phenomenon, totally foreign to the experience of its members, had not suspected these members were associated with charismatics. These were not divisives; they were revitalizers!

Is the Charismatic Movement an Evangelical Movement?

We noted earlier in this chapter that Rifkin and Howard deal with the evangelical renewal and the charismatic movement together. Clearly, however, the charismatic renewal cannot be regarded merely as a manifestation of renascent evangelicalism. It includes both evangelicals and liberals, emphasizes experience rather than theology, and tends toward piety rather than social action. Charismatics are not much interested—if at all—in fighting liberal-conservative battles regarding scriptural interpretation. The test for them is the authenticity of the experience of the Holy Spirit. Says Spencer C. Murray, reporting on the 1977 Kansas City Conference on Charismatic Renewal:

> A curious fact about the charismatic movement is that the old liberal-funda-mental dichotomy has little meaning. The pie is sliced differently. Old liberals would rejoice in their social concern, but would find them too conservative otherwise. Old fundamentalists would find them too liberal and too open to all the new fads. They are enthusiastic about new translations and versions of the Scriptures. The issues are different. No longer are they defined by doctrine or dogma. Nor does the social gospel present an issue for debate in the way it once did. Now the issue is continuity or discontinuity with the world. The concern is to be different, to provide an option in way of life and life style.[16]

Yet when all this is said, the significance of the charismatic movement for mainline Protestantism must be seen at least alongside, if not in continuity with, the challenge of the evangelicals. The Pentecostal denominations, with which mainline charismatics are asserting growing unity (in their conferences, for instance), are quite conservative and clearly part of evangelicalism. A very high percentage of the students at Fuller Theological Seminary are charismatics. Non-denominational parachurch organizations related to the charismatic movement, such as the Full Gospel Business Men's Fellowship, are also evangelical. The charismatic movement is essentially a lay movement with close ties to other evangelical parachurch organizations of the laity. It is a biblical movement which studies not *about* the Bible, but rather studies the Bible. The very nature of the charismatic experience makes it essentially incompatible with the scientific rationalism of contemporary religious liberalism. Within the mainline denominations, though persons of a wide variety of belief patterns are attracted, they tend to be evangelical and to become more evangelical as a result of their participation. On balance, the charismatic movement should probably be considered as at least allied with, if not part of, the evangelical renewal. A leading Catholic spokesperson, writing in a Protestant journal, said recently that he preferred to be known as a Catholic evangelical rather than a Catholic charismatic.[16]

The openness of this particular movement is important to mainline churches confronted with the evangelical challenge. As noted, we find little of the anti-institutionalism such movements usually have. Most mainline charismatics actively seek to remain within their churches and to cooperate rather than to withdraw. They are present in almost every community and in a great many congregations.

The potential for divisiveness is, however, certainly present. Charismatics are generally members of parachurch groups either within the congregation or across congregational and denominational lines and may be sensitive, guarded, and concerned about their own acceptance. They may be judgmental and exclusivist, measuring everyone by their own charismatic standards. There can be bitterness, suspicion, and dissension.

The bridging potential, however, is also present. With a foot in all camps, with their emphasis on feeling and experience rather than the jots and tittles of the law, with their openness and desire to cooperate, they can be a reconciling force with evangelicals generally. The attitude of the establishment is often the determinant. When loved, they can respond with a great deal of love.

the membership crisis and
the church growth movement:
evangelical tool
for mainline use?

From 1952 to 1968 the membership of my denomination, the Presbyterian Church, U. S., grew steadily every year, from 675,000 to just under 1,000,000—an increase of 33 percent over a sixteen-year period. Since 1968, the membership has steadily declined to a 1979 total of 852,711 communicant members (11 percent in eleven years).

A similar trend has affected nearly every mainline denomination in America. The United Methodists, the United Presbyterians, the Episcopalians, the United Church of Christ, the Reformed Church in America, the three major Lutheran Churches—all these grew steadily through the fifties and early sixties and crested in the middle sixties. Since, all have declined and are greatly concerned. Most of these denominations, as well as others (Southern Baptists have continued to grow, but at a declining rate), have conducted internal studies to determine the factors behind the decline and to identify ways to reverse it.[1] A 1978 study by the Gallup organization, sponsored cooperatively with the National Council of Churches by twenty-nine denominations and religious groups (including most of the mainline), probed attitudes of the unchurched. All the groups expressed awakening interest in reaching them. Researchers predominantly from mainline denominations, together with leading mainline sociologists, contributed in 1979 to a major study, edited by Dean R. Hoge and David A. Roozen, and published under the title *Understanding Church Growth and Decline, 1950-1978.*[2]

The studies show almost without exception that a decline in denominational membership has been preceded by a decline in baptism and then in Sunday School enrollment. In my own denomination, for instance, Church School enrollment began to decline seven years before membership. Church Schools peaked in 1961 and declined a massive 46 percent between then and 1979. Baptisms peaked all the way back in 1955. The 1979 total represented a decline since that year of 67 percent in adult baptisrs and 47 percent in infant baptisms.

Another "leading indicator" preceding membership decline in most denominations was a deemphasis on the organizing of new churches. In the relatively small Presbyterian Church, U. S. there was a drop from a high of about sixty new congregations a year in the mid-fifties (the highest single number was seventy, in 1955) to between ten and fifteen a year in the early seventies (with a low of eight in 1972). The twenty-one new churches established in 1978 was the largest number of any year up to that point in the seventies, but down a massive 70 percent since the high point.

By the end of the seventies nearly every mainline denomination had undertaken major programs of one kind or another to try to arrest the decline. Whether because of these programs or for other reasons, some statistical evidence suggests that the membership decline may have begun leveling off as the eighties began, but no clear reversal of the trend has been established. It is worth noting parenthetically that throughout all this period of decline, one mainline statistic has shown steady growth, namely, the number of ministers. In my own denomination the number went from 3,448 in 1957 to 5,431 in 1979—an increase of 57 percent. In fact, someone has facetiously pointed out that if present trends continue, Southern Presbyterians will have one minister for every lay member by the year 2011, and by 2087 the denomination will have no lay members at all and will be made up entirely of ministers![3]

Research on Causes of Membership Decline

The large quantity of mainline research on *causes* of membership losses has produced some common findings. One common focus in most of the research is the importance of demographic and sociological factors (sometimes called "contextual factors" in the research studies) in church membership trends.

Contextual Factors

In some local congregations, because of location, population shifts or social conditions, numerical decline is statistically predictable (despite rare exceptions) and growth is highly unlikely. In other congregations, numerical growth is clearly possible. The studies agree that four contextual factors are important:

1. Generally speaking, regional church membership trends have paralleled regional population changes. The greatest population growth has been in the West and Southeast. The Sun Belt, as the region of population growth, has shown a membership increase in churches of the same denominations that may be declining in other regions. Some denominations are adopting a "sun belt strategy" in initiating new church development programs to try to arrest their overall decline. There are, however, wide variations in growth patterns *within* the sun belt. The overall correlation between church trends and population trends is by no means consistent throughout the region. The Gallup study of the unchurched highlights the role of mobility itself in church membership losses. Many church people who move fail to affiliate with a church in the new area.

2. Another demographic factor has been the declining American birth rate, accounting for at least part of the decline in infant baptisms. The average age of the population is a related factor. The growing over-sixty-five segment of the population is not an age group with a high level of church participation.

3. A third factor is socioeconomic status. In general, the higher the socioeconomic status of the denomination, the less it has grown or the more it has declined. In a related factor, the Gallup study showed that highly educated people are less likely to be church-related than the less educated. Generally, the mainline denominations are middle class denominations with a relatively high educational level. Several studies indicate that socioeconomic homogeneity is an important factor in the growth of particular congregations. (This mainline research finding supports an important and controversial aspect of the Church Growth movement, the homogeneous unit theory, which will be discussed later.)

4. Many studies suggest that a changing value system in the American culture, accompanied by changing family patterns, contributes to membership decline. The effect has been especially strong with regard to youth and young adults, the age group in which the decline has been most striking.

William R. McKinney of the United Church of Christ, one of the most knowledgeable researchers in the field, estimates that perhaps 50 percent of the variance in church membership statistics is a result of purely demographic factors. Some studies assign even greater importance to contextual factors generally.

Internal Factors

In seeking to identify internal causes (sometimes called "institutional factors" or "faith components" in the research), conclusions have not been unanimous, though some generalizations can be made. Numerical growth or decline is not attributable to any single or simple formula, but is rather the result of a complex combination of factors:

1. Pastoral competence is found to be a decisive factor in several of the studies. A few of the studies found it to be only an indirect determinant of growth as a contributor to member satisfaction.

2. Member satisfaction with the worship, fellowship, and work of the congregation was found to be correlated with growth in practically all of the studies.

3. Congregational involvement in evangelism and other workable programs of outreach and enlistment is another important factor. An involved laity is regarded as particularly crucial in the Southern Baptist study.

4. Identification of the church with the community is found to be a significant factor by two of the studies.

5. A growing or declining Sunday School is found by most studies to be a direct predictor of future growth or decline of the congregation.

6. Smaller churches appear to have a significantly higher growth rate than larger churches. One study (Methodist) found a consistently higher rate of professions of faith per thousand church members in smaller churches than in larger churches.

7. Involvement of the congregation in social action as a possible factor in growth or decline was investigated by several studies. Conclusions were mixed, some finding it to be a positive and some a negative factor. Most concluded that it was not a strong determinant in either direction. (However, when social action is associated with conflict in a congregation, the conflict—rather than the social action itself—is regarded by some as a negative factor.)

Denominational Programs to Reverse the Trend

Programs adopted in an attempt to reverse the trend have focused generally on three areas:

1. Christian Education

Programs in this area concentrate on "biological growth" in church membership—entrance into the church through birth into a Christian family and Christian nurture, with the "rites of passage" of baptism, profession of faith, reception to communion and/or confirmation. The experience of the Southern Baptist Convention, which has *not* declined and which has a Sunday School centered church growth strategy, confirms the significance of this factor. Southern Baptist Sunday School enrolment peaked in 1964 and declined slightly for the next seven years, but has been increasing again since 1971.

Data on comparative sources of church members are hard to find, but a Methodist Church study shows that well over half the new members—perhaps as many as seventy or eighty percent—are children of church families brought into full membership through the Christian education system. In light of these data, renewed emphasis on Christian education and youth programs is one solution being explored by several denominations. The United Methodist Church adopted such a program ("Decision Point: Church School") in 1976, and after two years found the results to be sufficiently encouraging to continue it.

2. *New Church Development*

Practically all those denominations that have in recent years developed new strategies to deal with membership decline have instituted denomination-wide programs of new church development. This follows a period in which little attention was given to church development by mainline denominations. Patterns were similar to the one detailed earlier for my own denomination. A United Presbyterian study noted that in the 1960s a national strategy focusing on the development of "experimental" or "innovative" or "noninstitutional" congregations replaced the earlier conventional church development emphasis, and that few if any of these experimental congregations ever achieved a size beyond forty adult communicant members. The Southern Baptist Convention experienced some decline in new congregations (though not as great a decline as other denominations) and has continued to grow at a slower rate than earlier. It has renewed its emphasis on church development in recent years. Its "Bold Growing" program, initiated in the late seventies, was designed (along with increases in Christian education and baptisms) to establish fifty-five hundred church missions by 1982. In my own denomination, the awakening interest in church development in regional jurisdictions (presbyteries and synods) has been striking. The primary initiative has been there rather than in denominational headquarters, although a denominational capital funds campaign, designated largely for new church development, was scheduled to begin in 1985.

3. *Evangelism*

The need for a positive understanding of and commitment to evangelism is a third area of general agreement. What is meant here, however, is not always easy to pin down. This key issue will be discussed in detail later in this chapter.[4]

The Conservatism Factor

A striking contrast emerged in the decades of the sixties and seventies between the decline in membership of the liberal-ecumenical mainline denominations on the one hand, and the growth of the conservative denominations on the other. Attention of mainline Christians was first directed to this factor by Dean M. Kelley—a United Methodist minister and sociologist of impeccable mainline credentials, long on the staff of the National Council of Churches—with his 1972 book, *Why Conservative Churches Are Growing.*[5]

From an overall denominational standpoint the contrast is obvious. Membership trends in major denominations generally regarded as conservative, such as the Assemblies of God (1965–75 growth rate, 37.3 percent); the Church of the Nazarene (28.4 percent); the Seventh Day Adventist Church (35.9 percent); and the largest of the Protestant denominations, the Southern Baptist Convention (18.2 percent) have been in sharp contrast with the declining numbers of the mainline denominations.

Mainline studies focused on growing and declining congregations *within* the mainline denominations themselves have tended to play down this factor and do not show strong and consistent correlations between conservatism and growth. A United Presbyterian study of 681 churches indicated that some conservative and some liberal congregations are growing, and some of both kinds are declining. It concluded that conservatism is a very weak determinant. The conclusion of a United Church of Christ study was similar, if somewhat ambiguous: "While growing churches tend to be conservative churches, there is little evidence of a strong causal relationship between conservative theology and membership growth."[6] As David A. Roozen points out, most of the current studies of particular congregations have been conducted in liberal denominations, so we have no way of knowing what the findings would be in studies of more conservative denominations.[7]

Studies of trends in entire denominations (as distinct from studies of particular congregations) are also ambiguous. A comparative study of the Reformed Church in America (which is considered somewhat liberal, and which like other mainline denominations has been declining in membership) and the Christian Reformed Church (a more conservative denomination with similar Dutch Reformed roots which has continued to grow since the mid-sixties) was conducted in 1979 by a mainline-oriented researcher. The study did not find the cause of Christian Reformed growth in the denomination's conservatism; it found the cause mainly in geographical and immigration factors. The author struggled with the conservatism issue and did find that it may be a factor in the Christian Reformed Church's greater retention rate of those born into it.[8] Other denominational studies do show some positive correlation between theological conservatism and church growth.

Roozen and Hoge, in an essay entitled "Some Sociological Conclusions About Church Trends" included in their definitive volume, suggest that broadening the categories beyond "liberal" and "conservative" may be helpful. As we noted in Chapter Two in connection with terminology describing the two "parties" in Protestantism, they conclude that denominations can be seen on an axis with "conservative-disciplined-distinctive from culture" at one pole, and "liberal-pluralistic-culture affirming" at the other. In general, those denominations near the first pole have been growing. Not only theological conservatism, but also personal evangelism, distinctiveness of life style and morality, and maintenance of unitary beliefs all appear to have a direct impact on growth. Those denominations near the second pole (liberal-pluralistic-culture affirming) have been declining. These denominations tend to emphasize social action and ecumenism. Neither is seen by Hoge and Roozen as a *cause* of decline. They see social action as only indirectly related to declining membership since social action sometimes arouses church conflicts in reallocation of mission money and energy.[9]

In conclusion we might note that the entire approach of mainline denominations to the membership crisis has tended to be a *managerial* approach based on the technological, human problem-solving assumptions of a secular scientific-managerial age. To conduct research studies aimed at identifying causes of the churches' malaise, and to design "programs" based on the findings of those studies, is to treat the church as a human organization susceptible to the control of human managers. This is as true of the evangelical Church Growth movement (which makes widespread use of research findings and contemporary technologies) as it is of the liberal-ecumenical mainline leadership.

To *identify* a managerial approach is not to condemn it. Christianity—beginning with the New Testament—has always affirmed human responsibility to God to use talents, skills, as well as spiritual gifts for the upbuilding of the church. Christianity has never rejected the explorations of the human mind, the expansion of knowledge, or the use of tools and technologies devised by human ingenuity in this process. Church leaders have not only the right but the duty as persons responsible to God to use the management skills, the scientific methods, and the human technologies of the managerial age in dealing with church problems.

Yet one can reasonably ask whether the church, as an organization seeing itself as a community of persons called by God through the grace of Jesus Christ, has been giving sufficient attention to the role of the Holy Spirit in its numerical decline or growth. The church may need to place greater emphasis on some of the spiritual gifts and shared experiences with which it has been endowed since its beginning through the unique presence of the Holy Spirit.

The Evangelism Issue

The evangelism issue may be more central in the mainline membership problem than conservatism or liberalism of denominations. The fact that the new evangelicals prefer to be called "evangelicals" rather than "conservatives" says something about where they put their emphasis, and evangelicals in the mainline churches are inclined to view evangelism as the key to the membership crisis. It is an "issue" because of a low key but longstanding dispute within mainline circles over the meaning of evangelism. Liberal mainliners have been unwilling to draw a line between, on the one hand, the processes leading to an initial commitment to Christ, and, on the other, the demands of the gospel once the initial commitment is made. They have been unwilling to make a distinction between witness with words and witness with deeds and have been unwilling to regard evangelism as something distinct from social action.

In chapter six, concerning the crisis in overseas mission, we examined the unresolved issue of the nature of Christian mission. Liberal-ecumenicals and evangelicals define mission (whether overseas or at home) differently. Central in this divergence is the place—and the meaning—of evangelism in mission. David W. Bosch, writing for the jointly published Britsh-American New Foundations Theological Library, discusses at length the polarization between liberal-ecumenicals and evangelicals over evangelism and the contrasting models of mission derived from the different understandings.[10] Liberal mainliners have sought broad, inclusive definitions of evangelism which at times appear to embrace almost everything the church does.

For most evangelicals, the struggle over a definition of evangelism is a liberal problem, not theirs. They are quite clear about what evangelism means: spreading the good news in order to bring people into the Christian fellowship. It means converting people, making disciples, and "winning the world for Christ." They often turn the noun into a verb: "to evangelize" is to engage in activities that enable people to find Christ.

A 1967 paper on "A Theological Basis for Evangelism," prepared in the Presbyterian Church, U. S., described the inherent tension in its extreme form:

> There are some who feel that evangelism is almost solely concerned with the destiny of the individual in the next world. They feel that the concern of the church with social conditions in this world can be the enemy of evangelism and that it can interfere with the proclamation of the pure gospel and antagonize those whose souls need to be saved.
>
> Others are attracted to the view that evangelism is almost solely concerned with social change. The good news is that the secularization and urbanization of life are not to be resisted, but to be welcomed as gifts of God.
>
> We would reject either of these extremes as an inadequate theological basis for evangelism in our day.[11]

There has been much verbal sparring about evangelism between mainline liberal-ecumenicals and evangelicals in church courts and assemblies. The result, usually, is a compromise statement. Such compromises must include the explicit language of conversion or at least proclamation of the gospel to satisfy the evangelicals, but they must also be inclusive to satisfy the liberals. For instance, a 1975 Presbyterian Church, U. S. General Assembly action seeking to define evangelism affirmed that:

> The proclamation of the Kingdom of God is Evangelism. . . The love of Christians one for another in the fellowship of the Christian community is Evangelism. . . The life style of the Christian person and the Christian community in radical obedience to the biblical mandates of the Kingdom of God in the world is Evangelism. . . Effective evangelism includes all three dimensions and is incomplete when any one of three is not incorporated.[12]

These inclusive formulations of church assemblies do not, of course, solve the problem. The issues, however, are reasonably clear. The liberals know very well what the evangelicals mean by the term, and such a narrowly limited meaning is exactly what they are trying to avoid!

There is some evidence that the evangelical's definition of evangelism and insistence on its centrality in Christian mission is gaining strength in mainline denominations. A 1979 survey of attitudes among United Presbyterians, conducted by that denomination's Research Division, showed that while a small majority (53 percent) of the members still place "equal emphasis on winning people to Christ and changing society in his name," this majority had declined dramatically since 1974, when 79 percent held that view. The number of members leaning toward the view that the primary role of the church is solely that of winning people to Christ has increased correspondingly in the five-year period.[13]

The evangelical insistence on a traditional definition of evangelism has not generally been a rejection of social action (though liberal-ecumenicals tend to see it as a deemphasis of social action). They frequently agree that evangelism must be *accompanied* by social action. They have insisted, however, that social action is not the same thing as evangelism. Why the mainline's discomfort with this separation and with the traditional definition of evangelism? The reason is probably a quite basic one, inherent in the relativism of the modern scientific world view undergirding religious liberalism. It is inherent, from the liberal perspective, in the whole ethos of our culture. It is a world view that distrusts and avoids absolutes. And evangelism is an activity of absolutists who are convinced that "there is salvation in no one else, for there is no other name under heaven given among men by which we must be saved" (Acts 4:12). To evangelize (in the classic sense) is to imply that the views of others who have not accepted or do not agree with our own beliefs about Jesus Christ are not valid—or at least less valid than our own. To offer Jesus to others as a savior from sin is to suggest that the objects of evangelism are sinners. To want to evangelize the world is to claim that the religions of the Hindus, the Muslims, the Buddhists, are not as valid for them as Christianity is for us. The word "heathen" is extremely bad form today, and to want to evangelize is to suggest that there *are* such things as heathens. These are positions which the liberal is unwilling to take even by implication.

At a recent denominational conference on mission, the growing strength of Islam in the Middle East and Africa was the focus of much attention. Both the liberal-ecumenicals and the evangelicals in the group expressed concern, although the liberal concern was somewhat tempered by higher priorities elsewhere. The group agreed on the need for a "witness to the Islamic world," but such a witness meant something quite different to the two factions. To the evangelicals, Muslims are part of the "two-thirds of the world as yet unreached for Christ." While they would engage in many kinds of works of compassion and social change, their ultimate goal would have been to bring as many Muslims as possible into the Christian fold. The liberals at the conference were willing to engage in witnessing through works of compassion and social change in countries where Islam is present. Such acts would show forth the love of Christ. They were eager for dialogue and communication between the Christian and Muslim worlds, dialogue aimed at mutual understanding and improved relationships; but they rejected the idea of consciously and deliberately *seeking converts* from Islam to Christianity.

Despite the differences and disagreements, however, signs today suggest that liberal-ecumenicals and evangelicals are moving closer to each other on the evangelism issue. The movement is not in the conceptual area as much as in the area of practice. The church membership crisis of the mainline denominations has reached the point at which it can no longer be ignored. Institutional survival is beginning to be the issue. An organization that continues indefinitely to lose members ultimately disappears. The mainline could cease being the mainline in numerical terms alone.

Even in responding to the membership crisis, the mainline has often used terms and adopted goals that avoid the implication of explicitly seeking converts. It seeks "church development" rather than "church growth," spiritual depth rather than conversion, "renewal" rather than "revival." For some years it has been unfashionable in mainline circles to attach much significance to numbers. Among the "prophetic," involved in controversial forms of social change ministry, loss of members has even at times been regarded as a badge of courage calling forth admiration. The dictum that the ultimate demand on Christians is "not to be popular but to be faithful" has become a cliche.

We have been through a period in which we sought to deal with the need for renewal organizationally. All the tools of human technology developed by behavioral science, corporate management, and the human relations movement, have been placed at the disposal of declining churches in their quest for renewal. Organizational Development (OD), Management by

Objective (MBO), Planning, Programming and Budgeting Systems (PPBS), conflict management, group dynamics, change agentry, goal setting, team building, evaluation—the entire arsenal of management science—all have been offered as tools for renewal. In fact, most of the church-generated literature on organizational and managerial techniques has been written and published under the rubric of congregational renewal. One ecclesiastical version of Management by Objective is known as 'Renewal by Objective (RBO)." The most widely-used tool has been goal setting, which is at the heart of most organizational attempts at renewal.

As useful as these tools may be for specific purposes, however (and they are), they have not proved to be the answer to the kind of decline exemplified by membership losses. Indeed, the managerial revolution within the church, with the widespread adoption of the assumptions as well as the technologies of management science and organizational sociology, may have been one of the *reasons* for the decline.[14]

The Church Growth Movement

In seeking solutions to the membership decline, a number of mainline churches have been moving closer to the evangelical position at the practical level by embracing a program from evangelical sources. This is the Church Growth movement associated with Donald McGavran and Peter Wagner, Fuller Theological Seminary, and the Institute of Church Growth in Pasadena, California. According to Wagner,

> this approach operates within a set of theological presuppositions that decisively influence its goals and methodologies. In broad brush strokes this can be described as an evangelical theology. It takes seriously the sovereignty of God, the lordship of Jesus Christ, the absolute authority of the scriptures, the reality of sin and eternal judgment, the divine will that all men and women be reconciled to God through Jesus Christ, the need for a born-again experience, and the requirement placed on all believers to share their faith.[15]

Yet despite these evangelical assumptions, according to a National Council of Churches study of "What the Mainline Denominations Are Doing in Evangelism," the "big news of the past triennium is that the church growth approach, originated in Fuller Seminary, has been sweeping the mainline denominations."[16]

The United Methodist Church, the Episcopal Church, and the Reformed Church in America have placed heavy emphasis on it in denominational programs. The United Presbyterian Program Agency has published a pamphlet on it and is experimenting with its use. Others have been exploring it. In the Presbyterian Church, U.S., Church Growth workshops have been conducted and the approach used extensively in some presbyteries even though denominational agency leadership has resisted involvement.

Regardless of the attitudes of denominational leaders, evidence suggests widespread involvement of local mainline congregations in the movement. Growth Ministries, Inc., an independent Church Growth organization in Atlanta, Georgia, reported in November 1979 that churches of six mainline denominations were currently being assisted. One entire Atlanta Methodist District of twenty-five thousand members was involved, and the report noted that six out of seven of the quiescent or declining churches involved in an intensive year-long effort had begun to show significant growth.[17] The Church Growth approach has unquestionably made deep inroads into the mainline churches and considerable evidence suggests that this trend does represent some movement in the evangelical direction. An early 1980 reviewer of twelve new books on evangelism (mostly by mainline authors) under the title, "Protestantism Goes Evangelistic," said in summary, "almost all these books on evangelism take note of resurgent evangelicalism, evangelicalism's reawakened social interest, and the Church Growth Movement as fostered by Fuller Seminary."[18]

A prolific literature and widespread familiarity make it unnecessary to detail the Church Growth methods here. One aspect which has commended it to mainline churches is the emphasis on making disciples ("discipling" is the term used), rather than simply seeking decisions. Leaders in the movement have criticized the Billy Graham organization and Campus Crusade's "Here's Life" evangelistic effort for their emphasis on decisions. As far as Church Growth is concerned, the evangelizing process is not completed until persons are brought into active fellowship with some visible part of the church. A name on the roll is not enough; the evangelized must become active disciples. Such incorporation into the Body of Christ is a rigid measure of effectiveness for the Church Growth movement.

Perhaps the most controversial aspect of the approach for mainliners, as noted earlier, is the homogeneous unit principle which affirms that people are most likely to become Christian within their own racial or cultural group or social class. Many are suspicious that a concealed racism lies within this approach. John R. Hendrick, a Presbyterian, U.S., regional executive and writer on evangelism, points out that in their own work with racial minorities, mainline churches tend to "affirm the validity of cultural ethnicity as the basis of existing congregations and the establishment of new congregations," and that in overseas mission activities the principle is widely recognized.[19] Indeed, the assumption that only indigenous Christians can effectively bring persons of their own culture into Christianity is a major reason given by mainliners for their unwillingness to send evangelistic missionaries overseas. De-westernization and "indigenization" of churches in the third world countries is high on the agenda of socially active liberal-ecumenicals.

Mainliners using the Church Growth approach generally seek to modify and adapt it to their own theological posture and style. Arthur O. Van Eck of the Reformed Church in America has spoken of that church's effort to "reform the Church Growth movement." Hendrick, in one of a series of articles on adapting the approach for Presbyterian use, says, "when man's part and God's part in the work of evangelism are weighed, Church Growth tips the scale toward the human side. Historic Reformed theology, if not Presbyterian practice, would stress God's side of the scale." He does, however, find the approach adaptable and useful.[20]

Carl S. Dudley, who wrote a "popular" companion volume to accompany the scholarly *Understanding Church Growth and Decline,* concedes that the Church Growth approach "works" and refers to a number of its insights in his practical section on strategies for congregations. He seems, however, to find it basically incompatible with mainline Christianity. He says it has "misunderstood the nature of mainline theology," making "Private Religion" (Martin Marty's term for the traditional emphasis of conservative Christianity) its priority over "Public Religion." He also rejects the "homogeneous unit" theory, which, he says, "does not provide a description of the mainline churches, but that description is a judgment upon the church's failure to embrace as Christ's family 'all people who come in the name of the Lord.'"[21]

He is probably accurate, at least in part. The adaptation of Church Growth principles by mainline churches *does* represent a movement in the direction of evangelicalism in that it gives priority to the necessity of a personal faith in Jesus Christ. Its assumptions, as Wagner has made clear, are evangelical. Yet those mainliners who have embraced it are not simply borrowing from the evangelicals, but rather are recalling and renewing an aspect of their own historical identity. They, like the evangelicals who orginated Church Growth as a methodology, are responding to the spirit of the times, to the need for authority, for meaning, for recovery of roots. Church Growth has been espoused by those in mainline churches who are *willing* to see the mainline move in the evangelical direction—a movement which many of them see as a return to the center stream, to a balanced approach, to their own authentic heritage.

It tends to be rejected by those mainliners who are unwilling to see movement toward a more evangelical position and who identify it with movement away from social involvement. Dudley believes the uniqueness of mainline religion lies in its mediation of Christian values for the welfare of the whole society. He presents data to show that the society has large numbers of believers in these values (particularly the young) who share the mainline perspective but are not affiliated with the churches. He proposes the reclaiming of these non-affiliated mainliners as the answer to the membership crisis.

Some would disagree with Dudley in his assumption that Church Growth's emphasis on the "private" dimension (personal faith in Christ) means exclusion of the public dimension. Analysts like David O. Moberg, Donald R. Dayton, and Richard F. Lovelace, who find historical evangelicalism at its best when combined with strong social concern, and the "young" or "new" evangelicals who are deeply involved in social action, would take strong issue.

Despite the controversy, the Church Growth approach clearly has been widely adopted by mainline churches. Whether in adapting it the evangelical assumptions will be modified, or whether its widespread use will give those theological assumptions more currency and credence in mainline circles, its impact is sure to be significant. At this practical level it is certainly another signal of the renewal and recovery of the mainliners' own heritage, who, after all, have the same roots as the evangelicals. Potentially, it is a bridging movement which may serve to alleviate the polarization and provide a path toward the middle ground of a more balanced Protestantism.

fragmentation of denominational life: is "connectionalism" dead?

In the summer of 1979 I met with a small group of ministers in Charlotte, N. C. They had invited me, as a representative of the denominational Office of Review and Evaluation, to discuss the central agencies of the church. On the day I arrived they were irate about a denominational bureaucrat who had recently visited Charlotte and whose attitude they had regarded as arrogant. This initially clouded the issues; they had extended the invitation to me before that visit, however, and their concerns were deeper. They were troubled about the direction being taken by the denominational mission agencies. Again and again they reiterated their theme: "We still care. We still believe there is a role for denominational mission."

Their protestations made an impression. They were assuming, it seemed, that most people do not care. They talked as if they were unusual in still seeing a role for denominational mission. I began to question them on this score, and my impressions were confirmed. This group of ministers felt that very few people around them pay much attention to the denomination. To most, the Presbyterian Church is the local congregation. They have some awareness of the Presbytery in their area, but do not pay much attention to that either. They know, of course, that there is a denominational superstructure, but they are not interested. They just no longer care.

Fragmentation of denominational life may be as critical an issue for the mainline churches as the decline in church membership.[1] There is a sense in which the old established denominations appear to be disintegrating, though their congregations, of course, are not threatened. Some, indeed, are more vital than ever before and are deeply engaged in mission in their own communities, thriving spiritually as well as numerically and financially. Even as denominations, the danger is not immediate. No matter what happens, Annual Conferences, General Assemblies, and Conventions will continue to meet, go through the familiar motions, and carry on some residual functions as far into the future as we can project. Are the denominations themselves, however, disintegrating as significant institutions with meaningful roles to play? The signs are ominous, and we have already touched on a number of them in examining mainline crisis points.

Signs of Fragmentation

The first signs can probably be identified in the wave of restructuring which took place in the early seventies. As the sixties ended, nearly every mainline denomination was sensing so much stress, so much discontent, such a widespread feeling that its organs were not functioning properly, that something had to be done. We believed reorganizing would solve the problems. It did solve some, but it created others, and the denominational bureaucracies went through a period of great turbulence.

Another clue which began to be identified at about the same time and which became increasingly evident through the seventies, was growing alienation between the people in the pew and the social activist agency bureaucrats. We called it "lack of trust," and we thought restructuring would solve it. But it has only grown worse.

In the mid-seventies we began to be aware of the enormity of the financial changes that were taking place. Money which once went to "denominational causes" was being kept at home in the local churches, and much of what went beyond the local churches was being used in the local region as Districts, Dioceses, and Presbyteries became mission centers. These middle judicatories employed staffs of professional experts and expanded their budgets to carry out the mission intentions of the people within their bounds. We came to realize in the late seventies that this trend, combined with the effects of inflation, had brought a radical budget decline in the central agencies of all denominations. Retrenchment, termination of staff jobs, budgetary pressures, and fiscal problems generally became the major preoccupations of the bureaucracies.

Still, we viewed it simply as a realignment of the church's engagement in mission, with a greater emphasis on localism and regionalism, and we sought to adapt to the new patterns. We tried repeatedly to sort out the "appropriate functions" for the various levels—local congregation, regional, national.

As I watched these developments in my own denomination, I thought at least one denominational activity was safe: overseas mission. As long as Presbyterians wanted to engage in mission abroad—and my church historically has given high priority to overseas mission—this, at least, would be done denominationally. Yet in the late seventies, more and more presbyteries adopted their own overseas projects. Though nominally done through the Division of International Mission of the General Assembly Mission Board, some of them (and sometimes the most effective of them) have in reality been managed directly by the presbytery concerned. In 1978 one presbytery actually sent its own missionary overseas—unintentionally and through a fluke of circumstance, true, by this is the way it ended up. The seriousness of this dimension of denominational mission disintegration was brought home to me when one church leader, having read some of my articles, sent me copies of two papers prepared for consideration by his own presbytery. They proposed that the General Assembly *get out of the mission business entirely* except for coordination, leaving all mission activity—especially and specifically overseas mission—to presbyteries which would select and commission their own missionaries and engage in direct overseas church relationships.

Regional mission has much to commend it. The values of personal participation in mission by church members directly involved in close-to-home projects in their own regions seems self-evident. It must, therefore, be viewed as a desirable trend in this sense. Even though denominational mission has been seriously eroded in the process, the denominational model as such is not sacred. Historically there have been many patterns through which Christians have responded in mission to their experience of God's grace—the majority of them outside the official governing structures of denominations. In Chapter Five we looked at length at the history of the parachurch pattern.

Yet some question persists as to whether local congregations are much more interested in the regional judicatories now assuming responsibility for corporate forms of mission than they are in the denominational bureaucracies. A recent book on a congregational revitalization project—a project designed as a presbytery undertaking (Presbytery of Chicago, UPCUSA)—found that congregations had so little commitment to and concern for presbytery, and presbytery itself was so deeply divided and involved in power struggles, that it could not be done. Presbytery was simply by-passed and the project conducted directly with local congregations.[2]

Much of this has been confirmed by my own reflection on my experience in the congregation in which my family and I participate. It is a large and once prominent church (it entertained the denomination's General Assembly in the late fifties) located in a now-deteriorating neighborhood. It has risen to the challenge of its situation in what I consider a superb way by providing a wide range of services to the deprived—often hopeless—residents who now live in its immediate proximity and is welcoming them into its fellowship in a way I consider remarkable for a staid, upper class Presbyterian congregation. Its *local mission* is its focal point. Indeed I have not only applauded this trend, this is what attracted me—and some other General Assembly bureaucrats who have chosen it as a church home—in the first place. The congregation is involved to a modest extent in Presbytery mission—being a city church, much aware of its place in and the way it is affected by, its city. Presbytery, however, is peripheral, and General Assembly—with its headquarters ten blocks away on the same street—scarcely exists for the congregation. This is true despite a significant number of active members who work for General Assembly agencies.

This fiscal, organizational, and experiential evidence of disintegration has been mounting rapidly. So has plain talk. More and more reports have come to denominational headquarters reflecting the disinterest of the local church. As I have traveled around the church, I have heard with increasingly frequency what the Charlotte group was saying, and colleagues in other denominations report the same thing. "Folks around here are not interested in what's going on at headquarters. They just don't care any more."

Sociological Causes of Fragmentation

One can only hazard guesses and begin to shape a theory as to why this is happening. Certainly the striking parallel between the growing localism and regionalism in the church on the one hand, and similar trends in society at large on the other, is suggestive. All over the world the centrifugal effect of separatism, tribalism, and self-determination is apparent. Sovereign nations get smaller and smaller; tiny Caribbean islands scarcely capable of mounting a police force nevertheless insist on and are granted full sovereignty. The federal bureaucracy has remained fairly stable in recent years, but state and municipal bureaucracies have been growing rapidly. The states and counties have been the battleground of the tax revolt. Congressmen vote local interests so exclusively that the concept of "common good" seems almost lost.

We find, however, one essential difference between the effect of localism on civil society and the effect in the church. Federal power in the United States is so massive, federal taxation so enormous, federal regulation so ubiquitous, that localism can only peck away at the periphery. Federal structures are in no real danger (though in Canada they may be). In the church, however, the situation is quite different. The real powers of denominational structures are severely limited. Even in churches with an Episcopal form of government this is true. Only Methodist bishops, among Protestants, have real power, and that is limited to certain defined areas (having primarily to do with the assignment of clergy to parishes). Denominational mission agencies are almost totally dependent on the voluntary support and cooperation of local churches. The effect of localism and loss of interest in denominational programs has thus been strongly felt.

A second parallel with secular society is the proliferation of special interest groups, of "one issue" coalitions which apply enormous pressure solely in the interest of their own concern. Opponents of nuclear energy find all other issues unimportant. Pro- and anti-abortion forces vote for candidates solely in terms of their stands on abortion. Gun lobbies make opposition to gun-control legislation the sole litmus test. The National Organization of Women announced early in the 1980 presidential campaign that it would oppose President Carter's reelection bid, regardless of who opposed him, because his support of ratification of the Equal Rights Amendment had not been sufficiently strong. As the 1980s began, five major appropriation bills in Congress were stymied over the abortion issue alone. In such a climate, politics becomes a matter of putting together enough special interest groups to achieve a majority vote.

Churches, too, have seen special interest groups multiply. Public policy and overseas mission advocates jockey for position and funds. "Rightsmanship" is practiced by women, minorities, homosexuals, the elderly—and even by the clergy. "Professional" organizations of church employees multiply. Here again, the absence of recognized power, guaranteed funding, and a strong tradition of centralization leaves the denominational structure far more vulnerable than that of the federal government.

A third factor present in society and mentioned several times earlier in this book is the effect of the managerial-professional revolution. America is a society of large, corporate organizations managed by experts. In this technological age, Americans no longer really control their own lives and environment in many respects. We leave things to the technicians, the experts, the professionals, the managers. Even though the managerial age has brought a proliferation of "group processes," the groups—boards, committees, work units, task forces, liaison groups, ad infinitum—are narrowly focused, tightly organized, and dependent on "process management." A denominational power structure which follows the contemporary management model pays little attention to the non-professional, non-expert person in the pew.

Another factor, somewhat related, is the kind of mobility an urban-surburban society has produced. Today's church members move freely between denominations, and many who were brought up Methodists are now Episcopalians, Presbyterians, or Baptists. The laity has no strong sense of distinction between denominations. This has a positive effect in the fostering of an ecumenical spirit and a sense of identity with the *universal* church of Christ, also a negative one in the absence of a strong sense of identification with a *particular* larger group. The ecumenical commitment of mainline denominations is a treasured heritage and current reality that we do not want to deemphasize. Yet it inevitably brings with it some loss of the sense of denominational distinctiveness or uniqueness.

Supreme Court decisions in church property cases at the end of the seventies alarmed denominational leaders in connectional churches. They reflected—as court decisions often do—social conditions of the times. Several factors have undoubtedly contributed to the fragmentation of denominational life. We live in a society and are inevitably affected by cultural and social influences.

Is Denominational Fragmentation Related to the Evangelical Renascence?

The extent to which the evangelical resurgence and its challenge to the mainline churches plays a part in the fragmentation of denominational life is a major issue. Important as social and environmental factors are, they are not the whole story. The commitment of grassroots mainline evangelicals is to a dynamic, "Bible-believing" church life rather than to denominational church life. Given high mobility, when mainline evangelicals move they tend to seek a church that is "alive" whether or not it is of the same denomination as the one they left.

Certainly the pluralism of the mainline denominations is itself an important contributing factor. Consensus churches, with their shared commitment and relatively homogeneous outlook, have a cohesiveness which pluralistic churches, held together by the legal principle, lack. The move from a consensus pattern to pluralism, which most of the mainline churches have experienced in this century, may have made denominational fragmentation inevitable. What pluralism reflects is *the absence of any real denominational unity as to the mission and purpose of the church*. As noted earlier, the most prominent form of pluralism in the mainline is the divergence between the liberal-ecumenical and the evangelical wings. Cultural pluralism—with its efforts to open up and strengthen the place in the church of minorities and persons of all socio-economic classes—might be a more significantly divisive factor if we had been more successful in achieving it. Liberal-conservative pluralism, however, is present in abundance and is a major source of the disintegrative dynamic.

Each of the crisis points we noted in Part II of this book is, at least in part, an evidence and a symbol of the fragmentation of denominational life. The mainline youth crisis is an illustration. Young people who find their religious nurture in Young Life or Campus Crusade may be, as many believe, finding something which their own congregations are failing to provide. They are, however, missing the opportunity to develop a sense of identification with the denomination. Even those who remain in denominational youth programs often find this missing.

I find a personal illustration of this in a comparison between my daughter's experience in our congregation's Youth Fellowship, and my own in an earlier generation. As a youth, I was fully aware of my membership in the larger

church: presbytery (there were frequent "rallies"); synod (summer "conference" was synod-wide); and General Assembly (even though I never attended
an Assembly Youth Convention, I was well aware of them). Presbyterian
Youth Fellowship was for me the youth of the whole denomination. For my
daughter, participating in our congregation's youth program today, the sense
of the larger whole is missing. When she goes to the local presbytery's Camp
Calvin, she goes at a time the facilities have been reserved for a "retreat" of her
congregational youth group. The communicants' class that prepared her for
full membership dealt with the "presbyterian system" almost entirely in
terms of the session of the local church. In fact, the mainline young people
most likely to be gaining a sense of participation in a larger youth network are
those participating in Young Life or Inter-Varsity.

Each of the crisis points examined shows similar indicators. The
parachurch organizations by their very existence undercut denominational
"connectionalism." The electronic church not only diverts funds, it also
encourages a Christianity related to the larger whole only through the air
waves. The mission-oriented special cause organizations express the
wholeness of Christianity only in connection with the one cause they support
in isolation from other forms of wholeness. They suffer particularly from the
absence of opportunities for the "gatheredness" of Christians in community.
Their only form of contact often is the mail or broadcast through which funds
are solicited.

The internal denominational parachurch organizations which gained
strength in the decade of the seventies as expressions of growing evangelical
strength in mainline denominations, have had a direct effect. The Covenant
Fellowship of Presbyterians in my own denomination began in the late
seventies to sponsor its own denominational youth conference, an event
called "Fun in the Sun," to counter what was perceived as the absence of
biblical content and the failure to seek commitment of life in the conferences
sponsored by the denomination's liberal-ecumenical establishment.

The independents in overseas mission have already moved into the
vacuum left by the mainline denominations with their changed emphasis in
the mission of the church abroad. Mainline evangelicals feel this keenly. In a
letter to my office, a missionary said:

> the denomination must accept the fact that . . . in the pluralistic church
> overseas missions is the realm of the evangelical wing of the denomination—it
> always has been and always will be. In an attempt to more widely distribute its
> support base, the result has only further diluted it.[3]

The charismatic movement and the Church Growth movement demonstrate
the same liberal-evangelical fragmenting dynamic. Each has a bridging or
reconciling potential, but each is also perceived by many as divisive. What all

the mainline crisis points demonstrate is the *absence of a broad churchwide consensus* serving as a basis for a shared experience of wholeness.

Is the disintegration of the denomination as a meaningful part of church life inevitable under such circumstances? Is it desirable? Can anything be done? *Should* anything be done? The last is not a rhetorical question. In the area of mission, a valid case can be made for *allowing* denominational mission to disintegrate so resources can be devoted to local and regional mission where involvement is more direct and participation more meaningful. A valid case can be made for consciously turning things over to the managers and professionals who are presumably more effective than amateurs. (This is particularly true if the value of the church is seen in terms of its impact on society.) A valid case can be made for encouraging the demise of denominational identification and loyalty in order to permit the ecumenical church to come into being.

The decision concerning whether attempts should be made to arrest and reverse denominational fragmentation, then, must be based on value judgments. There are real values in denominations which are worth preserving. For all the gains from local involvement, for all the benefits of regional mission close to home and visible to congregations, the deterioration of the wholeness of the church is a serious loss. The sense of one's place in Christ's whole church cannot be derived solely from giving money to the World Council of Churches or from the knowledge that ecumenical negotiations are going on. It cannot be derived entirely from joint worship services with congregations of other denominations or races, or from participation in ad hoc coalitions, important as these things are. It must take institutional form and it must come from sensing one's part in a larger institutional whole. Denominations play a role that congregations, regional judicatories, and even ecumenical relationships, cannot entirely fill. Mainline Protestants will be much poorer without it. If there is to be a meaningful sense of the wholeness of the larger church for Protestantism in the foreseeable future, it must be found in the denomination.

We turn now, in Part Three of this book, to an examination of possible solutions. How can mainline churches at the operative level meet the evangelical challenge?

part three

manual for mainline ministers: how to cope with charismatics and deal with dissenters

chapter 10

mainline
decision point:
which option
for the future?

In Part Two we examined a series of crisis points for mainline churches. They are so labeled because each represents a point at which a renascent and vigorous evangelicalism has mounted a challenge to the mainline and has, at least to some extent, made a significant impact.

We looked both at the deterioration of youth programs in mainline churches and at the way non-denominational evangelical youth organizations have moved into the vacuum. Where have all the young folks gone? They are studying their Bibles over at Young Life and Campus Crusade. The alumni/ae of these organizations are showing up in the mainline seminaries, each entering class seeming more evangelical than the last. Even more pointedly, the young people are rejecting mainline institutions and attending independent evangelical seminaries in preparation for mainline ministry. They are showing up in the youth delegations to General Conferences and Assemblies and in the new generation of young congregational leaders.

The vehicle for this "youth takeover" has been the parachurch organization, and we looked at a whole range of these parachurch groups which have become a second home for mainline evangelicals. In particular, they have offered an attractive magnet for mainline money. As conservatives have virtually despaired of finding acceptable channels for mission outreach through the mainline bureaucracies, they have sought other channels. And they have found them readily available.

We looked at overseas mission, long a special concern of evangelicals within the mainline churches. We noted their consternation at the process by which "foreign missions" has been replaced by a more generalized—and less evangelistic—"mission of the church." We saw, however, how the decline of mainline overseas mission has been more than matched by the growth in mission activity sponsored by non-denominational, evangelical, parachurch organizations. Overseas mission is now largely in the hands of the conservative denominations and the independents.

We looked at the charismatic movement. This form of evangelicalism has made significant inroads into mainline churches, sometimes bringing dissension. It can, however, offer a means of bridging the gap between the two Protestant parties.

We looked at the numerical decline of the mainline churches in the past decade or two, and at the evangelism issue which evangelicals perceive as central in the decline. We examined the evangelical Church Growth movement in which desperate mainliners find a readily available vehicle offering some means of reversing the trend as well as of recovering part of their own heritage.

Finally, we looked at the fragmentation of denominational life and at the deteriorating sense of denominational identity and wholeness, both of which no doubt have many sources in secular movements and social trends, but which are also directly related to the evangelical renewal, to the massive changes in funding as evangelicals have looked outside their denominations for mission channels, and to the alienation between evangelicals and the denominational power structures.

What does it all signify? If the thesis of this book is correct, it reflects the impact on mainline churches of a renewed and vigorous evangelicalism.

The mainline tendency has been to deal with each of these movements and developments from a lofty pedestal in terms of whether "approval" can be granted. Listening to an Annual Conference debate on the Church Growth movement, one comes away with the impression that Church Growth will stand or fall on whether the United Methodist Church "supports" it. One would assume at a Presbyterian Synod meeting that Campus Crusade is waiting outside in fear and trembling at the prospect of a resolution questioning its methods. In fact, each of the movements, trends, organizations, and "renewals" discussed in Part Two has reached its present state of development and vigor *without mainline permission*. Presumably they will continue to do so regardless of whether mainline churches "accept" them or "approve" what they are doing. Indeed, if a challenge to mainline Protestantism is being mounted, it is a challenge which has already had a major impact. *It is the thesis of this book that mainline churches—for their own sakes and the sake of the health of the Body—must recognize the challenge and rise to it in a positive and affirming way.*

Whether they do so or not, the battle may already be half over. A generation of mainline youth has already received much of its Christian nurture from Young Life and Inter-Varsity; the products are already in our colleges and seminaries, on our Vestries and Boards of Stewards. We may respond by renewing our own youth programs as our members are begging us to do (and we probably will do this by imitating the parachurch groups, since no other successful alternatives seem to be before us). The problem is not "down the road." We are in the midst of it.

Similarly, the balance in overseas mission has already shifted to the conservative denominations and the independents. The parachurch agencies both outside and increasingly inside our denominations and congregations, and the charismatic groups—these are not possibilities on the horizon. They have already happened. What options are open to the mainline churches? The first chapter of this book suggested at least three.

Option One: Battle for Control

The obvious option, and the one most likely to be adopted (not necessarily by conscious choice, but by visceral reaction) is to fight for control. At the end of the seventies, a retired theologian who had earlier been identified with the centrism of neo-orthodoxy wrote: "What we really have in the churches today is a polarization between right-wing and left-wing fundamentalism." He said "the utopianism of the social activist may be just as legalistic and his dogmatism just as intransigent as any attitude exhibited on the right."[1] We may be in for a replay of the modernist-fundamentalist battle of the twenties.

The evangelical bid for adherents and for grassroots support, as we saw, has been under way for some time from the base of parachurch organizations outside the mainline and has therefore been out of the direct line of fire. In this contest the evangelicals have had considerable success. The battle for control for mainline church organizational structures, however, is yet to be fought. Such a battle in the 1980s would be much more sophisticated than in the 1920s. Applied behavioral science has made political control of groups and organizations a well-developed technology. It is one in which the liberal-ecumenicals have thus far excelled, having adopted the insights of the human relations movement earlier than the mainline evangelicals. Today's evangelicals, however, are more sophisticated than the fundamentalists of the 1920s, and their use of modern human technologies is greatly improved.

Will such a battle be fought? The signs—at least at the mainline denominational level—are not encouraging. A power establishment which insists on only one model of mission and maintenance and which manipulates political processes and budgets to support that one model (this is how many evangelicals perceive what is happening in mainline churches with liberal-ecumenicals in control), encourages the battle option. I personally come out of the liberal-ecumenical ethos. My background, education, training, and experience, have all been mainline liberal-ecumenical. By every instinct I respond to situations in liberal ways. Yet after six years of close, intensive observation in the heart of one mainline denominational bureaucracy, and with continual opportunities to observe others, I have come to the reluctant conclusion that the evangelical perception is, on the whole, accurate.

Mainline establishments are wide open to cultural pluralism, but not to liberal-evangelical pluralism. Out of the highest of motives—response to what they are convinced is God's claim on the church—they are manipulating every possible organizational, political, and budgetary process to maintain one unified model of church life and mission.

Considerable evidence suggests that evangelicals, were they in control, would do exactly the same thing. The one recent denominational schism in which the schismatic group was a liberal-ecumenical minority in a conservative denomination—the Lutheran Church, Missouri Synod—did not lead an outsider to believe there was any invitation to shared power, any search for middle ground, or any absence of manipulation of denominational machinery on the part of the evangelical power structure. Neither does political behavior of evangelical parachurch groups within the mainline denominations appear to offer reassuring contrast to the political behavior of the establishment. None of this, however, clouds the essential accuracy of the evangelical perception of what is now going on within the mainline churches.

The spirit of the times is an additional factor pushing us toward a battle for control. The loss of a sense of cohesiveness already noted in the mainline denominations reflects a general loss of such a sense throughout society. Contemporary political activity in the civil realm exhibits this fractiousness. The zealotry of one-issue groups willing to use almost any means to impose their viewpoint—whether the issue is nuclear energy, abortion, the environment, or homosexuality—on the larger society, is indicative of the general tone. The search for common ground, for compromise, for a meeting of minds, is out of fashion. Battling it out for control may thus well be the option chosen.

The outcome of an all-out struggle for power and control is difficult to predict. Like a president in office with all the powers of incumbency, the liberal-ecumenicals now control the machinery and until now have been more adept than evangelicals at using the political processes on which that control is based. However, all the developments described in Part Two have taken place despite—and to some extent because of—liberal control of the machinery and processes.

Liberal "victory," in light of these developments, could conceivably leave the machinery with little to pull. It could herald a further decline of the mainline until it ceases to be the mainline. A Roman Catholic historian, observing the Protestant scene, sees this as a probable outcome:

In purely historical and sociological terms, extrapolating from present trends, the following prediction seems not unreasonable: by the beginning of the 21st century most of what are presently considered the "mainline" Protestant denominations in America (Episcopal, Presbyterian, United Church of Christ, Methodist, along with some branches of the Baptists and the Lutherans) will either have ceased to exist or ceased to claim any distinctively Christian character for themselves. The Roman Catholic Church may continue in a condition of stagnation and confusion, although there are now hearty signs of revival. Whatever lively Christian presence exists in America (and it may be very lively) will be centered in those denominations presently considered peripheral and not quite respectable—those which are called, pejoratively, fundamentalist and which call themselves Evangelical.[2]

Dr. Dennis Oliver, a demographer and church growth coordinator for the Presbyterian Church of Canada, has suggested that rapidly multiplying evangelicals can already be regarded as the new "main-line" churches of Canada.[3] Such an outcome of a battle for control of American churches is by no means inconceivable.

The totally unpredictable element is the Holy Spirit. God has never left the church alone to go its own way, and God's will for the church has repeatedly baffled human beings who seek to use it for their own ends. There is some question that a power battle for control of church machinery is in accord with divine will. Even if such a battle should be fought, the final outcome, certainly, depends on far more than the strength, tenacity, and political adroitness of the antagonists. It would rest in God's hands.

The Pluralistic Alternative

A second option which mainliners may choose in the face of the evangelical challenge—an option suggested in the introductory chapter of this book—is a consciously planned pluralism. We have noted repeatedly that one of the distinctive characteristics of mainline churches is their pluralism. They incorporate great diversity and are economically, culturally, and socially pluralistic to some extent (though not manifesting nearly the kind of diversity the ideal would call for; absence of racial pluralism is a particular embarassment). In this period, however, their theological-missional pluralism, which takes the form of the liberal-evangelical confrontation, presents the major issue for them.

Theologically pluralistic churches have worked well in the past, but without voluntarism. The earlier patterns of both Roman Catholicism and Eastern Orthodoxy, when they flourished in one-church societies, were pluralistic. The classic "church" (as differentiated from the "sect") according to the analysis of Max Weber and Ernst Troeltsch was by its nature inclusive.[4] Everyone in the society belonged by birth to the universal church. In such an inclusive institution diversity was inevitable, and routinely accommodated.

The church demanded conformity in a few basic areas but permitted latitude elsewhere, as the rich diversity of the classic Catholic tradition demonstrates. A second reason the universal church worked as a pluralistic organization was its claim to use sanctions—usually spiritual sanctions but nevertheless perceived as potent by believers—to hold dissenters in line. The intellectual awakening of the Renaissance brought a deterioration in the effectiveness of the church's spiritual sanctions. This was at least one of the reasons the Protestant Reformation became possible.

Protestant pluralism—which because Protestant churches are voluntary organizations is a *voluntary* pluralism—is a relatively new experiment.[5] The birth of Protestantism represented a rejection of the Catholic version of internal pluralism in a universal church. Protesters, as generations of Reformation Day speakers have affirmed, "stood for" something they regarded as unique and essential. Their churches developed as self-limiting consensus groups. The consensus group pattern continued through most of Protestant history, with denominationalism as the escape valve when disagreements arose. Although larger denominations had some room for diversity (particularly in the European national church pattern), major disagreement usually resulted in schism and the formation of new denominations. Until the present century, internal consensus remained the pattern for these voluntary organizations. The wide range of belief and practice now seen in the mainline denominations is largely a twentieth century phenomenon. The question is, can such pluralism be maintained consciously and intentionally in voluntary churches?

A theological question arises concerning whether voluntary pluralism of belief and practice must mean indifference, lukewarmness, and the absence of religious certainty. Clearly religious pluralism is related to the rejection of absolutes—the relativism—which is characteristic of the modern intellectual climate and which the liberal-ecumenicals of the mainline establishment reflect. Voluntary pluralism could only have developed in a liberal climate.

Yet establishment liberals are faced with a dilemma as they confront the evangelical challenge within their churches. Their liberalism calls for tolerance of diversity, for a marketplace of ideas, for refusal to impose one's own vision of truth on others who disagree. The challenge, however, comes from an opposition which rejects this very liberalism. Evangelicals *do* have a vision of absolute truth derived from an infallible if not inerrant Bible. They are responding to an imperative which makes them insist on a church in which that vision of absolute truth is accepted as normative. The liberal dilemma is the fear that if they accept this evangelical attitude as valid and allow it to become dominant as evangelical strength grows, the very liberalism on which pluralism is based may be undermined. Accommodation requires moderation of extremes on both sides.

There is, however, a theological model for the pluralistic church on which such accommodation can be based: the biblical imagery of one body with many members, one Spirit with many gifts. While the church has never found the final answer to the problem of unity and diversity, biblical patterns clearly suggest that some answer must be found, that both unity and diversity are inevitably present in the Body of Christ. To succumb to a new "fundamentalism of the left" under pressure from liberal-ecumenical extremists, to return to sectarianism as the dominant form of diversity, would mean a major defeat for the mainline.

Lyle E. Schaller, in an article called "What Will the '80s Bring?" listed a number of challenges to the churches. His concluding word dealt with active pluralism:

> The continued growth of the new evangelical churches (and the word "new" may be as significant as the word "evangelical") plus the increasing acceptance of the homogeneous unit theory of church growth will force those churches which identified themselves as "pluralistic" to develop a coherent, consistent and systematic concept of creative and active pluralism to replace what is now a largely passive and defensive response.[6]

This "coherent, consistent and systematic concept of creative and active pluralism" must move beyond the de facto diversity which presently characterizes Protestant voluntarism, to a pluralism which is consciously sought and willingly encouraged. A *planned pluralism* is required. In the past, the mainline establishment has been willing to seek, encourage, and plan for a largely missing cultural pluralism. Regarding the kind of pluralism already present in abundance—theological and missional—however, more planning seemed to be devoted to suppressing it than to encouraging it!

If a consciously planned pluralism is to be chosen as an alternative to an all-out battle for control, the local congregation is the locus for such a choice. In the next chapter we shall examine the potential of this alternative.

chapter 11

strategy for congregational coping: planned pluralism

The congregation is the focal point for all the changes in church life Part Two of this book detailed as crisis points. The congregation is where the need for a viable youth program is intensely felt. Here the pressure of parachurch organizations—both independent and denominational—is experienced. Here the budgetary issues are fought. Here the charismatic groups and other internal consensus groups are formed. Here the need for leadership is most intense.

In some congregations the evangelical renewal is not experienced as a challenge to the status quo. Some congregations *are* thoroughly evangelical, while others are relatively untouched by evangelicals. Even in the most pluralistic denominations, local congregations tend to be self-selecting consensus groups. Nearly every mainline denomination in every city has its Grace Church, know for conservatism and overseas missionary involvement, and its St. John's, known for liberalism and involvement in environmental and social change issues. There are First Churches, staid and proper strongholds of the business and social establishment, and charismatic churches. Newcomers to a community often shop around until they find a congregation into which they "fit"—their own consensus group. The range of diversity is not likely to be as great within such congregations as it is in the denomination as a whole.

In a great many mainline congregations, however pluralism *is* a major factor. Suburban churches, chosen by parishioners for proximity rather than by "shopping around"; rural churches in areas where distances are great;

downtown churches operating on a market place model—for these diversity is the norm. Even in once relatively homogeneous mainline liberal congregations the tide of change is being felt. The present evangelical challenge is not somewhere "out there." It is taking place in the churches. Vestries, Sessions, and Boards of Stewards, long controlled by a liberal power structure, are being confronted with the election of evangelical "young turks." Ministers seeking associates are finding the seminary-graduate market heavy with alumni/ae of Youth for Christ and Inter-Varsity. Social activist congregations accustomed to operating from a liberal perspective are being joined by social activist new evangelicals. How do these congregations cope?

Living with Internal Diversity

Leaders in mainline congregations tend to think the way to handle all forms of internal diversity and disagreement is through parliamentary procedures. The vestry or session takes a vote, makes a decision, and the matter is considered settled. But is it? Evidence increasingly suggests that pluralism cannot be handled solely by majority votes and parliamentary victories. Some areas exist in which the dynamics of dealing with dissenters, coping with charismatics, and handling all our various kinds of pluralism must move beyond parliamentary majorities.

An initial step is to identify those areas in which majority vote rules, and those areas in which the convictions of the believer take precedence. The first category, for most mainliners, is the area of church government: the preservation of good order and discipline, confessional standards, the ministry—all those matters covered in Books of Church Order and Discipline. The long tradition of self-government by elected representatives and voluntary compliance with the rulings of governing bodies, taken for granted by mainliners, carries a great deal of weight.

Another whole area, however, concerning the response of Christians to the experience of God's grace in Christ Jesus—the way they go about expressing their faith in mission—probably cannot be legislated. It is no accident that mission is not dealt with in most denominational canons or books of order. Telling people who feel called by God to engage in evangelistic mission in Africa that because of a majority vote in a general convention they must devote their money to boycotting the Nestle company instead, is seldom effective. The teaching in a church school is not controlled solely on the basis of a majority vote by a session to support and use denominationally approved materials. People may be swayed, and may even be convinced, by these majority decisions. But they do need to be convinced.

A pluralistic congregation, finding that majority votes do not solve all problems and seeking ways to handle its pluralism of conviction, can move in either of two directions. One is toward becoming a consensus congregation.

Dissenters may be handled by getting rid of them. A demand for conformity, a careful screening of membership, and a high level of internal discipline, will achieve the goal. In some denominations this method of maintaining consensus within the congregation is official policy.

In most mainline churches, the same goal is more likely achieved by subtle excommunication of dissidents. We do it by carefully excluding them from positions of control, and by adopting a "love us or leave us" attitude. This, coupled with the natural desire of members to be with a like-minded group—the homogeneous unit principle—is nearly always effective. I once had close ties to a congregation with two polarized factions, and I watched the process operate. I received earnest invitations from the dominant faction: "Do come aboard and see and do things our way." "Our way" was clearly the only permissible way. The process was inexorable.

One after another, members of the opposing faction gradually gave up and moved their membership elsewhere. It is certainly possible to handle pluralism by becoming a consensus congregation, and at the congregational level it may even be the best way. Cumulatively, however, in the larger church, it is simply a disguised form of fighting for control.

The thesis of this book is that a more creative direction for a congregation is toward a planned pluralism. By this is meant a consciously adopted attitude of permitting, accepting, and living with diversity and dissent. Planned pluralism means "both-and" rather than "either-or." A church that welcomes all people must to some extent deliberately seek to be "all things to all people."

The Holistic Heresy

To live with diversity in the congregation is to recognize the *legitimacy* of diversity. Our churches have been through a period of idealistic unifying so admirable in theory but so dysfunctional in many of its results that one is tempted to label the movement a "holistic heresy." The goal has been to consolidate everything into one universal whole, eliminating the contradictions, competitions and dichotomies that characterize much of church life. Budgets have been unified so that we no longer deal separately with expenses of the congregation and benevolences. On the entirely reasonable premise that heating a room in which a kindergarten church school class meets is no less worthy and no less a form of mission than sending funds to operate a church school kindergarten class in Indonesia, we have eliminated most distinctions between maintenance or nurture on the one hand, and mission on the other. In the congregation with which I worship, everything contributed to the outreach of the larger church—regional, national, and overseas mission programs—is lumped into a single line item (less than 1 percent of the total budget) labeled "Presbytery, Synod, and General Assembly."

Governmental structures of congregations have been unified. In the

Presbyterian churches we have witnessed a wave of unicameralism. Church after church has eliminated the Board of Deacons (which once handled charitable and financial responsibilities) and the Board of Trustees (which once assumed responsibility for church property), combining them both with the Session, the official governing board.

One of the most far-reaching changes out of this period of unbridled holism was the deemphasis if not elimination of special consensus groups within the congregation differentiated on the basis of sex or age. We became convinced that to have women's groups or youth groups as major channels for Christian activity and witness for their members was to give them "second class status." A better alternative, we said, was to "fully integrate" women and young people into the "total life of the church."

Unity and wholeness are, of course, important values. The biblical call for oneness is a compelling one which cannot be ignored. Systems theory has taught us the interrelatedness of everything, and management science has taught us how to integrate our structures and coordinate our operations. Quite apart from these considerations, practical gains have resulted from the move toward holism in the church. The opening of all church offices to women has been a major accomplishment in terms of the good of the congregation. Church governing boards which were the preserve of males deprived the church of an enormous amount of talent and leadership ability. Leadership structures have frequently been given new ideas and fresh viewpoints by the participation of young people as well.

Yet the holistic approach, carried to its logical limits, leaves little room for dividing things up into manageable pieces. Sessions have become overloaded with work. Specific causes have lost their identity. Women's organizations were never really *for* women alone. They were for the church, and in deemphasizing them, congregations have lost a valuable resource. The unified mission agencies of denominational headquarters left constituencies in the local church no way to understand or identify the particular aspect of the mission organization with which they had business. As a result, the ink on the plans of restructure was hardly dry before the movement began to reintroduce some functional separations into the holism.

The theological-missional diversity of the church, however, has tested the holistic approach most severly and demonstrated its dysfunctional nature most clearly. To be intentionally pluralistic is to reject rigid conformity to a single pattern. Diversity as well as unity characterizes the biblical model of the Body of Christ.

Pluralism in Mission Funding

To a proper mainline establishmentarian trained in management and theologically committed to the holistic approach, a call for pluralism in mission funding is the ultimate scandal. Yet this is the point at which imposed holism is most obviously breaking down. Nothing is more indicative of mainline malaise than the radical decline in funding for the restructured and centralized denominational bureaucracies with their "one mission" and single budget dogmas. Whatever may have been the theological rationale for commitment to the "one mission" concept; whatever may have been the organizational and managerial justification for the single denominational budget; whatever may have been gained in elimination of duplication and competition for dollars, grassroots mainline evangelicals have not been convinced. Whatever may be the social and cultural causes of funding trends in an inflationary economy, with an endemic localism and a widespread distrust of centralized bureaucracies, internal causes are certainly also present. Funding for unified mainline denominational mission in the hands of the liberal-ecumenical establishment has gone into a disastrous decline.

The facts are too well documented to need lengthy repetition here. Every mainline denomination has suffered a radical decrease in the amount of money received from contributors in the pews. Every bureaucracy has been slashed. Every mission agency has had to cut programs. Mainline evangelicals have made no secrect of their role in this decline. They have expressed both their distrust of the liberal-ecumenical establishment running the mission bureaucracies and their disapproval of the ways in which funds are being used. They have pressed for channels through which they can designate their funds for particular uses and have made full use of the restricted channels available to them.

The Role of Prophets

Throughout the period in which all this has been taking place, social activists, calling for radically new directions in the face of the reluctance of the mass of people in the pew to change, have regarded their activities as prophetic. In many instances they have been right. Prophets, biblical and post-biblical, have seldom been popular and have often found themselves against the crowd. The abolitionists of the nineteenth century, the critics of unbridled privilege in the Gilded Age, the civil rights movement, the anti-war movement in our times—all these have had their share of prophets who have frequently suffered for their courageous stands.

In the managerial age of the late twentieth century, however, many who consider their ministry prophetic have migrated to the church bureaucracies, seeking the reins of power. There, insulated from the grassroots, they have pioneered a new form of prophecy which engineers budgetary victories in bureaucratic in-fighting and steers pronouncements through the parliamentary jungle of church conventions.

The church needs prophets, but the role of prophets is to confront and challenge the people, to lead them to reshape their responses to the experience of grace. The place for prophets is not the bureaucracies, but the pulpits, the press, and the front line of social change. The prophetic task is not to thwart the missional will and manipulate the monetary gifts of Christian people, but to lead and shape them. We shall examine this concept in greater detail in the next chapter.

A bureaucracy which says "our pronouncements and programs are prophetic and therefore you cannot challenge them," is spouting specious nonsense. Prophecy must confront and convince, not manipulate and coerce. A ruling establishment which says "53 percent of the delegates voted for this program, and therefore you, the remaining 47 percent, must contribute your money to support them," is naive. Prophecy has its visionary role; majority votes have their governing role. Neither, however, can control the stewardship of believers who experience God's grace in Jesus Christ and feel compelled to respond in particular ways with life, service, and money.

Far more persuasive than the complaints of evangelicals about unified mission establishments and bureaucratic prophets and about the actions taken within mainline churches to channel money for restricted purposes, are their suggestions for alternatives. The entire second section of this book was an account of the way mainline evangelicals have voted with their energies their commitment, and their pocketbooks—for the non-denominational youth organizations, for foreign missions through independent agencies, indeed for a whole range of parachurch movements engaged in all kinds of Christian nurture and mission activity. Christians respond in stewardship to their experience of grace. If they are not allowed to respond through mainline church channels, they will find other ways of responding; and they have, to the tune of millions of lives, hours and dollars.

Stewardship Structures

Pluralism in mission funding need not mean a breakdown of customary congregational stewardship patterns. The unified budget and the every-member canvas have for many years been standard in mainline churches, and the pattern is not likely to change. Few church members would want to change it. Membership implies assuming one's share of the common responsibility, and even divergent groups in pluralistic congregations routinely join together to support a common budget. Mission outreach, as we have seen, is where divergent groups insist on responding to their own sense of the gospel's imperative.

As this insistence has been frustrated, two things have happened. One is that congregational budgets have focused more and more on maintenance and nurture requirements of the congregation itself and on those local forms of mission on which agreement could be reached. In an earlier generation, a widely-shared measure of congregational health was the percentage of total giving which went to outreach and benevolences beyond the congregation compared with the percentage used for the congregation's expenses. A fifty-fifty division was often promoted as a guideline. Such a standard has almost disappeared. It is a rare mainline church in which more than a small percentage of the budget now goes beyond the congregation. Many reasons are given: inflation, recurring economic recessions, building funds, growing staff, and administrative costs. But the trend is certainly not unrelated to that second phenomenon, namely, the large amounts now by-passing congregational stewardship structures as direct gifts to independent causes. A certain amount of such by-passing has generally been tacitly encouraged—direct giving to church colleges (particularly by alumni/ae), United Way campaigns, various now-secularized charitable organizations. Tithing Christians often regard such gifts as part of their tithes. The proliferation of the parachurch organizations we examined in Part Two, however, and the enormous range of activities now funded through them is a direct indication of how substantively the congregational stewardship structures have been changed.

Such a pattern may be entirely acceptable. Certainly, as we saw earlier, the independent parachurch organization has been the normative way of carrying on Christian mission through much of Christian history. However, the planned pluralism alternative—that of establishing a variety of channels through which persons and groups in the congregation can give in ways consonant with their own sense of stewardship—has much to commend it. It offers a means of insuring that gifts are accounted for and used in accord with the wishes of the donors. Some parachurch organizations have questionable records in regard to accounting for funds, and others subject themselves to no public accounting at all. More important, however, it builds toward a unity transcending the diversity within the congregation.

Mission, including the giving of money, is and probably will remain a voluntary activity which cannot be coerced. It can be led, organized, directed toward unity, and urged to join in corporate wholeness, but not coerced. Mission is a response to a sense of calling, and this sense of calling varies. A church seeking to be consciously pluralistic can provide for pluralism in mission funding and thereby respond to the concerns of the whole range of its members.

Legitimating Internal Consensus Groups

A second strategy for pluralistic survival is the acceptance of internal consensus groups—and of their legitimacy. We have already examined the unsatisfactory experience of mainline denominations in the period of the "holistic heresy" as they sought to deemphasize internal groupings based on age or gender. Women and young people were to be "fully integrated" into "the whole church," we said. Women's groups never fell for it. Even though in some mainline denominations they were deprived of centrally-provided resources and leadership, they refused to die and have remained a major source of congregational vitality. For a while they were regarded by feminists in the church as strongholds of traditional female submissiveness, to be discouraged if not stamped out. The battle for equality of women has, however, been won in most mainline denominations—in principle if not yet in practice—and the polarization is ending. The value of women's groups is widely affirmed.

Youth groups, with less continuity than that enjoyed by women's groups and with a higher level of dependence on adult leadership, suffered gravely from the holistic heresy. The mainline youth vacuum which set the stage for the non-denominational parachurch youth organizations probably began with the deemphasis resulting from the "integration" of youth into the "life of the church." Determined efforts are now being made to revive mainline peer group youth programs, and to give them greater meaning and substance.

Men's organizations, never strong, gave up the ghost without a struggle when called into question by the holistic approach, though a modest revival appears to be in progress now. Indeed, the need is perhaps even greater now than before, since the earlier sexism made male preserves of the congregational governing structures, and these structures functioned partially as small consensus groups for men. Overall, a consciously planned pluralism should affirm the legitimacy of all such sodality groups based on age or gender.

Accepting and encouraging consensus groups which reflect theological and missional differences is more difficult. We noted earlier the insight of Lon L. Fuller regarding the two principles of human association: shared commitment and a legal principle (constitution, by-laws, accepted traditions). Both principles, he says, are present in almost all voluntary organizations. Maturing organizations tend to move from the first principle toward the second. This is perhaps particularly true of churches, which move from the intensely shared commitment of the early stage of a spiritual movement toward the routine of institutionalization. Organizations dominated by the first principle—shared commitment—cannot tolerate internal groupings. When they are dominated by the legal principle, he says, they not only can tolerate, but in fact *need* internal groupings based on deeply shared commitment.[1]

Because religious commitment is the central dynamic of church organizations, groups based on shared commitment are quite essential to church life. In consensus churches this sense of shared commitment pervades the entire membership. In pluralistic churches, with their internal diversity, smaller internal groupings are also necessary. Traditionally, conservatives within a liberal congregation have been permitted to gather for "prayer groups" or for Bible study, but with great care that the activity extend no further than these relatively innocuous forms of piety. Yet a consciously planned pluralism must probably be open to more active forms of involvement, involvement based on shared commitment to a particular form of mission or devotion which may well be different from that of the congregational majority.

Church power structures which resist such groupings on the grounds that they are divisive are not being realistic. Only when the entire church is *itself a consensus group*, sharing the same commitment, can they be avoided. The alternative may be a church devoid of deep commitment. Indeed, some data suggest that the level of commitment—measured by the self-appraisal of the strength of one's religious identification and by frequency of church attendance—is considerably lower in mainline than in non-mainline Christians.[2] There is no certainty that internal consensus groups would heighten such commitment, but common sense supports Fuller's principle.

In today's context, accepting internal consensus groups probably means conceding the legitimacy and constructive role of evangelical parachurch organizations. Whether this necessity can be recognized by the power establishment is an open question. The tendency of those in power is to say, "I accept you; you must therefore stop all these disruptive things you have been doing and start supporting *my* program, *my* priorities, *my* way of doing things." This, of course, is really an attempt to eliminate diversity. To accept their legitimacy is to accept the right of these organizations to be different. The option of fighting it out for control is always available to mainliners, but if the choice is planned pluralism instead, internal parachurch organizations constitute one reality that must be recognized.

Coping with Charismatics

It is the charismatic movement which has brought the issue of internal consensus groups most forcefully to the attention of mainline ministers and congregational governing structures. Charismatics in a non-charismatic congregation are often suspected of being potentially divisive. Everyone knows of congregations which have been—as the establishment usually expresses it—"split wide open by the charismatics."

One must recognize that this factor of potential divisiveness is real, though it is probably not correct to blame it entirely on the charismatics. The blame is shared by both sides. It is characteristic of the charismatic experience that it is deeply felt and matters enormously to the person involved. It engenders both great conviction and great enthusiasm. As Christian history knows, it is difficult to deal with the zeal of enthusiasts. There is a pressing desire to share the conviction and enthusiasm with others. With an intense sense of vitality and renewal, charismatics tend to see themselves as over against the perceived "deadness" of non-Spirit-filled Christians. So the tendency for divisiveness is there.

On the other side, the ruling establishment often sees such a group as a threat to the status quo. Conventional Christians react defensively to the implication that "my Christianity" is not as deeply felt or as authentic as "yours," that the Holy Spirit has given you a gift I have not received. The potential for conflict is built in. Charismatics are not the only divisive element. The potential is present on both sides.

As we have seen, however, the contemporary charismatic movement as a whole is notable for its absence of anti-institutionalism. Despite obvious exceptions, the contemporary charismatics are by and large trying hard to stick with the mainline churches and to cooperate. The question is, can we accept them? And that means even more specifically, can we accept them as charismatics? Can we accept them as participants in charismatic groups, since group participation is an important element in the contemporary movement? Accepting them does not mean saying, "I accept you as long as you give up speaking in tongues and limit your communion with God to reciting the Lord's Prayer, as I do." It does not mean, "I accept you if you stop meeting with that bunch of kooks on Thursday nights and limit your group participation to official organizations." That is not acceptance; that is a demand for conformity.

There are four simple steps the non-charismatic leadership of a congregation can take to legitimate this form of pluralism. First, leaders can seek out the charismatics in the congregation in a spirit of oneness and love. There may be far more of them than the establishment realizes. Often they keep a low profile, unsure of their reception, until the leadership makes the first move.

Second, the official structures can affirm and cooperate with them—or allow them to cooperate. That means learning about their experience, affirming the legitimacy of their spiritual gifts and of the consensus groups in which they find spiritual nourishment. By and large they are willing and eager to work with others, if others will work with them.

Third, church leaders can help them in their own spiritual experience by reinforcing its non-exclusivist dimensions. Sometimes they do have a tendency to pull apart, and toward spiritual pride. Glossalalia, according to Scripture, is only one of the spiritual gifts—not given to all, but clearly part of the New Testament image of the Body of Christ made up of many members with different functions. Congregational leadership can help them understand their own experience in the larger context of the church.

Finally, the congregation can tap into the enormous reservoir of vitality, spirituality, energy, and renewal which those with such spiritual gifts can bring to it. They are eager workers and, in a cooperative situation, can be trusted to cooperate in return. Few congregations today are not in need of the presence and work of the Holy Spirit, even if the channel is a new and strange one.

Recognizing and Countering Win-Lose Tactics:
A Primer on Church Politics

Accepting a range of choices in mission funding, accepting internal consensus groups, accepting the legitimacy of the charismatic experience for those to whom it is meaningful—all these are ways of living with congregational diversity in consciously planned pluralism. None is easy. We noted in the last chapter that a win-lose battle for control may be a more likely response to the evangelical challenge than planned pluralism. Churches seldom, however, make clearcut choices between the two options. In reality, both responses are likely to go on at once. Even within the same congregation, the two dynamics—battling it out and striving for a planned pluralism—may operate simultaneously.

Win-lose battles in the church depend heavily on political control mechanisms. The techniques are widely known and frequently employed—nearly always, in church circles, from impeccable motives. After a great deal of observation of church politics, I am convinced that persons who set out to establish political control almost always do so for worthy reasons. They do it because they are sincerely convinced that the position they support is God's will for the church and that the opponents they seek to defeat would harm the church. Yet the results are not always as wholesome as the motives. Those committed to a consciously planned pluralism as an alternative to win-lose battles need to recognize the techniques and be prepared to counter them. Partisans seeking political control are likely to operate in predictable ways.

1. *Elections*

The vehicle for control is the representative governing body. Elections, therefore, are a key element in gaining control—not only elections of members of the Session, Vestry, Board of Stewards or Deacons, but also representatives to regional or national governing structures. In a stable, non-polarized congregation, most elections are polite and genteel affairs, models of courtesy—and poorly attended. Members are grateful for the willingness of those who are nominated to assume responsibility and are reluctant to challenge them. *When control is an issue, however, political operators will have been busy behind the scenes.* The election will have assumed great importance, and those seeking political control will be counting not only on their own behind-the-scenes planning, but also on the lethargy and gentility of others.

2. The Nominating Process

Control of the nominating process is extremely important to control seekers. If the "right" people can be put into nomination, the battle is half won, and control of the nominating process is always a key political plum. *Recommendations of a nominating committee are generally accepted by most groups.* If additional nominations come from the floor, those proposed by the nominating committee have considerable advantage, since the general presumption is that they have been carefully selected and are the best qualified for the positions to be filled. When there is no nominating committee, and the process is genuinely open, the *political operative will be quick to gain the floor to make the first nomination.* The first candidate nominated has a significant advantage, since the field is empty. Later nominees must face the disadvantage of being proposed "instead of" the first.

3. The Presiding Officer

Besides the nomination process, the other major control point is the parliamentary leadership—the presiding officer. In many systems of church government, the pastor of the church is automatically the presiding officer of the governing board, a position of great power. Few chairs of church organizations would actually preside over meetings in an openly partisan way. Opposition speakers will almost always have a full opportunity to be heard, and rulings will be even-handed. *The power, however, lies in organizing and controlling the agenda and the process.* If the chair appoints the nominating committee, this is a particularly important control mechanism.

4. Committees and Work Groups

Apart from the parliamentary process itself, the key vehicles for those seeking political control are the committees, task forces, and work groups in which the real work is done. The assignment of work to such groups is an important element in manipulation. *Key business must be assigned to the right small group where control can be exercised.* There are always plenty of "throwaways"—items of business that do not really matter to the political operative—which can go to other committees. This, as a matter of fact, is a favorite device for keeping opponents occupied and out of the way.

5. Small Group Control

The key committees must, of course, be controlled. Within these work groups, manipulators have golden opportunities. Such groups are usually small, intimate, and depend heavily on one or two workhorses who organize the work for the committee, prepare recommendations to be considered, provide information when needed, and write up the report. *An astute political operative has the right workhorse on the right committee at the right time.* The small committee is also the ideal environment in which to "tame" a member of the opposition—*provided* he or she is outnumbered and preferably isolated from other like-minded persons. As numerous social psychologists have demonstrated, small group pressure is a powerful tool.

6. *Input of Information*

Another key control device is the input of information. A committee or governing body *deals largely with whatever information is placed before it.* In addition to preparing agendas and resource materials, the person seeking to control the information input may call on a variety of "professionals," "experts," or "consultants." Available experts naturally represent a wide range of viewpoints, opinions, and techniques. Selection of the *right* experts is therefore a critical point of influence.

7. *Compromises*

When compromise is in order, those seeking to exercise political control may opt for a committee representing both sides. They will, however, seek to *hand-pick the representatives of the opposition.* A committee made up of an equal number of Democrats and Republicans is a pushover—provided the Democrats can select the Republicans who serve on it!

8. *Planning*

A political operator leaves nothing to chance. A strategy is always planned if the outcome matters. Only the throwaways are left unplanned.

9. *Homework*

The single most important element in exercising political control is doing one's homework. *Most political victories are the product of nothing more arcane than knowing more about the business at hand than the opponents do.*

Is There a Core of Unity?

A basic question for the pluralistic mainline churches is whether a sufficiently substantial core of unity underlies their diversity. Obviously a core of unity exists. All Christians have a common allegiance to Jesus Christ, and all members of a particular denomination share a common set of church traditions. Unity is often most strongly affirmed and most real to the participants when people worship together.

But is the core of unity substantial enough to hold things together in today's pluralistic churches? Are the various interpretations of the meaning of allegiance to Jesus Christ and of the validity of the church traditions close enough together to provide common ground for joint endeavors?

Disparate traditions, commitments, and beliefs are most readily held together from a position in the center, as a long history of political processes in free societies, as well as in mainline churches, demonstrates. Unity requires a center core from which no one feels so far distant as to be alienated. We have been through a period of significant alienation between conservatives outside the major denominations and liberals inside who control the denominational machinery. Now, as the evangelical challenge moves with a surge of strength into mainline territory, the question is whether the evangelical dissenters on the one hand and the liberal establishment on the other are too far from the center for the core of unity to assert itself. The leap of faith now before the mainline churches is the assumption that the core of unity is sufficiently strong and that a planned pluralism can be based on it. We shall look at the possibility of reestablishing a consensus of the middle in the final chapter.

At the congregational level, however, where planned pluralism must actually operate, a major question remains to be examined. Whether consciously planned pluralism is a viable strategy may depend primarily on the kind and quality of *leadership* provided.

chapter 12

the leadership factor:
pulling it all together

"You make it sound hopeless," a minister said to me in a workshop on pluralism and strategies for coping. "I agree with you that these things are happening. They are happening in my congregation. I know we've got to accept and live with the dissidents—I don't want to get rid of them. But I don't want to be just a ringmaster presiding over a three-ring circus either. What about leadership?"

He was pointing to a critical element in any strategy for planned pluralism. Living with diversity does not mean abdication of leadership. Acceptance of a variety of internal consensus groups, coming to grips with church politics, willingness for stewardship to take different directions in response to different perceptions of Christ's claims—none of this is incompatible with leadership which has its own clear vision of Christ's claims and which strives for and builds unity. In fact, a power structure which presides over a collection of disparate groups all heading in different directions, but which does not hold before them the biblical model of diversity *with* unity, is failing in its responsibilities. Diversity in a congregation intensifies both the need and the challenge for leadership.

Background Principle: Voluntarism in the Local Church

A starting point in building toward such leadership is an understanding of the voluntary nature of the church. Every congregation depends on volunteers to perform much of its work, but a more basic principle than the use of volunteers in programmatic activity is involved here. Voluntarism is a central organizational dynamic for the church. Churches are volunteer organizations. We looked in the last chapter at the voluntary dimension of contemporary mainline pluralism, but far more is involved. Building toward a creative leadership in dealing with dissenters and coping with charismatics requires an appreciation of at least three aspects of voluntarism in congregational dyamics.

The first is the *voluntary nature of membership and participation*. The motivation behind church membership is not voluntary; it is a sense of God's call, a divine imperative. But sociologically—that is, from the human perspective—members are completely free to join or withdraw, to participate or not to participate. The church does have the characteristics of a voluntary organization in the membership-participation sense.

Second, the *funding is voluntary*. With a few exceptions (income from endowment and collateral business activities), church financial support comes from voluntary contributions. Once again, the motivation is not necessarily voluntary; givers are often responding to a sense of divine imperative. The strength of that motivation is indicated by the fact that the largest category of voluntary giving in the United States is money given to and through churches and synagogues ($18.4 billion in 1978, or 47 percent of the total).[1] In the human (sociological) sense, however, funding is clearly voluntary.

The third aspect of congregational voluntarism is a variation from the norm of voluntary organizations. Despite the voluntarism of membership and funding, churches are among the few voluntary organizations in which *every local unit (congregation) has a professional staff*, even if it consists of only one person. Ministers, as salaried employees, are non-volunteers in their relationship to the congregation. Further, in most denominational polities, the clergy participate in a larger non-voluntary system. The minister's relationship to the bishop and membership in the annual conference, presbytery or classis, is far less voluntary in its dynamics than is the member's participation in the congregation. This means that some of the minister's basic assumptions and perspectives are likely to be quite different from those of members. The same is true of other employees on the church staff. Professionals and volunteer members may tend to think "we are all in this together, working for the same God, toward the same ends, so we should all see things the same way." At the operative level, however, such an assumption is probably inaccurate. No matter how dedicated a Christian may be, there is a significant difference in one's perspective toward those activities in which participation is voluntary, and one's job, which is non-voluntary.

Power and Authority

Against this sketchy background of observations about the voluntary nature of the church, a few implications may be examined. One is the issue of power and authority. Social scientists have engaged in a great deal of study of power and authority in social organizations, and many definitions of the terms are current. One simple distinction between the two, however, is most important for our purposes. Power involves coercion. Power means being able to force someone to do something. The major form of coercive power encountered in modern organizations (apart from law enforcement with the power of the state behind it) is monetary. Monetary coercive power is real; whoever pays the salary has a great deal of power.

Authority, on the other hand, is non-coercive and involves voluntary compliance. Max Weber, in a classic analysis of authority, identified three kinds: traditional, which is the kind of authority centuries of church practice and the mystique of the clergy give to the minister; legal, which is the kind of authority derived from church canons or books of order or discipline; and charismatic, which is the force of one's own personality and persuasiveness.[2] In voluntary organizations, authority, not power, is what counts.

A very real and quite unique form of power operates in churches—the transcendent power of God. Ultimately churches are far more dependent on the operation of that power than on their own authority. There is one area where *human power* in the church is very real: the power of monetary coercion through payment of staff salaries. Between human beings, however, in the organizational life of the church, we are primarily concerned with authority, not power. Voluntary compliance rather than enforced obedience motivates church members in their organizational life.

A second area concerns clergy and lay roles in church organizations. Because they are voluntary organizations (sociologically), congregations are groupings in which the members—the laity—play the dominant role. The classic pattern of a voluntary association is that of a small group of people who band themselves together for some particular purpose. The closer the congregation is to the classic pattern, the stronger is the lay role. In terms of the traditional church/sect paradigm, the lay role is stronger in a congregation of the sect type. In terms of the traditional congregational/presbyterian/epis-copal church polity paradigm, the lay role is strongest where the polity is congregational. Although there are variations in degree, it is important to recognize that in *every* case at the level of the local congregation, the lay role is likely to be dominant. Even in Roman Catholic parishes today (except in particular areas like the sacramental, where the authority of the clergy is carefully guarded), the laity has a strong voice. Only at hierarchical levels is clergy dominance clearly established. The size of the congregation has much to do with the dynamics of lay dominance, as noted below. The funding, however,—based on voluntary giving—is what assures lay dominance. The power of the purse is persuasive power, and in this particular period it is being exercised with increasing boldness and effectiveness.

The size of the congregation has considerably more effect on clergy and lay roles than is sometimes recognized. The difference between large churches and small churches is not just quantitative. There is a qualitative difference as well; they are different creatures. This is one reason a highly successful pastor of a small church, called to a large church, sometimes encounters difficulties; or why an effective associate on a multiple staff of a large church, when called to be pastor of a small church, is sometimes disappointing. A large church is not just a larger small church. The dynamics are different. As a rule of thumb, the smaller the group, the closer it will conform to the basic model of a voluntary association and the more dominant will be lay participation and control. The larger the church, the closer it will conform to the corporatized model, the more highly structured it will be, and the more professional control will be exercised. A ten-person Board of Stewards is quite different from a sixty-person Board both in the way it operates as well as in its size.

The professionals in church organizations—the clergy—have a great deal of *authority*. Traditional authority, derived from clerical status, has waned considerably in society at large, but it is still significant within the church. The polity of most mainline denominations gives the clergy a great deal of legal authority. Apart, then, from whatever measure of personal charisma a minister may have, there is a considerable measure of authority which elicits voluntary compliance. Further, an additional source of authority which has become quite important in our technological society is professional expertise. In our corporatized and professionalized society, there is a widespread tendency to let professionals dominate those areas of our lives in which they claim to have expertise. The church is no exception.[3] This is the temper of our times.

Yet strong counterforces are now in operation. A general reaction against the corporatization of life, against dominant institutions and professionalization of services, is evident. This reaction as yet has little impact on big business, big labor, big medicine, big school systems, big regulatory commissions, and especially big government. Their power is too great to be challenged successfully. The reaction is, however, making itself strongly felt in those segments of life in which the individual person can have an impact. Because churches are voluntary organizations, the impact here is significant.

A final factor influencing clergy and lay roles in the contemporary church is the trend toward "privatized" or "laic" religion. While undoubtedly related to the institutional, managerial and social factors we have been noting, the privatization of religion is a phenomenon of increasing importance. With a marketplace model of religions—not only a broad range of denominations with easy transfer from one to another, but also the electronic church, the parachurch groups, and a plethora of cultic alternatives—individuals feel free to pick and choose. Martin Marty has labeled privatization of religion the most basic trend of the seventies, underlying all others.[4] While "laic religion" (Marty's term) is not the same thing as "lay religion," the movement away from institutionalized clergy authority in the direction of increased lay power—even within institutional churches—is an obvious outcome of the trend.

One additional note: while the local congregation is a lay stronghold, presbyteries, dioceses, and various higher courts and conferences are clergy strongholds. The further from the local congregation a minister gets as a delegate to a church court or convention, the more likely will he or she reflect the professionalized attitudes and corporate perspectives of the denominational power structure. This has nothing to do with conscience and authenticity; it is simply an organizational fact of life. We are in a period, however, of fragmentation of denominational life, as we noted in chapter nine. In such a period, clergy control of the higher ecclesiastical reaches has less and less effect on local congregations.

Mainline churches, then, appear to be in a period when the pendulum is swinging from dominance by clergy authority to dominance by lay power. This swing illuminates much that is happening in the churches today. Churches reflect some things that are going on in the whole society, but in an intensified way. People cannot control government, or taxes, or corporatized institutions in a substantive way; they are too massive and impervious to constituency influence. Churches, however, are voluntary organizations, and people can control them. Localism and the waning of hierarchical authority, the power of the purse, privatized or laic religion—all these are factors contributing to a shift from clergy to lay dominance.

Leadership and Management

In my 1979 book, *Wheel Within the Wheel,* I wrote on the management crisis of the pluralistic church. One of the most controversial sections, a chapter called "The Minister as Manager," focused on church leadership. Management, I suggested, is the ultimate technology of a technological age—the technique of manipulating personnel, budgets, technologies, and organizational structures to achieve goals. Its *human* technology is "applied behavioral science." (The term is used in a generic sense; "applied behavioral science" is sometimes used as a technical term for group processes.) This human technology is a particularly potent tool. Congregational management places the emphasis on the goals to be achieved and utilizes all available congregational resources (including human resources) to reach its goals.

There is a signficant difference, I suggested, between management and leadership. Leadership was defined as a function of the *relationship between persons,* those in charge and those who voluntarily follow. Leadership both shapes and is shaped by those who follow. The one thing it *cannot* do is ignore the constituency. It articulates what people are feeling and saying. At the same time, it lifts them beyond their present level of living and responding, to a new vision of where they might be and what they might become. The contemporary church, I charged, has fallen into the error of adopting the managerial mode for ministry. Certainly there is a place for management in the local congregation and particularly in denominational bureaucracies where good management is highly prized. The basic model of ministry, however, should be leadership rather than management.

Shortly after the book came out, a church journal published a symposium on the issues it raised. One critical article was entitled "Managers or Leaders—A Misplaced Debate."[5] The writer rejected the dichotomy. Particularly with regard to denominational executives, he called for vision and consensus-creation as well as management. As I read the critique, I could find nothing with which I disagreed. Yet it did seem clear to me that I had not pursued the analysis of leadership far enough in that book. In the period since, whenever I have heard the malaise of the church debated (as it frequently is in the circles in which I move), the leadership issue has tended to surface. So much has been said and written about the "leadership vacuum" in our times, both in the church and in the larger society, that it is an inescapable issue.

Three Types of Leadership

Type A: Managerial

There are basically three kinds of leadership; all are shaped by the context within which they take place. For convenience I shall call them Types A, B, and C. Type A leadership takes place where the controlling structures (organizational and behavior-governing) are already established, where roles (leader and led) are already determined, where goals are understood, and where voluntarism is not a major element.

This is the context of leadership in most segments of a corporatized society. Its extreme form is the military organization, and its normative form is the business organization or governmental bureaucracy (which differ very little in their essential dynamics). Certainly elements of vision and inspiration are called for in such an environment. On the whole, however, this form is what we know as management. (I probably erred in my earlier treatment in making such a sharp distinction between leadership and management.) "Personnel" are the most important tools at the managers' disposal, to be used along with appropriate technologies, funds, and structures in reaching the established goals. Such utilization of personnel, however, is not necessarily dehumanizing, and much of modern management technique tries to prevent it from becoming dehumanizing.

Nearly all the empirical research on leadership has taken place in Type A situations. We have been through a period in which we thought of management and leadership pretty much as interchangeable categories. In that we were wrong.

Type B: Leadership in Voluntary Situations

Type B leadership takes place in a more fluid situation where structures, roles, and goals are not as clearly defined and *voluntarism* is a major element. It requires mobilizing and maintaining a *constituency* around a *cause*. The constituency and the cause are both essential elements along with the leader. Since important causes are seldom created ex nihilo, the leader usually reflects or buys into causes that are already present, even if dormant and unrecognized. Since important constituencies, likewise, are hard to find, most leaders place themselves at the head of constituencies already present even if amorphous. As James McGregor Burns so clearly demonstrated in his important book on *Leadership*, real leadership does not just pick up and consolidate the opinions and feelings of the constituency; it starts there and lifts them above themselves, giving them a vision, inspiring them, and moving them forward.[6]

Type B leadership does not necessarily occur in organizations and institutions different from those in which Type A leadership is required. It must often energize and set in motion established organizations accustomed (or previously, by abdication, forced) to get along with "management" of established processes only. In the sectors of such institutions where a fluid situation obtains and where voluntarism is important, it becomes necessary.

Illustrations are readily found in the political arena. The decline of the perceived legitimacy and power of traditional parties has led to a far more fluid political situation than existed in an earlier day. Structures are shaky; roles and goals are not clearly defined. Both Jimmy Carter and Ronald Reagan were establishment outsiders who rode to power by mobilizing constituencies around causes. To an astonishing degree, the outward form of the cause was the same in each case: the failure of the ruling establishment or presidential predecessor to deal with pressing problems, and the promise of change. Each found an existing constituency—Carter a coalition of disenchanted liberals and underprivileged groups; Reagan a coalition of conservatives championing rightist causes. Each mobilized his constituency through the campaigning process, and was elected president.

The problem for contemporary Type B leaders in the political arena has been that of providing the vision, of lifting these constituencies, once mobilized, above one-issue self-centeredness toward united action or movement in the common good. At one point in his presidency, Jimmy Carter approached it. Near the beginning of 1980, after a period of extraordinarily low standings in the public opinion polls, he found himself in the midst of a double crisis with the seizure of more than fifty diplomatic hostages in Iran and the Soviet invasion of Afghanistan. With the help of some skillful alarm-clock ringing on the part of Carter, the crisis awoke in the citizenry long-dormant feelings of patriotism, of having an American cause. President Carter sensed precisely the reaction of the electorate: the urgent need to "do something," to take a strong stand, coupled with an equally urgent unwillingness to do anything rash, to "get us into another Vietnam." His firm but calm and measured response not only articulated what was there, but helped to shape it as well. It gave a moral and rational note of restraint to a situation that could easily have gotten out of hand—in either direction. Thus he not only mobilized the constituency and seized on the cause; he formed and shaped both, lifting an angered America above itself to a level of rational measured response. The subsequent inability to bring about any real movement, over an extended period of time, may ultimately have lost him the election, but for a brief period it was a case study in leadership. The result, at least for a time, was the most spectacular turnaround in public opinion in the history of polling.

Churches are more firmly structured than political parties. The traditional roles of minister and congregants are clear, and churches are therefore often perceived as needing Type A leadership only. The critical element, however, is voluntarism. The givenness of ministerial leadership is confined largely to liturgical and sacramental functions. In mission or goal-achievement, churches are voluntary organizations. Movement in any direction requires the articulation of a vision, and the mobilization of the ready-made constituency around a cause or causes.

Type A and Type B leadership rarely occur in total isolation from each other. Almost all situations contain elements of both. Churches, in particular, require elements of both, and it is important for the sake of understanding to treat them separately. One of the problems of society in the managerial age has been our failure to distinguish between these two forms and contexts of leadership. We have universalized Type A, attempting to place *managers* in organizational chairmanships, public office, and congregational pastorates. In particular, we have failed to understand the importance of the *voluntary element* in Type B leadership and followership. It cannot be coerced by management but must be mobilized around a cause—even in highly structured situations.

Type C: Entrepreneurial-Prophetic

There is a third kind of leadership which in general terms may be labeled entrepreneurial leadership. It occurs where structures and roles are extremely fluid or non-existent. The leader mobilizes the constituency de novo around a chosen cause. This is the pattern by which most of the parachurch organizations we examined earlier in this book were established. We have noted that they generally start from scratch and focus on one charismatic leader and one cause.

The classic religious variant of Type C leadership is that function which in church circles we label "prophetic." The prophet is the leader who confronts and calls into radical question the status quo, and who charts a different course. Prophets in the classical tradition speak for God to a misguided, wayward, or sinful people. They pronounce God's judgment in oracular form.

The object of prophecy is always people, and in its essence it is pure proclamation, not goal-seeking. The prophet prophesies, and whether or not the people respond, God's word has been spoken. Prophecy merges into leadership when a response does come, when a new vision emerges and a constituency is created around a new, renewed, or purified cause.

A minor twentieth century heresy has been a creation of the managerial age: "bureaucratic prophecy," the fallacy of which we examined in the last chapter. Church agencies have been filled with social activists proclaiming a new vision but seeking to make it a reality through the manipulation of budgets, meetings, political processes, and bureaucracies. Attempts at radical action *in spite of* the people, rather than through *leadership of people,* have been the result.

The classic form of prophecy in the church has been the prophetic role of the preacher in the local congregation. When Riverside Church in New York City sought a new senior pastor in the late seventies and called the Reverend William Sloane Coffin, Jr., to its pulpit, a spokesman articulated that role: "We were looking for someone to stand in the line of prophetic preachers," said the Reverend Eugene Laubach, the church's top administrator, "to continue the tradition of an open, liberal pulpit, and to stimulate some controversy."[7] While few churches are willing to select a preacher explicitly for challenge and controversy, the prophetic dimension of preaching is well-established and widely expected. The prophetic pulpit is a remarkable institution in a voluntary organization and is one of the ways in which the church as an organization transcends its purely human possibilities. The persistence of prophetic preaching, and the willingness and even insistence of voluntary members that it function without hindrance, is perhaps one of the surest signs of the presence of the Holy Spirit in the church. This may be affirmed despite those all-too-frequent times when pulpits have been shackled and preachers muzzled.

At its worst, such prophecy may take the form of radical proclamation from the pulpit on Sunday morning which is contradicted by weekday behavior and management of the pastor in question and ignored by a complacent congregation. Such prophecy obviously is not intended to be taken seriously. At its best, prophetic preaching renews the conscience and vision of a congregation and provides leadership for a new constituency on behalf of a new cause.

Clearly there is room in the local church for all three types of leadership. Congregations have certain established structures and roles which call for a considerable measure of Type A leadership. As I suggested in my earlier book, management has much to teach the pastor. In particular, certain management techniques such as team building and conflict resolution can be extremely helpful to the leadership of a pluralistic congregation. Human technologies developed by behavioral science can be learned and applied like any other technology. There are management and human relations courses in which these principles are taught, and books from which they can be learned.[8]

Voluntarism, however, is an extremely important element in church organizations, and mobilizing constituencies around causes is its basic form of leadership. This becomes especially important in pluralistic situations where a number of constituencies, pursuing divergent interests, are present. To identify unifying causes around which the whole congregation can be mobilized is the leadership challenge in such situations.

Some fairly simple steps can be followed in constituency building:

1. Be clear about the cause or causes.

2. Seek out the constituency and place the cause before it.

3. Establish a *personal* relationship with the constituency around the cause; it is not a matter of "managing a process" but of leading people.

4. Clarify the feelings and longings already present or inherent in the constituency relative to the cause.

5. Articulate a vision which can lift the constituency above its present status in relation to the cause.

6. Help the constituency establish its goals relative to the cause.

7. Help the constituency mobilize its resources to reach those goals.

Goal setting, as a tool for congregational revitalization, often fails because it leaves out all the steps except 6 and 7. Its failure is its assumption that Type A conditions—in which the cause and the leader/follower roles are givens—are present. The voluntary nature of church organizations generally means that the first five steps are necessary to establish those conditions.

Pointing Toward Unity

The prophetic role of the minister is crucial in leadership of the pluralistic church. The freedom of ministers to proclaim from the pulpit the word of God as they understand it—even the demand that they do so—saves them from the indignity of doing nothing more than coping with charismatics and dealing with dissenters. The inherent and generally recognized need for prophetic preaching, for prophetic challenge to long-accepted and comfortable ways of doing things, for a call to a higher vision of Christian responsibility—this is unique to the church. Prophetic leadership in the congregation not only can but must encourage divergent groups to examine their assumptions and move in the direction of a Christ-mandated unity.

The most basic and essential leadership role is that of pointing beyond human leaders to the Lordship of Christ as ultimate leader. In pluralistic congregations the minister is usually found to be closer to one of the divergent groups than to the other. The same is often true of lay leadership. The leader's personal vision of the *shape* of unity may for that reason be perceived by others as a partisan position. The classic test of authenticity in Protestantism—faithfulness to the biblical record with the Holy Spirit as interpreter—may be the most effective safeguard against a partisan view of the shape unity must assume. Ultimately common worship, with proclamation of the Word and celebration of the sacraments pointing to the Lordship of Christ, is a far more effective means of leading toward unity than the techniques of conflict management and team building.

From the human perspective, leadership must recognize that *unity is most likely to be achieved somewhere in the middle of the spectrum*. A meeting of minds and spirits somewhere between the extremes represented by various internal consensus groups is more likely than is some process through which one group—whether liberal or conservative, activist or pietistic, ecumenical or exclusivist—becomes convinced of the error of its ways and accepts the premises of the other.

Such movement toward the middle need not reflect a sacrifice of conviction, nor a partial compromise satisfying no one. It reflects rather the necessary and continuing tension of a faith which calls for *both* contemplation and action, pietism and prophecy, affirmation of the holy in human society and confrontation of the demonic, social action and evangelization, faith and works. It represents a striving for *balance*. Living with divergent groups that make no move toward meeting each other halfway can be organized chaos. Other things being equal, it is the role of leadership to lead toward balance and acceptance and toward the middle ground. Is that possible? We shall examine the viability of a new consensus of the middle for today's polarized Protestantism in the concluding chapter.

chapter 13

a new consensus
of the middle:
is it possible?

In an article labeled "Fractures in the Future?" Douglas W. Johnson wrote in the *Christian Century* near the end of 1979 of his pessimism regarding the decade ahead. He recounted the splintering of denominations in the 70s—the schisms in the Presbyterian Church, U. S.; the Lutheran Church, Missouri Synod; and the Episcopal Church. He cited the control of national agencies by social activists beginning back at the end of the 60s, the opposition that developed within the churches in response, the clergy-laity gap that widened, the dissenters who entered the 70s as a silent majority but who organized within the denominations and became increasingly effective. He concluded:

> Given the history of the past two decades the future appears likely to be one of fractures. The optimism of the early 60s is a faded dream. The current interest in smallness, the emphasis on self-fulfillment, and the desire by grass-roots people to control organizations to which they belong are forces that will further the splintering.[1]

Yet there are those with a more optimistic view. Diogenes Allen of Princeton Theological Seminary wrote at the end of the seventies of his hope for reconstitution of what he calls the "central channel" in Christianity. Nearly a decade earlier he had written that he considered the most significant event in the churches in the sixties to have been the collapse of the middle ground between liberalism and fundamentalism. Dean Hoge, in his book *Division in the Protestant House*, quoted Professor Allen and presented an array of research findings to confirm the polarization and collapse of the middle.[2] Allen said, however, as the seventies ended:

There are signs that a middle ground or a central channel, as I prefer to call it, is being reconstituted in a new way today. This middle ground or central channel once set the pace for American Christianity. . . It can be a channel in which diversity, instead of being a source of antagonism, can strengthen us and make us grateful for each other.[3]

At the beginning of this book three options for mainline Protestantism in the face of the evangelical challenge were outlined. Two of them, the basic choices open to mainline church people, have already been examined in detail. One choice is to fight it out for control; the other is a consciously planned pluralism. The third option may not be available through conscious choice. Perhaps it can come about only through the action of the Holy Spirit. However, the rebuilding of a consensus of the middle probably offers the best chance of a creative solution.

An all-inclusive pluralism for mainline Protestantism probably is impossible. Centrists must accept the reality that extremists at either end will not be satisfied, and will look elsewhere for channels of Christian expression. Yet extremism in mainline Protestantism tends to be a matter of degree rather than substance. Even the most rock-ribbed conservatives still believe for the most part that their faith calls for active response of some kind. And even the firebrand activists of the Christian left still, for the most part, root their activism in faith in a transcendent God. So the centrism called for is one of *balance*. None of the polarities discussed in this book—between nurture and outreach, evangelism and social action, ecumenical inclusiveness and disciplined distinctiveness—represents an "either-or" for Christians. Each of them calls for a balanced "both-and." The broadest range is encompassed when a centrist position reflects such balance. "Mainline" in the past has meant "mainstream"—the central channel. The historic mainline churches have flourished when they have represented a consensus of the middle. The core of unity which may hold together the mainline churches today—if it exists in a sufficiently substantive way—will necessarily be in the center.

Where Is the Middle?

One's perception of where the center lies is likely to depend to a considerable extent on where one stands. Few of us perceive ourselves as being very far from the middle of the road. A liberal is likely to place the center a good bit to the left of where a conservative would place it.

One such liberal view of an emerging consensus of the middle comes from theologian Robert A. Evans of Hartford Seminary Foundation, in an essay included by religious sociologists Dean Hoge and David Roozen in their definitive study *Understanding Church Growth and Decline*.[4] Writing about the recovery of what he calls "the church's transforming middle," Evans defines the middle ground in terms of the balance between faithfulness and effectiveness. His own liberal perspective is clear from his first presupposition, namely, that the church is called by Christ to transform culture. His is therefore a social action-oriented analysis. Evans describes liberalism as "culture affirming" (a Christ-of-culture model), as opposed to fundamentalism, described as "culture denying" (a Christ-against-culture model). His is a middle which neither affirms nor denies, but rather transforms culture—a transforming middle.

Contributing to a book on church growth and decline, Evans offers a somewhat negative appraisal of the evangelically-oriented Church Growth movement based on the conviction that "what God requires of the church is not growth but faithfulness." While calling for both faithfulness and effectiveness, he tends to identify church growth with effectiveness and to juxtapose it with the transforming of church and culture (which he identifies with faithfulness) almost as if the two were mutually exclusive. He is unwilling to accept a "balance" between the two if growth comes at the expense of culture-transformation. The vision of the "transforming middle," therefore, is one with far more emphasis on transforming than on the middle. In impact it is a fairly uncompromising call for social change in the liberal-ecumenical tradition.

A far more conservative vision of the middle comes from Richard F. Lovelace, a leading evangelical spokesperson from Gordon-Conwell Theological Seminary. He sees American Protestantism as having been split into two halves after the end of the nineteenth century, but he sees the difference between the two not in terms of affirmation or denial of culture; each half, in its own way, is "enculturated":

> Half of it emulated the ostrich, turned its back on the culture, immersed its head in the biblical word and almost became an enculturated folk religion. The other half grappled with the task of integrating modern and biblical thought but often lost its biblical moorings and slipped away into another kind of enculturation: conformity to the secular mind.[5]

The time may now be ripe, says Lovelace, for a "reunification of the tribe within the Christian movement." He finds the basis of the new middle ground in what he calls live orthodoxy. "If dead orthodoxy is the brittle fault which leads to the splintering of Christendom, perhaps live orthodoxy is the element which can bridge and heal its divisions." This live orthodoxy focuses on "applied biblical truth" rather than biblicism. It uses doctrine as an implement of spirituality, a means of healing the ills of modernity rather than an end in itself. Lovelace sees biblical doctrine used in this way as essential to both evangelism and the church's prophetic social witness. His is a call to a conservative version of the middle, the basis of which, though live, is also "orthodox."

Social Concern and Biblical Theology

These two very different views of the middle point to the difficulty in defining the central channel. The center seen from my perspective may be far removed from the center seen from yours. One consistent element, however, is the fact that Evans *looks for* the center in terms of cultural transformation—action, change, results of faith—while Lovelace looks for it in terms of orthodoxy—belief, convictions, the faith-basis from which results come. This is true of most calls for a return to the middle. Those coming from the left are action-oriented; those coming from the right are belief-oriented.

A supportable hypothesis is that the periods in American church history when the center has held have been those when classic biblically-based theology has been *combined* with a lively social activism. If there is hope for a revival of a consensus of the middle today, room must be found both for Evans' transformation of society and Lovelace's live orthodoxy. One of the encouraging signs of return to the central channel seen by Allen was the "recognition by evangelicals of the social dimension of the gospel." We noted earlier in this book Drew Seminary Professor Thomas Oden's report that "the sons and daughters of modernity are rediscovering the neglected beauty of classical Christian teaching"—his claim that mainliners are reaching for "postmodern orthodoxy."[6] If both these signs are accurately read, there may indeed be hope.

A combination of classic biblical theology and social activism was the pattern set shortly after American independence which held throughout most of the nineteenth century. The evangelical theology and piety of the Second Great Awakening provided the impetus behind the social change activism of the abolitionist movement, the social work movement, the prohibition movement, and a variety of other attempts to influence society.[7] Toqueville's commentary on the activism of Americans with a "society for everything" reflected a period in which an evangelical Protestant consensus existed. The legendary "do-goodism" of Americans, the great social organizations such as the American Red Cross which are now secular (surely its central symbol is indicative), the Christian origins of hospitals and educational institutions—all these are classic reflections of the inherent social activism of centrist Protestant America.

The center no longer held after the radical polarization of the early part of the twentieth century. American Christianity became a battleground with extremists on both sides fighting for control.

The short-lived neo-orthodox consensus of the middle once again brought social action (with social gospel roots) and classical theology (though without biblical literalism) together in mid-century. Certainly the neo-orthodox consensus of the middle was not a return to the "good old days" of mid-nineteenth century evangelical activism, but was rather an expression of the dynamics of its own times—the disillusionment with liberal utopianism brought on by two World Wars, the social challenge of a historic crisis, and the irrevocable acceptance of the contemporary scientific world view. The new period of polarization which followed the mid-century neo-orthodox consensus of the middle may possibly be healed through the mainline's recovery of a new center. If this is to be the case, however, the new consensus of the middle can be neither a return to nineteenth century classic evangelicalism, nor to twentieth century neo-orthodoxy. Historically, there is never any going back.

Hopeful Signs

There are some signs that a new, late twentieth century consensus of the middle may be emerging. This emerging consensus is appropriate to the conditions and challenges of this difficult age; at the same time, it is recovering the biblical theology and the social dynamism which have historically characterized mainstream Christianity at its best.

Third World Influence

One of the most hopeful of these signs comes out of the worldwide interdependence of peoples and the emergence of the third world as a potent social force. Thus it is very much a product of late twentieth century conditions. The "Third Church"—Christianity in third world nations—is in many ways clearly the church of the future.[8] Numerically, Christians in the Southern Hemisphere where the third world is developing have already passed those in the Northern Hemisphere, the stronghold of the first and second worlds. Their influence in world Christianity is growing rapidly, and it may be characteristic of the late twentieth century that their growing influence on the American mainline offers one of its brightest hopes.

I mentioned earlier one of the exciting opportunities afforded me in recent years by my work at the head of the Office of Review and Evaluation of the Presbyterian Church, U. S., namely, the chance to visit leaders, ministers, parishes, and members of several third world churches. No impression was more striking to me than the relative absence of the kind of dichotomy between evangelicalism and social activism which marks so much of American mainline Christianity. By and large, the churches I visited were *both* more biblical in orientation and more actively involved in their developing societies than the churches to which I am accustomed. Their biblical orthodoxy tends to be more down-to-earth than ours—more like Lovelace's "live orthodoxy" than the propositional theology of much of the American Protestant right. At the same time, their social change activism also appeared more down-to-earth than ours. It reflected actual involvement in developing societies rather than the interminable meetings, conferences and consultations, process designs and strategies, networks and linkages, papers and pronouncements, which are the stock-in-trade of mainline social activist bureaucrats.

There is, of course, some evidence in the Third Church of the kind of polarization with which American Protestantism lives, especially in Latin America and some countries in the Far East. In most of the third world, however, and especially in Africa, the absence of polarization is striking. Christians generally—mainline and indigenous denominations alike—combine evangelicalism with social commitment. The churches, though theologically conservative, have worked with the new governments in creating their societies and have often assumed a major part of the responsibility for educational and social welfare systems. A dichotomy between evangelical Christianity and social activism is thus quite foreign to them.

The major channel through which the Third Church influences American mainline Protestantism has been the so-called liberation theology, which originated in the third world. It has had mixed results. Some of the most famous Latin American liberationists are social radicals whose theology has been shaped by the secular humanism of western liberals, and whose social orientation is Marxist. Theirs is the liberation theology best known in American liberal-ecumenical circles. Gustavo Gutiérrez, a liberal Catholic and a Marxist, has taught at Union Theological Seminary in New York.[9] Rubem Alves, whose *Theology of Hope* is regarded as one of the major works of liberation theology (though he himself rejects the label), has been widely read. He has reacted strongly against the fundamentalist separatism of his background in the Presbyterian Church of Brazil and questions whether he should identify himself as a Christian.[10] He is also a source of the popular identification of liberation theology with extreme liberalism. Salvation for these thinkers tends to be interpreted politically and economically. American versions of liberationism—black theology and feminist theology—have also contributed the far left image of liberation theology in this country.

Because of the ultra-liberal image, evangelicals have tended to reject liberation theology. Yet there is an evangelical theology which finds its major sources in the Third Church and which could readily be labeled a form of liberation theology. Orlando E. Costas, whose works have been widely read by American evangelicals, combines a classically conservative biblical orientation—an emphasis on evangelism and an identification with the Church Growth movement—with a radical call (out of his third world experience) for liberation from oppressive social and economic structures. In summarizing the "comprehensiveness of the missionary mandate," he says:

We are called in Christ to share with men and women, personally and collectively, the good news of God's kingdom. We are sent to call them to enter into this new order of life through faith in Christ and his gospel. *At the same time*, we are sent to proclaim, in word and deed, the good news of the new order of life *in* the multitudinous structures of society—family and government, business and neighborhood, religion and education, etc. In doing so, we must stand as Christ did, in solidarity with the poor and oppressed. Further, we must engage actively in their struggle for life and fulfillment. No dichotomies here: not a vertical vs. a horizontal emphasis of mission; not a redemption vs. humanization—but a holistic vision of God's mission to the world and the church's role in it.[11]

The Evangelical Seminary in Costa Rica with which Costas was earlier associated has been a fountainhead of such thinking in Latin America. The extent to which a merger of evangelical theology with a call for liberation from oppressive social structures is increasingly permeating Latin American Protestantism was illustrated by the "CLADE II Letter" issued at the end of the Second Latin American Congress on Evangelism held in Lima, Peru, late in 1979. Representatives of forty denominations from twenty-two countries saw evangelical faith as inseparable from radical discipleship in the present Latin American context.

This perspective is shared by many African and Far Eastern theologians as well, and is increasingly shared by American evangelicals. Ronald J. Sider, a professor at Eastern Baptist Theological Seminary in Philadelphia, and president of Evangelicals for Social Action, has called on his fellow conservatives to recognize an evangelical theology of liberation. Without deemphasizing personal salvation, he insists (on biblical grounds) that the liberation of poor and oppressed people is a central and essential biblical theme. Holding conventional conservative theology up to the same scriptural standard, he finds it heretical in its failure to take this central biblical theme seriously. Indeed, he accuses such theology (in its identification with rich oppressors rather than the poor oppressed) of "theological liberalism"—the error of allowing theology to be shaped by the views of the surrounding society rather than by biblical revelation.[12]

The Lausanne Congress, Covenant, and Committee

Entirely apart from the influence of liberation theology as a body of literature and conceptual frame of reference—whether liberal or evangelical in orientation—one of the most important channels of influence from the third world churches on American Christianity (particularly its evangelical wing) has been the 1974 Congress on World Evangelization, the Lausanne Covenant that came out of it, and the Lausanne Committee which continues to embody its concerns. We noted before the importance of the Congress in renascent evangelicalism. Attended by 2,437 participants from 150 countries and 135 Protestant denominations, it was described by *Time* magazine as "possibly the widest-ranging meeting of Christians ever held."[13] Though the original impetus for the Congress came from Billy Graham and though American evangelicals were well represented, it was the third world participants who combined an urgent socio-political concern with the more personalistic spiritual concern of many American evangelicals and placed the Covenant in the classic center stream of Protestant Christianity. C. Rene Padilla, in his introduction to an international symposium on the Covenant, suggests that its great achievement is the elimination of the dichotomy between evangelism and social involvement.

The fifth article of the Covenant, on "Christian Social Responsibility," is a direct and forthright product of third world influence on evangelical Christianity:

> We affirm that God is both the Creator and the Judge of all men. We therefore should share his concern for justice and reconciliation throughout human society and for the liberation of men from every kind of oppression. Because mankind is made in the image of God, every person, regardless of race, religion, colour, culture, class, sex or age, has intrinsic dignity because of which he should be respected and served, not exploited. Here too we express penitence both for our neglect and for having sometimes regarded evangelism and social concern as mutually exclusive. Although reconciliation with man is not reconciliation with God, nor is social action evangelism, nor is political liberation salvation, nevertheless we affirm that evangelism and socio-political involvement are both part of our Christian duty. For both are necessary expressions of our doctrines of God and man, our love for neighbor and our obedience to Jesus Christ. The message of salvation implies also a message of judgment upon every form of alienation, oppression and discrimination, and we should not be afraid to denounce evil and injustice wherever they exist. When people receive Christ they are born again into his kingdom and must seek not only to exhibit but also to spread its righteousness in the midst of an unrighteous world. The salvation we claim should be transforming us in the totality of our personal and social responsibilities. Faith without works is dead.

In commenting on the elimination of the dichotomy between evangelism and social involvement, Padilla noted that in this article of the Covenant the expression "social action" was replaced by "socio-political involvement," a considerably stronger phrase. He suggested that the Covenant also eliminates the dichotomy between evangelism and Christian discipleship, and between evangelism and church renewal (particularly with reference to Christian unity, to which the Covenant issues a summons). "Over against an unbiblical isolation of the proclamation of the gospel from the total mission of the church," he says, "there emerged a concept of evangelism in which the proclamation was seen as inextricably connected with social responsibility, discipleship and church renewal."[14]

The Lausanne Committee on World Evangelization joined with the World

Evangelical Fellowship in 1980 to sponsor an International Consultation on Simple Lifestyle in Hertfordshire, England. There were eighty-five participants from twenty-seven countries. The statement adopted by the consultation was perhaps the strongest stand thus far taken by an evangelical group against economic injustice and in support of a "redistribution of world wealth." It called for Christians to take part in "political action to bring about a radical change in the present unjust trade and economic structures."[15]

The New Evangelicals and Social Action

The new evangelicals in the United States have for some time shown a commitment to social action and a determination to recover this emphasis in the conservative wing of Christianity. Some—such as the Sojourners community in Washington, D.C.—are quite radical in their commitment to social change. A strong evangelical dimension has been added to the peace movement, which during the Vietnam War period had become highly secularized as liberal pacifists made common cause with non-religious war resisters. A poll of evangelical leaders, conducted at the beginning of the 1980s by *Evangelical Newsletter*, identified the "increased impact of Christian social concern" as one of the three most encouraging developments they saw in the contemporary world.[16] These leaders covered the spectrum of evangelicalism.

The significance of the Lausanne Covenant has been the breadth of its support, its accomodation to diversity (not only diversity within the evangelical camp, but also its acceptance of the authenticity of the input from non-evangelical sources), and its broadly based movement toward the middle. Together with parallel developments within the American evangelical community, it constitutes an assertion, from the evangelical side of the Protestant polarization, that a new consensus of the middle may be possible.

Changing Evangelical Attitudes Toward Ecumenism

Changing evangelical attitudes toward ecumenism can also be detected. The influential journal *Christianity Today* commented early in 1980 in a lead editorial that "there were no conservative evangelicals among the 100 delegates attending the recent meeting of the Consultation on Church Union" (COCU). Ascribing the absence more to evangelical suspicion of ecumenical projects than to liberal blackballing, the journal called for participation in such movements from conservative churches. While recognizing theological problems, *Christianity Today* insisted that "to be indifferent to the biblical mandate for unity" is not permissible. "Evangelicals have no more right to pick and choose what biblical commands they will obey than liberals have to pick and choose what biblical truths they choose to believe."[17]

We noted earlier the changing attitude toward church union on the part of evangelicals in some mainline Protestant denominations and saw the grassroots ecumenism of the charismatic movement. This changing state of affairs was illustrated early in 1980 by David du Plessis, an Assemblies of God leader long known for ecumenical activities. (In 1962 he was "disfellow-shiped" by the Assemblies of God for "hobnobbing" with the World Council of Churches and Roman Catholics, but was recently restored to full standing.) Du Plessis described a recent conversation with Philip Potter, World Council of Churches General Secretary, who asked whether the charismatic movement today is the real ecumenical movement. According to du Plessis, he replied, "My dear Philip, we [charismatics] are so far ahead of you we can't even see if you're still coming."[18] Although du Plessis, who is rarely given to understatement, may be overly optimistic in this assessment, mainline Protestantism cannot afford to ignore all these signs of reaching out.

Signs from the Liberal-Ecumenical Camp

Are there similar signs of reaching toward the middle from the liberal-ecumenical camp? Though not as readily apparent, such signs are discernible. One evidence is in the liberal seminaries where future church leadership is being shaped. In the summer of 1979, sociologist Barbara Hargrove, moving to another seminary after four years on the faculty of Yale Divinity School, reflected on the changes in that liberal stronghold during her period on the campus. She had been told that earlier the campus had been a hotbed of social activism, with a corresponding decrease in practices of personal piety and corporate worship (chapel attendance had dwindled to a handful of the faithful). She noted that by 1975, when she arrived, that picture was already changing. Throughout the late seventies she observed a steady climb in interest in spirituality, in chapel attendance and other worship activities. She identified three trends in Yale Divinity School during her four years there. The first was that of personalism—an assumption that ministry is directed at individual persons. The second involved a renewed interest in biblical and theological studies. (She noted a decline in interest in courses in her own field—sociology.) The third trend was a growing number of evangelicals on the campus.[19] These represent significant shifts in a seminary long known as one of the fountainheads of the liberal-ecumenical tradition in American Protestantism.

Another prominent sign already noted is the response of mainliners to the church membership crisis. Though adoption and adaptation of the principles of the Church Growth movement is by no means the universal mainline reaction, this evangelically-grounded approach has gained widespread acceptance. On an even more basic level, the liberal-ecumenical mainline establishment is being forced by the membership crisis to turn its attention toward bringing persons into the Christian community, and to reexamine a theology of evangelism.

A third sign already noted is the charismatic renewal in the mainline churches. The charismatics are not "out there"; they are all around us and among us, joining us in our work and our prayer, showing forth the power of the Holy Spirit in individual lives and groups. Many come from the orientation we have called liberal-ecumenical and still accept its world view. Though we all too often perceive them as a threat, we are being given opportunities, in congregation after congregation, to work with them, allow them to work with us, and to deepen our own spirituality in the process. There is evidence of progress. A "communicator" report to denominational headquarters early in 1980 reads:

> One executive commented that the uproar caused by the "charismatic" movement seems to be waning. While some Presbyterians continue to express their faith this way, they seem to be less divisive in their approaches. Those who are not attracted to this form of worship also seem to be less upset by the presence of charismatics within the Presbyteries.[20]

Other signals can be found if we look for them. We noted a rising evangelical interest in ecumenical conversations. There has been some hopeful liberal response. In my own denomination, the goal of reunion with the United Presbyterian Church for two generations has been the rallying cause of the liberal-ecumenical establishment—almost the litmus test of liberal credentials, with opposition to union being almost as universal a test for conservatism. The negotiations looking toward union have been the preserve of the liberal leadership. In 1979, however, when evangelicals of both denominations showed some interest in joining the negotiations, the establishment reached out. The test lay not in the appointing of "conservatives" to the joint committee on union, but in permitting the evangelical parachurch organizations in both denominations to name persons who could authentically represent them. Similar overtures in the past had been handled by hand-picking "conservatives" who could be trusted to accommodate to the liberal-ecumenical position.

The result of this negotiation toward a centrist position by representatives of both sides remains to be seen. Even the attempt, however, is a hopeful sign.

Others are to be found throughout the mainline churches, where a return toward classic Christian roots from the humanistic excesses of the sixties and seventies can be seen in a number of areas. After the long seige in which "doing theology" was the only acceptable form of "theologizing," propositional theology is no longer quite so unacceptable. Proclamation of the biblical Word is making a comeback in homiletical discourse after an era of dialogue sermons and insistence on "two-way communication" in preaching. Biblical modes of pastoral care are making a comeback, enriching the psycho-therapeutic model so long in vogue. There is a growing interest in traditional forms of piety and devotion. Donald E. Miller, an avowedly liberal professor at the University of California's School of Religion, has called for liberal commitment to daily prayer, meditation, and Bible study. "The inner reserves of liberal Christianity are largely depleted," he says. Liberalism is "in the doldrums," and rescue must come from personally encountering "the Source."[21] There is an upsurge of interest in the Bible, in biblical studies, in the church fathers, and in the recovery of our roots. Dean Peter M. Schmiechen of Elmhurst College, asserting that "the precarious middle ground is precisely where ecumenical Protestantism should be," suggests not only that we "lay claim to the truly evangelical heritage of the Reformation," but also that we develop "our own form of piety, consistent with the biblical and Reformation tradition."[22]

Liberal scholars show increasing openness to evangelical scholarship. At the 1980 meeting of the liberal-dominated Society for Biblical Literature, which meets jointly with the American Academy of Religion each year, evangelicals found a surprisingly warm reception. Liberal scholars Paul Achtemeier of Union Theological Seminary of Virginia and James Sanders of Claremont College, California, were joined in a panel discussion by leading evangelical Clark Pinnock. In a subsequent telephone interview, Achtemeier spoke warmly of Pinnock:

> I find nothing that he's written that I can't accept. He and I pretty much view the Bible in the same way, and apparently we have found that out, which means either he's going to lose his credibility as a conservative or I'm going to lose mine as a liberal.

Mark Branson, of Inter-Varsity's Theological Students Fellowship organized an "evangelical consultation" as a beachhead for conservative scholars at the American Academy of Religion meeting, and it was attended by a number of liberals as well. In light of the success of the "consultation" and the apparent openness to evangelical scholarship, Branson made plans to expand with an evangelical "group" with three sessions instead of one at the SBL/AAR program in future years.[23]

Carl S. Dudley's book on the church membership crisis has been referred to earlier. We noted that he is a defender of the present mainline stance and that he finds the evangelical emphasis on the Church Growth movement somewhat incompatible with mainline Christianity. He also tends to reject the approach of Dean Kelley, in *Why Conservative Churches Are Growing*, labeling Kelley's analysis a call to sectarianism. Yet Dudley, near the conclusion of his book, has a section on "Faith in the Middle" which defines mainline Christianity in a centrist way:

> The theological task of the mainline pastor is to affirm the necessity for a personal faith in Jesus Christ, for congregational and denominational diversity in the ways that faith is understood, and for religious pluralism in the public arena.[24]

Preservation of the Liberal Spirit

Dudley's centrism, however, reflects an insistence on the preservation of the liberal spirit. Some evidence, as we have seen, suggests a movement toward the middle. It would, however, be a mistake to regard these as a rejection of those aspects of liberalism in which mainliners have a heavy investment.

Pluralism

The very fact that they seek to be pluralistic in their churches, that they are willing to be inclusive rather than exclusive, bespeaks a movement beyond narrow denominationalism which mainline Protestants insist on preserving. *Conscious and willing pluralism is a liberal position,* soundly rooted in the biblical image of the one body with a diversity of members and gifts. Pluralism's inclusive tendencies, its insistence that acceptance of others (love) is the greatest spiritual gift, its model of unity with diversity, may be more biblical than conservatism's exclusive nature based on the search for doctrinal and missional purity.

Ecumenism

Pluralism is reflected in the ecumenical movement, which has also flourished in the liberal ethos. Ecumenism need not mean watering down of the confessional positions or commitment of those who engage in it, but is simply a broader form of unity with diversity. It does, however, mean commitment to the oneness of the church, and a continuing quest for ways in which the spiritual unity of the Body of Christ can be given institutional form.

A reaching for the center may bring forms of ecumenism somewhat different from those of recent past as well as a wider variety of institutional forms. The World Council of Churches is so identified as the vehicle of the far left in Christianity and as the opposite pole from evangelicalism that it may need to be joined by newer symbols of a mainline Protestantism closer to the center. As we have seen, however, there are forms of ecumenism for which evangelicals also strive. Even large federations of churches, says leading evangelical Richard Lovelace, are "genetically rooted in earlier evangelical unity movements." He notes that the World Council of Churches is a fusion of two separate unity movements, one of which, represented in the Life and Work Conferences, was liberal, while the other, represented in the Faith and Order Conferences, was evangelical.[25]

Ecumenism, as an attempt to give visible form to the unity of the church, is so central to the liberal view of Christianity, so appropriate to twentieth and twenty-first century conditions, and so expressive of the reality of the contemporary global village, that it must be an element in the centrist mainline Protestantism of the future.

Social Concern

Finally, the social emphasis of liberal Christianity must not be lost in a reach for the center. In view of the prominent and growing social concern of today's evangelicals, there is no reason to believe that a recovery of the middle today would bring such a retreat. Post-secular Christianity will not "let the world set the agenda," but neither will it retreat into an inward denial of the world. From the base of a secure meaning structure centered in the saving act of God in Jesus Christ, the church faces outward in service to society. The range of that service can be as wide as are the concerns of a consciously pluralistic church. Liberal Christians reaching for the center will, however, encounter evangelicals with the same concern for Christian witness in society.

Importance of a Meaning Structure

The base of a secure meaning structure is important. The present evidences of a reach toward the middle in mainline Christianity focus attention on what Dean Kelley has called the "indispensable function of religion" which is to explain life in ultimate terms.[26] We noted earlier that the search for a meaning structure is seen by many as a central dynamic leading a new generation of young people to turn to the evangelical parachurch youth organizations—and sometimes to extremist cults. Young people are not alone in this search. The scientific study of religion as a universal human phenomenon which has persisted in spite of all obstacles as long as human beings have existed, points consistently to this indispensable function as its common strand. The uniquely Christian answer to the question of life's meaning, the life view and style resulting from the Christian answer, and the demands placed on the believer by that answer—these are the reasons the evangelicals and mainliners in the classic tradition have regarded Jesus Christ not as an option among many, but rather as an embodiment of ultimate truth, and have regarded Christianity not as a means to social ends, but rather as a self-validating end. The evangelical purpose—the imperative to share the good news, to make available to others the only fully satisfactory answer to the question of life's meaning—is grounded on this base.

An instructive exercise is to question leaders of the liberal-ecumenical power structure about their own background. I have been struck again and again by the remarkably high percentage who came out of conservative, evangelical backgrounds. The prototype grew up in a conservative Christian home with Sunday School, church, and family prayer. He (or she; despite major strides toward inclusive policies, today's mainline leader is usually male) went to a good church college or university, encountered the secular scientific world view, and intellectually rejected the conservatism of his background, particularly its lack of social concern. Nevertheless, at some point he had an intensely religious experience of the kind fostered by his background. The commitment growing out of that experience has led him to devote his adult Christian life to leading the church toward, or bringing about, the kind of social change the gospel requires. He now discovers, however, that his own children, brought up in an atmosphere of intense concern for the social requirements of the gospel, have inherited the social concern but not the gospel. They have left the church and wandered off into the secular left, or have entered the business world with a little dabbling in social concerns on the side. And he wonders why.

A reasonable hypothesis is that today's liberal-ecumenical establishment acquired its own meaning structure out of an evangelical tradition, but in taking that meaning structure for granted has failed to provide a church in which that meaning structure now receives sufficient attention. The evangelical challenge to the mainline churches may be history's (or the Holy Spirit's) way of bringing it back in.

The Role of the Spirit

Ultimately, neither the evangelical challenge nor the mainline response can create a new consensus of the middle. Richard Lovelace, in his analysis of current divisions in the church and his call for reconstitution of the central channel, speaks of the "delta effect." He describes an earlier main channel encompassing renewal, nurture, evangelism, mission, ecumenism, and social reform. In the delta effect, he suggests, this main channel splits into a number of smaller channels running on either side of what would be the "main channel of balance." Now, he says, the delta effect seems to be yielding to a pattern of convergence.[27]

The metaphor of the river channel, also implied by Allen's call for return to the "central channel," suggests more than a floating in mid-stream. For the course of a river—its delta effect or its convergence—is not under human control. The return to the middle, for the contemporary church, may not be a product of human endeavor at all, but of divine providence. Perhaps the most important sign, then, is the recovery of awareness of the unique presence of the Holy Spirit in the church. The charismatic movement is only one—if the most dramatic—evidence of the Spirit's work.

Institutionally, the bankruptcy of the idea that human management controls the present and future of the church and the fresh awakening to the reality of the *element of surprise* in God's dealing with his covenant community are important signals. Throughout the worldwide church, and especially in the churches of the third world, there are others. The absence of polarization in much of the Third Church; the evidences of healthy growth; the surprising development of independent indigenous churches without influence from the west—these point to the Spirit at work elsewhere in the world. The recovery of authority; the renewed awareness of the divine initiative in evangelism, in church growth, and in witness—these are evidences here at home. Even the crisis points explored in this book may suggest that when we—the mainline churches—fail, the Spirit still finds ways within the parameters of the larger church. As disconcerting as they may have been and may continue to be for middle-class, middle-aged, middle-American liberals, we can hardly deny that through the independent youth organizations, the parachurch groups, and the independent overseas missions, the Holy Spirit has maintained a certain vigor in the church. The mainline parents of a teenager turned off by home church and brought back into its fellowship by Young Life, are not likely to let their institutional disapproval prevent their personal gratitude. Thank God for the Spirit's surprises!

Perhaps the most that can be done by human initiative to create the conditions in which a consensus of the middle may be reconstituted is to live creatively within our pluralism. As we make our plans and develop our strategies, unless we want to opt for a power struggle, we have little choice but to strive for a consciously planned pluralism. Our mainline pluralism is a reality, but it must be accepted, affirmed, and provided for if the way is to be open for reconstitution of the center.

It is no doubt too much to expect that the mainline churches, in opting for a planned pluralism, might consciously establish themselves at the midpoint of their range of diversity. Who knows where the middle is? If the mainline finds its way back to the historical position in the middle of the Protestant spectrum, it will be more by the action of the Holy Spirit than by conscious planning, goal-setting, or charting a course toward a carefully plotted center point. Even at the congregational level where it is a practical necessity, reaching for the center involves a leap of faith.

The most important strategy of all, ultimately, is to recognize the limitations of any strategy. Liberal-ecumenicals and evangelicals alike may be reaching for the center. A conscious pluralism may open the way, but we cannot bring it about by ourselves.

This being the case, perhaps the most important thing the diverse elements in a pluralistic church can do is to pray together. In committee meetings, in congregational gatherings, in worship services, in leadership groups, in conferences and conventions, in ecumenical gatherings, the *most effective single method of coping with diversity* is to pray. Prayer for unity, prayer for understanding, prayer for a spirit of love, prayer for adversaries, prayer for dissenters, prayer for the particular congregation, prayer for the whole church—an atmosphere of continuing and earnest prayer places the responsibility for creating a constructive pluralism where it belongs. Regardless of options perceived, choices made, and human successes or failures, the church is God's. Its future is in God's hands.

notes

Chapter 1

1. George M. Conn, Jr., "King College: Maybe Institutions Need Living Wills," *Presbyterian Outlook*, May 14, 1979 (161:20), p. 8. A legal settlement between the synod and the new Board of Trustees was reached late in 1979. The three presbyteries (regional judicatories) in the Appalachia region later entered into a support relationship with the college, but as of the time of this writing no relationship had been reestablished with the synod.
2. See "The Decade in Religion: 1970–1979" (Religious News Service), *Presbyterian Outlook*, January 14, 1980 (162:2); "As Nation Enters 1980s: 10 Key Trends in Religion in U.S.," *Emerging Trends*, Princeton Religious Research Center, November 1979 (1:9), p. 2; Martin Marty, "After Ten Years: The Shape of the Decade in Religion," *Context*, October 15, 1979. Marty's analysis concludes that "at the heart and core of all trends there has developed what I have come to call *laic religion*." By this term he means a privatized and individualized approach to religion developed primarily by lay people, outside the classic church institutions. He refers to "parachurch" or "extra-ecclesial religiosity." While this is by no means identical with evangelicalism, there is much overlapping between the two concepts.
3. *Emerging Trends*, Princeton Religious Research Center, November 1979 (1:9), p. 2.

Chapter 2

1. The following books have been the major sources for this discussion of evangelical self-definition: Donald G. Bloesch, *The Evangelical Renaissance* (Grand Rapids: Eerdmans, 1973); Donald W. Dayton, *Discovering an Evangelical Heritage* (New York: Harper and Row, 1976); Morris A. Inch, *The Evangelical Challenge* (Philadelphia: Westminster, 1978); Robert K. Johnston, *Evangelicals at an Impasse* (Atlanta: John Knox Press, 1979); Harold Lindsell, *Battle for the Bible* (Grand Rapids: Zondervan, 1976); Richard F. Lovelace, *Dynamics of Spiritual Life: An Evangelical Theology of Renewal* (Downers Grove, Ill.: InterVarsity Press, 1979); David O. Moberg, *The Great Reversal* (Philadelphia: Lippincott, 1972); Ronald H. Nash, *The New Evangelicalism* (Grand Rapids: Zondervan, 1963); Rene C. Padilla, ed. *The New Face of Evangelicalism* (Urbanna: InterVarsity Press, 1976); Bernard L. Ramm, *The Evangelical Heritage* (Waco: Word Books, 1973); Richard Quebedeaux, *The Young Evangelicals: Revolution in Orthodoxy* (New York: Harper and Row, 1974) and *The Worldly Evangelicals*

(New York: Harper and Row, 1978); David F. Wells and John D. Woodbridge, eds., *The Evangelicals: What They Believe, Who They Are, How They Are Changing* (Nashville: Abingdon, 1975).

2. Moberg, *The Great Reversal: Evangelism versus Social Concern* (Philadelphia: Lippincott, 1972).
3. Martin E. Marty, *Righteous Empire* (New York: Dial Press, 1970), 177-87.
4. Dean R. Hoge, *Division in the Protestant House* (Philadelphia: Westminster Press, 1976).
5. Dean R. Hoge and David Roozen, eds., *Understanding Church Growth and Decline, 1950-1978* (New York: Pilgrim Press, 1979).
6. Bernard L. Ramm, *The Evangelical Heritage*, 64-68.
7. Ramm, 64-66.
8. Sydney E. Ahlstrom, *A Religious History of the American People* (New Haven: Yale University Press, 1972).
9. Marty, *Righteous Empire.*
10. Ahlstrom, 763-787.
11. Richard V. Pierard, *The Unequal Yoke: Evangelical Christianity and Political Conservatism* (Philadelphia: Lippincott, 1970).
12. Martin E. Marty, "Born Again," *Presbyterian Survey*, September 1979 (69:8), pp. 11-16.
13. Richard Quebedeaux, Introduction to Arthur Carl Piepkorn, *Profiles in Belief* vol. IV, *Evangelical, Fundamentalist and Other Christian Bodies* (San Francisco: Harper and Row, 1979), p. xvii.
14. Richard Quebedeaux, *The Young Evangelicals*, pp. 7-9.
15. Robert K. Johnston, *Evangelicals at an Impasse*, p. 3.
16. Piepkorn, pp. 8-9.
17. See Harold Lindsell, *Battle for the Bible*, and Johntson, *Evangelicals at an Impasse.*
18. See Richard Quebedeaux, *The Worldly Evangelicals.*
19. Quebedeaux, *Young Evangelicals.*
20. Ramm, p. 20.
21. Quebedeaux, *Young Evangelicals*, p. 144.
22. Bloesch, *Evangelical Renaissance*, pp. 7-8.
23. *Ramm, p. 122.*

Chapter 3

1. James H. Smylie, "Church Growth and Decline in Historical Perspective" in Dean R. Hoge and David Roozen, eds., *Understanding Church Growth and Decline, 1950-1978* (New York: Pilgrim Press, 1979), pp. 76-82.
2. Martin E. Marty, Foreword, Hoge and Roozen, p. 12.
3. See Richard G. Hutcheson, Jr., *Wheel Within the Wheel: Confronting the Management Crisis of the Pluralistic Church* (Atlanta: John Knox Press, 1979), pp. 63-140. This book deals extensively with the effect of the managerial revolution on church organizations.
4. For instance, Amitai Etzioni, *Modern Organizations* (Englewood Cliffs, N. J.: Prentice-Hall, Inc., 1964), p. 3; Charles Perrow, *Organizational Analysis* (Belmont, Calif.: Brooks/Cole Publishing Co., 1970); Peter Drucker, *Management,* (New York: Harper and Row, 1973), p. 46.
5. Hoge and Roozen, pp. 325-327.

Chapter 4

1. See, for instance, *Minutes of the 119th General Assembly,* Presbyterian Church, U.S., Part I, p. 316.
2. Richard Quebedeaux, *The Worldly Evangelicals* (San Francisco: Harper and Row, 1978), p. 107.
3. Joanna Bowen Gillespie, "Meditation of a Middle-Aged, (Upper) Middle-Class, White, Liberal, Protestant Parent," *Christian Century,* August 15-22, 1979 (96:25), pp. 792-94.
4. *Minutes of the 118th General Assembly,* Presbyterian Church, U.S., Part I, p. 162.
5. A survey by the Institute of Church Growth of 400 churches which participated in the program in two cities, Indianapolis and Fresno, California, showed that 29,000 telephone calls were made, 1,665 made decisions for Christ, but only 101 completed the follow-up study, and only 55 (of whom 23 had some previous church involvement) joined churches.
6. "Missions Sunrise, Not Sunset, Is Seen," *Presbyterian Journal,* Jan. 16, 1980 (38:38), p. 4.
7. Most of the information on the evangelical youth movements comes from Quebedeaux, *The Wordly Evangelicals,* pp. 55-59 and 100-105, and from *Para-Church Groups,* a brochure prepared by the Council on Theology and Culture, Presbyterian Church, U.S. (Atlanta, 1980).
8. Lyle E. Schaller, "Public versus Private School: A Divisive Issue for the 1980s," *Christian Century,* Nov. 7, 1979 (96:36), p. 1087.
9. Schaller, p. 1090.
10. "Evaluation of Overseas and Domestic Mission," prepared for 1978 Mission Consultation of Presbyterian Church, U.S., by Office of Review and Evaluation.
11. Princeton Religious Research Center, *Religion in America, 1979-80,* p. 64-65. Also reported in *Emerging Trends,* June 1979 (1:6).
12. "Interest in Religion on Rise, Survey Shows," *Presbyterian Journal,* June 20, 1979, p. 5.
13. Princeton Religious Research Center, *Religion in America, 1979-80,* p. 71.
14. *Emerging Trends,* PRRC, June 1979 (1:6), p. 3.
15. "High School Leaders Turn Conservative," *Presbyterian Journal,* Jan. 16, 1980, p. 4.
16. Martin Marty, *Context Newsletter,* June 1, 1979 (quoting from Gerald L. Klerman, "The Age of Melacholy," in *Psychology Today*).
17. Dean M. Kelley, *Why Conservative Churches Are Growing* (New York: Harper and Row, 1972).
18. Richard F. Lovelace, *Dynamics of Spiritual Life: An Evangelical Theology of Renewal* (Downers Grove, Ill.: InterVarsity Press, 1979), p. 317.
19. Research conducted by Donald Campbell, Staff Associate for Professional Support Services, for the Office of Professional Development, General Assembly Mission Board, Presbyterian Church, U.S., 1979.
20. Thomas C. Oden, *Agenda for Theology* (San Francisco: Harper and Row, 1979), p. 3.
21. Haddon Robinson, "A Profile on the American Clergyman," *Christianity Today* May 23, 1980, pp. 27–29.

Chapter 5

1. Arthur F. Glasser, "Discovering Mission," mimeographed paper for Mission Consultation, Presbyterian Church, U.S., January 1978.

2. Ralph D. Winter, "Protestant Mission Societies and the Other Protestant 'Schism'," in *American Denominational Organization,* ed. Ron Scherer (Philadelphia: Fortress Press, 1977); also Winter, "The Two Structures of God's Redemptive Mission" (American Society of Missiology, 1974).

3. William G. McLoughlin, "Changing Patterns of Protestant Philanthropy, 1607-1969," in *The Religious Situation: 1969,* ed. Donald R. Cutler (Boston: Beacon Press, 1979), pp. 538-614.

4. Jeremy Rifkin with Ted Howard, *The Emerging Order: God in the Age of Scarcity* (New York: G. P. Putnam's Sons, 1979), p. 148.

5. Sidney E. Ahlstrom, *Religious History of the American People* (New Haven: Yale University Press, 1972), p. 422.

6. Ahlstrom, p. 423.

7. Ahlstrom, p. 858.

8. Ahlstrom, p. 859 ff.

9. For a more thorough discussion of this trend and the dynamics underlying it, see Richard G. Hutcheson, Jr., *Wheel Within the Wheel: Confronting the Management Crisis of the Pluralistic Church* (Atlanta: John Knox Press, 1979), Chapter 6, p. 99 ff.

10. J. Richard Bass, "Some Stewardship Thoughts to Ponder," Savannah Presbytery, Fall 1979.

11. Charles E. Swann, "The Electric Church," *Presbyterian Survey,* May 1979 (69:5), p. 9; J. Thomas Bisset, "Religious Broadcasting: Assessing the State of the Art," *Christianity Today,* December 12, 1980 (24:21), pp. 28-31.

12. This account is based on information in Charles E. Swann, "The Electric Church"; Russ Williams, "Heavenly Message, Earthly Designs," *Sojourners,* Sept. 1979 (8:9), pp. 17-22; Rifkin and Howard, *The Emerging Order,* pp. 105-112.

13. This account is based on Swann; Rifkin and Howard; Philip Yancey, "The Ironies and Impact of PTL," *Christianity Today,* Sept. 21, 1979 (23:22), pp. 28-33.

14. Charles E. Swann, "Is the 'Electronic Church' a Church?" *Presbyterian Outlook,* March 10, 1980 (162:10), pp. 5-6.

15. Dean R. Hoge, *Division in the Protestant House* (Philadelphia: Westminister Press, 1976), pp. 74-91.

16. Ron Sider, *Rich Christians in an Age of Hunger* (Downers Grove, Ill.: InterVarsity Press, 1977).

17. Quoted by Martin E. Marty in *Context Newsletter,* November 15, 1979, p. 4.

18. See David Morrison, "Evangelical Christians Turn GOP Platform into a Pulpit," *Atlanta Constitution,* July 16, 1980, p. 8A. Most of the information about Christian Voice and Moral Majority in this section is based on Edward E. Plowman, "Is Morality All Right?" *Christianity Today,* Nov. 2, 1979, pp. 76-85.

19. Information on these four groups comes primarily from "Para-Church Groups," brochure prepared by the Council on Theology and Culture, Presbyterian Church, U.S., 1980.

20. Interview with Paul McKaughan, Executive Secretary, Mission to the World, Presbyterian Church in America, December 20, 1979.

21. "United or Untied?" *Christianity Today,* Sept. 7, 1979, pp. 54-55; John Maust, "Methodists Grope for a Common Center," *Christianity Today,* May 23, 1980, pp. 40-42.

22. Lon L. Fuller, "Two Principles of Human Association," in *Voluntary Associations,* eds. J. Roland Pennock and John W. Chapman (New York: Atherton Press, 1969), pp. 3-23.

23. Fuller Theological Seminary, *Theology News and Notes*, June 1979.
24. "Former Crusade Staffers Find Need for Discipline," *Presbyterian Journal*, Nov. 28, 1979 (38:31), pp. 4-5.
25. "Para-Church Groups," p. 13.

Chapter 6

1. David J. Bosch, *Witness to the World: The Christian Mission in Theological Perspective* (New Foundations Theological Library). (Atlanta: John Knox Press, 1980), pp. 28-29.
2. Dean M. Kelley, *Why Conservative Churches Are Growing* (New York: Harper and Row, 1972), p. 10. Other statistics are from Edward R. Dayton, ed., *Mission Handbook: North American Protestant Ministries Overseas*, 11th edition (Monrovia, California: Missions Advanced Research and Communication Center, 1976), pp. 61 and 382.
3. *International Review of Mission*, April 1969 (63:230), p. 141; cited in Ralph D. Winter, "Ghana: Preparation for Marriage," *International Review of Mission* July 1978 (67:267), pp. 338-353.
4. See discussion in Richard G. Hutcheson, Jr. *Wheel Within the Wheel: Confronting the Management Crisis in the Pluralistic Church* (Atlanta: John Knox Press, 1979), pp. 69-71.
5. Leslie Newbigin, "Mission and Missions," *Christianity Today*, Aug. 1, 1960, p. 23; cited in Ralph D. Winter, "Ghana: Preparation for Marriage," p. 340.
6. Richard Quebedeaux, *The Young Evangelicals: Revolution in Orthodoxy* (New York: Harper and Row, 1974), p. 4.
7. See Hutcheson, *Wheel Within the Wheel*, Chapter 4, "Churches as Goal-seeking Organizations," pp. 63-81, for a discussion of important issues.
8. Tim Stafford, "The Church in Kenya: A Catch 22," *Christianity Today*, Jan. 25, 1980 (24:2), p. 20.
9. Walbert Buhlman, *The Coming of the Third Church* (Maryknoll, New York: Orbis Books, 1977).
10. See Orlando E. Costas, "Churches in Evangelistic Partnership," in *The New Face of Evangelicalism: An International Symposium on the Lausanne Covenant* (Downers Grove, Illinois: InterVarsity Press, 1976), pp. 143-162.
11. *Mission Handbook*, p. 61.
12. *Mission Handbook*, p. 62 and 58.
13. Data in this section on parachurch agencies come primarily from *Mission Handbook*.
14. John Maust, "Jungle Identity Crisis: Auca Country Revisited," *Christianity Today*, Jan. 4, 1980 (24:1), pp. 48-50.
15. "Mission Sunrise, Not Sunset, Is Seen," *Presbyterian Journal*, Jan. 16, 1980 (38:38), p. 4.
16. Harvey T. Hoekstra, *The World Council of Churches and the Demise of Evangelism* (Wheaton, Illinois: Tyndale House Publishers, 1979).
17. Phil Butler, "Europe's Surprise Groundswell for Missions," *Christianity Today* Feb. 8, 1980 (24:3), pp. 82-86.
18. C. Rene Padilla, ed., *The New Face of Evangelicalism* (Downers Grove: Ill.: InterVarsity Press, 1976), p. 87 ff.
19. Arthur F. Glasser, "Two Rubrics: 'Your Kingdom Come' vs. 'How Shall They Hear?'" *Missiology*, April 1980 (8:2), pp. 133-140.

Chapter 7

1. Much of the material in this chapter is a revision of the author's earlier treatment of "The Charismatic Movement: Conflict of Challenge," *Chaplaincy*, 2nd Quarter, 1979 (2:2), pp. 23-30. Major sources include Edward D. O'Connor, *The Pentecostal Movement in the Catholic Church* (Notre Dame: Ave Maria Press, 1971); John B. Healey, "Some Questions About Catholic Charismatics," *America*, Dec. 9, 1978, pp. 429-31; Charles E. Hummel, *Fire in the Fireplace: Contemporary Charismatic Renewal* (Downers Grove, Ill. InterVarsity Press, 1978); Kevin and Dorothy Ranaghan, *Catholic Pentecostals* (Paramus, N.J.: Paulist Press, 1969); Wayne A. Robinson, *I Once Spoke in Tongues* (Wheaton, Ill.: Tyndale House, 1973); James H. Smylie, "Testing the Spirits in the American Context," *Interpretation*, Jan. 1979, pp. 32-46; J. Rodman Williams, *The Pentecostal Reality* (Plainfield, N.J.: Logos International, 1972); and Albert C. Winn, "The Holy Spirit and the Christian Life," *Interpretation*, Jan. 1979, pp. 47-57.
2. According to a survey by the Gallup organization, only abut 2/5 (38 percent) of those who consider themselves charismatics speak in tongues. *Emerging Trends*, Jan. 1980 (2:1), p. 2.
3. Richard Quebedeaux, Introduction to Carl Arthur Piepkorn, *Profiles in Belief*, Vol. IV, *Evangelical, Fundamentalist and Other Christian Bodies* (San Francisco: Harper and Row, 1979), p. xvii.
4. Henry Pitney Van Dusen, "Third Force in Christendom," *Life*, June 9, 1958, pp. 113-122. The article popularized the "third force" concept.
5. *Evangelical Newsletter*, Nov. 2, 1979 (6:22). For the first time, this gathering of denominational Pentecostals had a mainline neo-charismatic on the program.
6. Jeremy Rifkin with Ted Howard, *The Emerging Order: God in the Age of Scarcity* (New York: G. P. Putnam's Sons, 1979).
7. J. I. Packer, "Charismatic Renewal: Pointing to a Person and a Power," *Christianity Today*, March 7, 1980 (24:5), p. 16.
8. William G. McLoughlin, *Revivals, Awakenings and Reform* (Chicago: University of Chicago press, 1978), p. 192. McLoughlin labels the revivalist movements of the nineteenth century a "Third Great Awakening," and the present movement a possible fourth. Some other commentators are suggesting that the present movement is a "third awakening."
9. Hans Küng, *The Church*, tr. Ray and Rosaleen Ockenden (London: Burns and Oates, 1967); Jürgen Moltmann, *The Church in the Power of the Spirit*, tr. Margaret Kohl, (New York: Harper and Row, 1977).
10. Richard G. Hutcheson, Jr. *Wheel Within the Wheel: Confronting the Management Crisis of the Pluralistic Church* (Atlanta: John Knox Press, 1979), pp. 10-11.
11. Smylie, "Testing the Spirits in the American Context."
12. This summary of the beginnings of the pentecostal denominations is based on the treatments of Ranaghan and O'Connor.
13. Dr. Everett Fullam, quoted in *Evangelical Newsletter*, Sept. 7, 1979 (6:18).
14. "The Catholic Charismatic Renewal," *America*, Oct. 6, 1979 (141:9), p. 165.
15. Morris G.C. Vaagenes, Jr. "Is Renewal for the Whole Church?" *PCC Renewal News*, Nov. Dec. 1980 (63), p. 4.
16. Spencer C. Murray, "Report on the Kansas City Charismatic Conference," mimeographed paper, September 9, 1977.

17. Ralph Martin, "A Catholic Assesses Charismatic Renewal in His Church," *Christianity Today*, March 7, 1980 (24:5), pp. 18-19.

Chapter 8

1. These denominational studies include: "Study of Church Renewal and Growth at General Assembly, Synod and Presbytery Levels—Church Membership Trends (UPCUSA)"; Ruth T. Doyle and Sheila Kelly, "Church Membership and Church Participation Trends in the Episcopal Church 1950-1975"; Warren J. Hartman, "Membership Trends: A Study of Decline and Growth in the United Methodist Church, 1949-1975"; Warren J. Hartman, "Mid-Quadrennium Report on Church Membership Trends and Decision Point: Church School"; "A First Look: LCA Trends During the Period 1963 to 1974" (LCA); Kathy Whipple, "A Report on Selected Trends for Use in Churchwide Planning" (LCA); Phillip B. Jones, "An Examination of the Statistical Growth of the Southern Baptist Convention Through 1976"; Gary D. Bouman, "The Real Reason One Conservative Church Grew," *Review of Religious Research*, Spring 1979 (20:2) (RCA and CRC); Wade C. Roof, Dean R. Hoge, John E. Dyble, and C. Kirk Hathaway, "Factors Producing Growth or Decline in United Presbyerian Congregations"; Foster H. Shannon, *The Growth Crisis in the American Church: A Presbyterian Case Study* (Pasadena: William Carey Library, 1977) (UPCUSA); William R. McKinney, Jr., "Performance of United Church of Christ Congregations in Massachusetts and Pennsylvania," *Understanding Church Growth and Decline* 1950-1978, ed. Dean R. Hoge and David Roozen (New York: Pilgrim Press, 1979) (UCC); Dan Martin, "The Church-Growth Questions," *Home Missions*, Dec. 1977 (48:11) (SBC); Ruth T. Doyle and Sheila M. Kelly, "Comparisons of Trends in Ten Denominations," *Understanding Church Growth*. The unpublished reports were obtained from the denominations concerned.
2. Hoge and Roozen, *Understanding Church Growth and Decline.*
3. Statistics in this section from Minutes of General Assemblies, Presbyterian Church, U.S.
4. Most of this analysis of mainline church membership decline is taken from a report written by the author for the Office of Review and Evaluation, and included in that office's report to the General Assembly. See *Minutes of the 119th General Assembly*, PCUS, pp. 307-319.
5. Dean M. Kelley, *Why Conservative Churches Are Growing* (New York: Harper and Row, 1972).
6. McKinney, "Performance of United Church of Christ Congregations."
7. David A. Roozen, "Church Membership and Participation: Trends, Determinants, and Implications for Policy and Planning" (The Hartford Seminary Foundation, 1978).
8. Bouman, "The Real Reason One Conservative Church Grew."
9. Hoge and Roozen, "Some Sociological Conclusions About Church Trends," *Understanding Church Growth and Decline*, pp. 315-333.
10. David J. Bosch, *Witness to the World: The Christian Mission in Theological Perspective* (New Foundations Theological Library). (Atlanta: John Knox Press, 1980), pp. 11-40.
11. "A Theological Basis for Evangelism," unpublished paper, Presbyterian Church, U.S., 1967.
12. *Minutes of the 115th General Assembly*, Presbyterian Church, U.S., p. 130.

13. "Social Policy: Activities and Attitudes Among United Presbyterians," Research Division, Support Agency, United Presbyterian Church in the USA, reported in *Monday Morning*, Nov. 5, 1979, p. 18.
14. The author's book, *Wheel Within the Wheel*, does not make this claim directly, but such a conclusion may be inherent in the analysis of the management crisis in this church which the book puts forward.
15. C. Peter Wagner, "Church Growth Research: The Paradigm and Its Applications," *Understanding Church Growth and Decline*, pp. 270-287; especially p. 270.
16. Alfred C. Krass, "What the Mainline Denominations Are Doing in Evangelism," *Christian Century*, May 2, 1979 (96:16), p. 49; originally published as a report of the Evangelism Working Group, Division of Church and Society, National Council of Churches.
17. Church Growth Ministries, Inc., brochure, November 1979.
18. Dale Sanders, "Protestantism Goes Evangelistic," *Christianity Today*, January 25, 1980 (24:2), pp. 34-36. The reviewer is a mainline minister.
19. John R. Hendrick, "The Church Growth Movement: Its Principles Analyzed," *Presbyterian Outlook*, June 4, 1979 (161:23), p. 7. The quotation is from a Presbyterian Church, U.S., General Assembly directive to its Council on Theology and Culture regarding the preparation of a paper. Hendrick is the author of *Opening the Door of Faith: The Why, When and Where of Evangelism* (Atlanta: John Knox Press, 1978).
20. Hendrick, "The Church Growth Movement," p. 8. The same article cites the Van Eck and United Presbyterian Program Agency attempts at adaptation.
21. Carl S. Dudley, *Where Have All the People Gone?* (New York: Pilgrim Press, 1979), pp. 56-57.

Chapter 9

1. Much of the material in this chapter was first published in "What's Happening to the Tie That Binds?" *Presbyterian Survey*, December 1979 (69:11), pp. 24-29.
2. Rhea Gray, Douglas Lewis, Norman Shawchuck, and Robert Worley, *Experiences in Activating Congregations: A Cross Denominational Study* (Chicago: Institute for Ministry Development, 1978), pp. 88-95.
3. Letter from Richard S. Dole, October 26, 1979.

Chapter 10

1. John Newton Thomas, in a letter to the editor, *Presbyterian Outlook*, October 15, 1979 (161:37), p. 2.
2. James Hitchcock, "Does Christianity Have a Future?" *New Oxford Review*, June 1980, p. 8.
3. Quoted in *Evangelical Newsletter*, November 22, 1979 (6:22), p. 1.
4. Max Weber, "The Protestant Sects and the Spirit of Capitalism," in *From Max Weber: Essays in Sociology*, eds. Hans Gerth and C. Wright Mills (New York: Oxford University Press, 1946); Ernst Troeltsch, *The Social Teachings of the Christian Churches*, tr. Olive Wyon (New York: The Macmillan Co., 1931). Many others have elaborated on this typology.
5. See discussion in Richard G. Hutcheson, Jr., *Wheel Within the Wheel* (Atlanta: John Knox Press, 1979) on "Churches as Voluntary Organizations," pp. 82-89.

6. Lyle E. Schaller, "What Will the '80s Bring?" *The Christian Ministry*, January 1980 (11:1), pp. 17-18.

Chapter 11

1. Lon L. Fuller, "Two Principles of Human Association," *Voluntary Associations*, eds. J. Roland Pennock and John W. Chapman (New York: Atherton Press, 1969), pp. 3-23.
2. Data from opinion sampling of the National Opinion Research Center (NORC) of the University of Chicago. For present purposes, those denominations affiliated with the National Council of Churches are considered mainline, and those not affiliated non-mainline. Even this division is not precise. Respondents identified themselves by denominational name, and in some cases, such as Baptist, the alignment is not clear. The differences, nevertheless, are suggestive. 32.2 percent of mainline affiliated Christians labeled their religious identification as "strong," compared with 45.5 percent of the non-mainliners. 57.6 percent of the mainliners considered their religious identification "not very strong," compared with 44.7 percent of the non-mainline Christian respondents. (Peggy L. Shriver, "Profiles in Faith," privately circulated to National Council of Churches member denominations by the NCC Office of Research, Evaluation and Planning, January 1980.)

Chapter 12

1. Carl Bakal, *Charity USA* (New York: Times Books, 1979), p. 85. This estimate, made by the American Association of Fund-Raising Counsel, is probably conservative, according to the author.
2. Max Weber, *The Theory of Social and Economic Organization*, tr. A.M. Henderson and Talcott Parsons (New York: Oxford University Press 1947), pp. 324-386.
3. Paul M. Harrison, *Authority and Power in the Free Church Tradition* (Princeton, N.J.: Princeton University Press, 1959) develops this theme in terms of "rational-pragmatic authority" based on technical qualification and competence, with particular reference to denominational agency bureaucrats. For a discussion of the effects of professionalization, see Richard G. Hutcheson, Jr., *Wheel Within the Wheel* (Atlanta: John Knox Press, 1979), pp. 114-139.
4. Martin Marty, "After Ten Years: The Shape of the Decade in Religion," *Context*, October 15, 1979.
5. Joseph Harvard, "Managers or Leaders: A Misplaced Debate," *Presbyterian Outlook*, November 28, 1979.
6. James McGregor Burns, *Leadership* (New York: Harper and Row, 1978). Especially pp. 18-22.
7. Kenneth A. Briggs, "Coffin and His 'Liberal Pulpit' Renew a Legacy of Controversy," *New York Times*, December 31, 1979, p. B1.
8. For instance, James D. Anderson and Ezra E. Jones, *The Management of Ministry* (New York: Harper and Row, 1978); Speed Leas and Paul Kittlaus, *Church Fights: Managing Conflict in the Local Church* (Philadelphia: Westminster Press, 1973); and numerous books and church management by Lyle E. Schaller.

Chapter 13

1. Douglas W. Johnson, "Fractures in the Future?" *Christian Century*, October 10, 1979 (96:32), p. 967.

2. Dean Hoge, *Division in the Protestant House* (Philadelphia: Westminster Press, 1976), p. 46.

3. Diogenes Allen, "The Central Channel," *Presbyterian Outlook,* September 3, 1979 (161:3), p. 5.

4. Robert A. Evans, "Recovering the Church's Transforming Middle," Dean R. Hoge and David Roozen, eds., *Understanding Church Growth and Decline, 1950-1978* (Boston: Pilgrim Press, 1979), pp. 288-314; p. 291.

5. Richard F. Lovelace, *Dynamics of Spiritual Life: An Evangelical Theology of Renewal* (Downers Grove, Ill.: InterVarsity Press, 1979), p. 281.

6. Thomas C. Oden, *Agenda for Theology* (San Francisco: Harper and Row, 1979), p. 3.

7. David O. Moberg, *The Great Reversal* (Philadelphia: Lippincott, 1972).

8. Walbert Buhlmann, *The Coming of the Third Church* (Maryknoll, N. Y.: Orbis Books, 1977).

9. Gustavo Gutiérrez, A *Theology of Liberation,* tr. and ed. Sister Caridad Inda and John Eagleson (Maryknoll, N. Y: Orbis Books, 1973). This is probably his best know work in the United States.

10. Based on an interview of the author with Dr. Alves in Campinas, Brazil, March 1977.

11. Orlando E. Costas, *The Church and Its Mission: A Shattering Critique from the Third World* (Wheaton, Ill.: Tyndale House Publishers, 1974), p. 309.

12. Ronald J. Sider, "An Evangelical Theology of Liberation," *Christian Century* March 19, 1980 (97:10), pp. 314-318.

13. Quoted in C. Rene Padilla, ed., *The New Face of Evangelicalism: An International Symposium on the Lausanne Covenant* (Downers Grove, Ill.: InterVarsity Press, 1976), p. 9.

14. Padilla, p. 11.

15. "Lausanne, WEF United Ask Simple Lifestyle," *Presbyterian Journal,* April 16, 1980 (38:51), p. 4.

16. Susan Lutz, "Evangelical Leaders Poll, Part I," *Evangelical Newsletter,* January 25, 1980 (7:2).

17. "Evangelical Unity Is Not One Option Among Many," *Christianity Today,* March 21, 1980 (24:6), pp. 12-13.

18. John Maust, "Charismatic Leaders Seeking Faith for Their Own Healing," *Christianity Today,* April 4, 1980 (24:7), p. 44.

19. Barbara Hargrove, "Reflections on YDS and the Society," *Reflection,* November 1979.

20. Report of William L. Pauley, Regional Communicator for Synod of the Virginias, January 4, 1980.

21. Donald E. Miller, "Spiritual Discipline: Countering Contemporary Culture," *Christian Century,* March 19, 1980 (97:10), pp. 319-323.

22. Peter M. Schmiechen, "The Challenge of Conservative Theology," *Christian Century,* April 9, 1980 (97:13), pp. 402-406.

23. Tom Minnery, "Evangelical Inroads Trim Bible Forum's Liberal Set," *Christianity Today,* December 2, 1980 (24:21), pp. 62-64.

24. Carl S. Dudley, *Where Have All Our People Gone?* (New York: Pilgrim Press, 1979), p. 109.

25. Lovelace, p. 333.

26. Dean M. Kelley, *Why Conservative Churches Are Growing* (New York: Harper and Row, 1972), pp. 36-37.

27. Lovelace, pp. 320-321.

index

191